D1094871

WITHDRAWN
UTSA LIBRARIES

International Control
of Investment

edited by
Don Wallace, Jr.
assisted by
Helga Ruof-Koch

Published in cooperation with
the Institute for International
and Foreign Trade Law,
Georgetown University Law Center

The Praeger Special Studies program—
utilizing the most modern and efficient book
production techniques and a selective
worldwide distribution network—makes
available to the academic, government, and
business communities significant, timely
research in U.S. and international economic, social, and political development.

International Control of Investment

The Dusseldorf Conference on Multinational Corporations

PRAEGER SPECIAL STUDIES IN INTERNATIONAL ECONOMICS AND DEVELOPMENT

Praeger Publishers   New York   Washington   London

Library of Congress Cataloging in Publication Data

Dusseldorf Conference on Multinational Corporations,
    1973.
    International control of investment.

    (Praeger special studies in international economics
and development)
    "Published in cooperation with the Institute for
International and Foreign Trade Law, Georgetown
University Law Center."
    1. Investments, Foreign—Congresses.
2. International business enterprises—Congresses.
I. Wallace, Don, 1932-   ed. II. Georgetown
University, Washington, D.C. Institute for Inter-
national and Foreign Trade Law. III. Title.
HG4538.D765   1973   332.6'73   73-16897

LIBRARY
University of Texas
At San Antonio

PRAEGER PUBLISHERS
111 Fourth Avenue, New York, N.Y. 10003, U.S.A.
5, Cromwell Place, London SW7 2JL, England

Published in the United States of America in 1974
by Praeger Publishers, Inc.

All rights reserved

© 1974 by the Institute for International
and Foreign Trade Law, Georgetown University

Printed in the United States of America

FOREWORD
Kurt Biedenkopf

The preparation of this volume was supported by the Institute
for International and Foreign Trade Law of Georgetown University
Law Center. The Institute was founded to promote greater understanding—in both Western Europe and the United States—of the legal
problems of international trade and other international economic relations. The Institute's present geographic and substantive scopes
embrace the legal problems of development, such as foreign investment in and procurement of basic goods and services by less developed
nations, as well as more traditional international economic and legal
transactions.

The current activities of the Institute can be divided into the
following categories: (1) fellowship, study, and exchange programs;
(2) research and training projects; (3) conferences; and (4) supervised
research.

The Washington, D.C., Institute is part of the Georgetown University Law Center. It is under the general supervision of a board
of trustees chosen from the Georgetown academic community, the
law faculties of other U.S. universities, local private practitioners,
and European sponsors. It has a permanent staff of professorial,
professional, and student members and is augmented by the Association of Adjunct Law Professors, which has special competence in
the Institute's areas of concern. The Director is Don Wallace, Jr.,
Professor of Law at Georgetown University Law Center.

The Washington Institute has a sister Institute at the University
of Frankfurt, Germany, the Institut fuer Auslaendisches und Inter-
nationales Wirtschaftsrecht.

In 1962 the Washington Institute cosponsored two international
conferences: one with the Frankfurt Institute on restraints of competition between the European Economic Community and the United
States; the second with the Brookings Institution on the extraterritorial
effects of trade regulations.

In 1964 the Washington Institute undertook an extensive study
of cartels in cooperation with American and European experts.

Kurt Biedenkopf is a member of the Board of the Institute for
International and Foreign Trade Law, Georgetown University Law
Center, Washington, D.C.

In 1968 the Institute sponsored a conference on trans-Atlantic investment and the balance of payments, including discussions of American restrictions on foreign investment in light of the balance of payments problems and the impact of such problems on American investment in Europe and European investment in the United States.

In 1970 a conference on foreign direct investment in the United States was held under the auspices of the Institute and its new director, Professor Wallace. The conference considered financial and securities regulations, antitrust problems, factors determining the economic relationship between the United States and Europe, and taxation problems of foreign direct investment in the United States. The proceedings of that conference have been printed and a resulting book-length study, Legal Environment for Foreign Direct Investment in the U.S., has been published. The present study is the result of still another conference sponsored by the Institute—the Düsseldorf Conference on International Control of Investment.

The Institute plans to hold further colloquiums and conferences on significant legal and economic issues and to regularly publish the results of these projects.

Exchange rates and other international monetary problems—
international trade negotiations, the multinational corporation, and
private foreign investment—have been much in the news in recent
years.

The subject of the Düsseldorf Conference—on the papers and
proceedings of which this book is based—has not been as widely discussed. The subject is the current feasibility, likelihood, and form
of possible international action with respect to the much debated
phenomenon of foreign investment. This book does not deal merely
or even principally with the nature of the multinational enterprise
or whether private foreign investment is good or bad, although these
subjects are certainly touched upon. Rather, it asks whether these
phenomena should be regulated and, if so, how; the conference was
largely at the level of policy statements and the book should be considered in that light.

The conference was called to "examine whether there is a need
for a 'GATT [General Agreement on Tariffs and Trade] for investment.'" We hoped to analyze the need for an international response
to investments made by multinational enterprises, the likelihood of
an international response in the foreseeable future, and the form of
that response.

A memorandum prepared for the participants before the conference stated the scope of the discussion as follows:

> There is a good deal of talk about the need for in-
> creased international organization in the economic area
> including some framework for the multinational corpora-
> tion. The conference will address the question of whether
> there should be something like a "GATT for Investment."
> There are some related themes. Many insist that there
> must be increased facilities for dialogue between the
> developing countries and the developed and their inves-
> tors. Some urge that negotiations among developed
> countries with respect to trade, finance and investment
> be coordinated. One even hears from a few about the

Don Wallace is Director of the Institute for International and
Foreign Trade Law and Professor of Law at Georgetown University.

vii

necessity of joint planning by the United States, Europe, and Japan. Concern about the environment and limits of growth may also be relevant.

The multinational corporation has entered our consciousness; much international trade takes place within its confines and much money moves because of it. We have the GATT dealing with trade (with proposals to broaden its scope) and the IMF [International Monetary Fund] dealing with short term money matters. There is no international organization dealing with investment or capital flows as such. The Düsseldorf Conference cannot address itself to all the questions suggested by the above. It will address itself to whether there is in fact a need for increased international organization in the investment area. If there is, what actually may be covered by such international organization? What might be the form of such organization? Most important, would any of this be realistic and feasible at this time?

In response to this call, the participants considered a range of possible alternatives: an international organization limited to informational activities; one that would seek to establish rules, presumably for both the multinational enterprise and the host (and sometimes home) state—the "GATT for investment" idea; even institutions that would seek to assist in the progressive disinvestment of foreign private capital. All possibilities were open.

The discussion carried beyond the problems of the multinational enterprises and their conflicts with nation-states to a consideration of concrete possibilities for international action in this area.

One matter of definition should be noted. The conference was designed to address itself to the international control of investment, that is, foreign investment or investment across national borders. However, a number of the speakers considered the activities of the multinational enterprise in general; reconciliation lies in the fact that many of the most vital activities of multinational corporations are indeed investment activities.

The conference took two days and was divided into three parts. Panels I and II on the first day analyzed the situation in the developed countries, considering both present economic and political factors, and the relationship between the developed and developing countries, again considering both economic and political factors. The information developed during these panel sessions was the basis for the discussion on the second day when the plenary session considered the possibilities for international organization.

The first day's proceedings do not offer too many surprises. Many of the participants thought the problems between the developed countries were rather different from the problems between developed and developing countries. It was generally thought that the developed countries did not have as much need for international organization, and yet there were suggestions that some effort might be reasonable, especially in the area of concentration and mergers. There also were some suggestions with respect to tax and other matters, but not much was said about international regulation of the Eurodollar market and related phenomena.

With respect to the developing countries it became clear that many Americans, and some Latin American participants, thought the problem of U.S. investment in Latin America was representative of foreign investment in all developing countries; however, it is obvious that Asia, Africa, and even the Middle East are not Latin America and the problems and the political responses may be quite different there.

With respect to both developed and developing countries there was some confusion as to factual premises: What is the foreign exchange effect of direct investment in the developing countries? Was U.S. investment in Europe entirely financed by local funds and does this have any significance? There was the usual disagreement as to whether foreign investment is good or bad in employment and other effects.

One surprise for some participants was that the developing countries, weaker countries by many criteria, distrust solutions through international organizations—presumably because they think they will be dominated by the developed countries. This is somewhat inconsistent with received notions that the weak seek refuge in the law, in this case the international law and its related international organizations.

The plenary session on the second day was the focal point of the conference and dealt with the actual prospects for international organization. Almost everyone seemed to agree that international investment takes place in the framework of two kinds of laissez-faire: the laissez-faire of the international economy in which the multinational corporation proceeds fairly free of control, and the laissez-faire of the nation-states which respond to international investment free of international control. The conclusion recorded during the plenary session was not wholly surprising: A GATT for investment or a disinvestment agency was thought to be neither feasible nor desirable at present. There was a feeling, however, that something probably should be done. In the words of Seymour Rubin, chairman of the second day's meeting, "some movement toward a new international organization or toward increasing the powers and the role of the existing organizations is likely."

Rubin has suggested the form that the new international effort might take. In his words, "it would seem sensible now to establish a forum or perhaps forums without attempting to formulate GATT-like rules. Within such a forum, with a disinterested secretary and a regular program of discussion, there might be generated not the heat that often characterizes these matters but a considerable amount of light." There seemed to be a fairly widespread sympathy at the conference for such a development. Whether it will transpire and, if so, when, remains a question.

We believe the main result of the Düsseldorf Conference is that it afforded serious students of this subject and policy-makers an opportunity to exchange ideas and proceed with the intellectual ground-work that must precede any new international effort with respect to the control of foreign investment.

I wish to thank Kurt Biedenkopf, Robert Neuman, Samuel Stern, and Seymour Rubin, who assisted in the preparation of this conference and in chairing the individual panels. I also wish to thank my assistant, Helga Ruof-Koch, who was responsible for the administrative organization of the conference and who, together with me, edited the conference papers and proceedings for this book.

CONTENTS

LIST OF TABLES

LIST OF ABBREVIATIONS

DEPI	direct foreign private investment
ECOSOC	Economic and Social Council of the United Nations
EEC	European Economic Community
ENI	Ente Nazionale Idrocarburi
GATT	General Agreement on Tariffs and Trade
GEPI	Study Group on Industrial Productivity
IBRD	International Bank for Reconstruction and Development
ICC	International Chamber of Commerce
ICSID	International Centre for Settlement of Investment Disputes
IET	interest equalization tax
IMF	International Monetary Fund
IMI	International Marketing Institute
IRI	Institute for Industrial Reconstruction
LDC	less developed country
MNE	multinational enterprise
MNC	multinational corporation
OECD	Organization for Economic Cooperation and Development
OFDI	Office of Foreign Direct Investment (Department of Commerce)
OMPE	Organization for Industrial Property
OPEC	Organization of Petroleum Exporting Countries
OPIC	Overseas Private Investment Corporation
SEC	Securities and Exchange Commission
UN	United Nations
UNCTAD	United Nations Conference on Trade and Development
UNIDO	United Nations Industrial Development Organization
UNITAR	United Nations Institute for Training and Research
WIPO	World Intellectual Property Organization

CONFERENCE PARTICIPANTS

Miss Peter Ady
St. Anne's College
Oxford, England

Tugrul Ansay
Max Planck Institute
Hamburg, Germany

Mr. Albrechtskirchinger
VCI
Frankfurt, Germany

Willis C. Armstrong
Assistant Secretary for Economic
   Affairs
Department of State
Washington, D.C.

Franz Ballman
Bank of America
London, England

Jack N. Behrman
University of North Carolina
Chapel Hill, North Carolina

Raymond Bertrand
Organization for Economic
   Cooperation and Develop-
   ment
Paris, France

Kurt Biedenkopf
Henkel GmbH
Düsseldorf, Germany

Fernand Braun
Department of Industry
European Economic
   Communities
Brussels, Belgium

Duncan Cameron
Cameron & Hornbostle
Washington, D.C.

Carsten P. Claussen
Gerling Global Bank AG
Hamburg, Germany

Edgar Cruft
Nord Resources Corporation
Albuquerque, New Mexico

John Dunning
University of Reading
England

Kristian Ehinger
Volkswagen Werke
Wolfsburg, Germany

Peter Eigen
Attorney General's
   Chambers
Gaborone, Botswana

Luis Escobar
International Bank for Reconstruc-
   tion and Development
Washington, D.C.

John Evans
Consultant
Washington, D.C.

Edward F. Farrell
Counsel
Madrid, Spain

Robert K. Foley
Law Offices of George F.
   Foley
New York

Milton Freeman
Arnold and Porter
Washington, D.C.

Lincoln Gordon
Woodrow Wilson Inter-
   national Center for
   Scholars
Smithsonian Institution
Washington, D.C.

Eckhard Gottschalk
Deutsche Unionbank
Frankfurt, Germany

Franz Grumbach
Hessische Landesbank
Frankfurt, Germany

B. Grossfeld
Juristisches Seminar der Univer-
   sität Göttingen
Göttingen, Germany

Robert Haeger
U.S. News and World
   Report
Bonn, Germany

Rainer Hellman
Chief Editor
Vereinigte Wirtschaftsdienste
Brussels, Belgium

Hans-Jürgen Hellwig
Müller Law Firm
Frankfurt, Germany

Robert L. Hirshberg
U.S. Embassy
Bonn, Germany

Pat M. Holt
Senate Foreign Relations
   Committee
Washington, D.C.

Norbert Horn
Max Planck-Institut für europäische
   Rechtgeschichte
Frankfurt, Germany

William Hui
Faculty of Law
Singapore, Malaysia

Yves-André Istel
Kuhn, Loeb & Co.
New York, New York

Harry Ivey
Department of Trade and
   Industry
Industrial & Commercial
   Policy Division 2
London, England

Richard Janssen
Economic Editor
Wall Street Journal
London, England

D. J. Jones
Standard Oil Company
   of New Jersey
New York, New York

Masao Kanno
BIAC
Tokyo, Japan

George Kelly
Consulate General of the
United States
Düsseldorf, Germany

Charles Kindleberger
Massachusetts Institute of Tech-
nology
Cambridge, Massachusetts

Norbert Kleber
McKinsey Company, Inc.
Düsseldorf, Germany

Udo Kollatz
Hessisches Kultusministerium
Wiesbaden, Germany

Edward M. Korry
Association of American
Publishers
Washington, D.C.

R. Krishnamurti
Manufactures Division
United Nations Conference on Trade
and Development
Geneva, Switzerland

K. Kuno
Japanese BIAC Secre-
tariat
Tokyo, Japan

Toro Kusukawa
The Fuji Bank, Limited
Düsseldorf, Germany

Milic Kybal
Inter-American Develop-
ment Bank
Washington, D.C.

Mr. Langbein
BASF
Ludwigshafen, Germany

Mr. Langer
Bundesministerium f.
Wirtschaft u. Finanzen
Bonn, Germany

Mr. Lehmann-Richter
Bundesministerium f. Wirtschaftl.
Zusammenarbeit
Bonn, Germany

Hans-Christoph Leo
Esso AG
Hamburg, Germany

Jerome Levinson
Senate Foreign Relations Committee
Washington, D.C.

Mr. Matthöfer
Bundesministerium f.
wirtschaftl. Zusamme-
narbeit
Bonn, Germany

Edwin M. Martin
Development Assistance Committee
Paris, France

Robert McCoy
Esso Europe, Inc.
New York, New York

George McIssac
McKinsey Company, Inc.
Düsseldorf, Germany

Hans-Joachim Mertens
University of Frankfurt
Frankfurt, Germany

P. W. Newton
TRW, Inc.
Washington, D.C.

D. L. T. Oppe
Kleinwort, Benson Limited
London, England

John R. Petty
Lehman Brothers
Washington, D.C.

Harald Rieger
Metallgesellschaft AG
Frankfurt, Germany

Roger Rosendahl
Curtis, Mallet, Prevost,
   Colt & Mosle
New York, New York

Helga Ruof-Koch
Institute for International
   and Foreign Trade Law
Georgetown University
   Law Center
Washington, D.C.

John J. Scoblick
Bendix International
New York, New York

Lot J. Seacat
European Finance Office
Rockwell Standard Company
London, England

Robert Neuman
Arent, Fox, Kintner, Plotkin & Kahn
Washington, D.C.

Alfred Northacker
Deutsche Kellog Industriebau GmbH
Düsseldorf, Germany

J. Ade Oyelabi
University of Ibadan
Ibadan, Nigeria

Raul Prebisch
Economic Commission for Latin
   America
Washington, D.C.

William D. Rogers
Arnold and Porter
Washington, D.C.

Seymour J. Rubin
Surrey, Karasik & Morse and Amer-
   ican University
Washington, D.C.

L. H. Sandberg
International Association for the
   Promotion and Protection of
   Private Investments in Foreign
   Territories
The Hague, Holland

Wilhelm Schulte zur Hausen
Mülheim-Ruhr, Germany

Piero Sella
International Bank for Reconstruc-
   tion and Development
Washington, D.C.

Philippe de Seynes
Undersecretary-General
  for Economic and
  Social Affairs
United Nations
New York, New York

Ibrahim F. I. Shihata
Kuwait Fund for Arab
  Economic Development
Kuwait

Ezekiel Solomon
Foreign Investment Board
Jakarta, Indonesia

Samuel Stern
Wilmer, Cutler &
  Pickering
London, England

Earle Teitler
Bechtel Corporation
London, England

Constantino Vaitzos
Junta del Acuerdo de
  Cartagena
Lima, Peru

Lord Wakehurst
Brown Harriman Interna-
  tional, Ltd.
London, England

Gisbert Wolff
European Economic Com-
  munities
Brussels, Belgium

Robert Shaffer
Bank of America
London, England

Anthony Solomon
Special Consultant to Chairman
  Wilbur Mills and the House of
  Representatives Ways and Means
  Committee
Washington, D.C.

Richard Steinig
Deutsche Bank
Düsseldorf, Germany

Mr. Stoermann
International Labor Organization
Geneva, Switzerland

Detlev Vagts
Harvard University Law School
Cambridge, Massachusetts

Don Wallace, Jr.
Institute for International and
  Foreign Trade Law
Georgetown University Law Center
Washington, D.C.

Kristian Watrin
University of Köln
Köln, Germany

To our regret, the following persons who had accepted
were unable to attend the conference:

Aron Broches
Vice President and General Counsel
International Bank for Reconstruction
  and Development
Washington, D.C.

Antonio Carillo Flores
Director
Fondo de Cultura Eco-
  nomica
Mexico City, Mexico

Enrique Iglesias
Executive Secretary
Economic Commission
  for Latin America
Santiago, Chile

Senator Jacob K. Javits
Washington, D.C.

Nicholas deB. Katzenbach
Director, Vice President and
  General Counsel
International Business Machines
  Corporation
Armonk, New York

Giuseppe Petrilli
President
Institute for Industrial
  Reconstruction
Rome, Italy

Judd Polk
Economist and Director of Program
  and Studies
Council of the International Chamber
  of Commerce
New York, New York

Germanico Salgado
Member of the Board
Andean Group
Lima, Peru

Walter Sedwitz
Executive Secretary for Economic
  and Social Affairs
Organization of American States
Washington, D.C.

1

THE DÜSSELDORF
CONFERENCE
Helga Ruof-Koch

The Conference on International Control of Investment was held in Düsseldorf, Germany, on January 5 and 6, 1973. It consisted of three panel sessions in which formally prepared papers and comments were presented, followed by a general discussion. The panel papers were distributed prior to the meeting and were only summarized by the speakers at the meeting itself. Commentators evaluated and criticized the papers. The panel sessions were recorded and edited from the transcripts.

Most of the papers are reproduced in this volume with some alterations by the respective authors and the editors. In many cases participants were kind enough to review and revise their comments and discussion at the panel sessions. In order to stay within our space limitations and present as tight a summary of the discussions as possible, we were forced to make substantial cuts in the panel presentations and to include only some comments from the floor.

The first section contains opening remarks made at the conference by Kurt Biedenkopf and a summary paper by Seymour Rubin, prepared at the conclusion of the conference. Biedenkopf points out the problems to be discussed and Rubin seeks to synthesize the ideas that emerged. These two papers, recommended as an initial overview of the conference, provide a general assessment of the ideas discussed in the course of the various sessions.

2

OPENING REMARKS
Kurt Biedenkopf

The Düsseldorf Conference on International Control of Investment is one of a sequence of conferences organized by the Frankfurt Institute for International and Foreign Trade Law and its Washington D.C. counterpart since the time of the initiation of the European Economic Community (EEC).

The first of these conferences, from which came two volumes of published papers in German, English, and French, was conducted in 1960 in Frankfurt. This conference directed its attention primarily to restraints on international trade. The focus of the meeting was not investment but contractual, behavioral, or structural restraints on international trade. This emphasis on restraints on trade was natural at a time when handicaps to international commercial traffic—the flow of goods and money—were still looked at primarily in the area of cartel agreements and less in the area of international enterprises. Although the multinational corporation was a well-known phenomenon in the early 1960s and late 1950s, it was not in the center of interest.

The next conference, in 1962, also directed its attention primarily to the trade problem, although it began to involve monetary matters. At that time the first disturbances in the international monetary picture became apparent and of interest also to the academic discussion.

As development proceeded in Europe and the United States, as well as in the developing countries, increasing attention was focused on the effects that multinational corporations and international investment were having on international trade, on the balance of payments, and on international monetary organizations. It became apparent that the nonacceptance or nonratification of the Havana Charter, which was part of the overall effort to organize international trade after World War II, was having repercussions. Although the General Agreement on Tariffs and Trade (GATT) was serving an important function in

4

keeping international markets open, it seemed more and more obvious that certain phenomena were not covered by GATT and that disturbances and imbalances were developing.

In the last several years the institutes, both in Frankfurt and Washington, have directed their energies increasingly toward the effects of international investment on international trade and commerce, and the problems resulting from the flow of money and capital between both the industrialized areas and industrialized nations of the northern hemisphere and between the industrialized and the less developed countries. The first part of the 1973 conference is concerned with investment control problems within the area of the developed countries on the one hand, and between industrialized and less industrialized nations on the other hand.

This is apparent in the splitting up of this subject into two panels. One panel is concerned primarily with the problems of investment control between developed countries. And it is no surprise that one of the major problems focused on in this first panel is the relationship between the United States and Europe. Special attention also is given to the effects of the European Economic Community in this area. The second panel is concerned with the relationship between the industrialized nations and the less developed nations, the countries that are receiving capital investments from industrialized nations.

In the third panel these problems of investment control are discussed in terms of the kinds of organizational arrangements, if any, that may be feasible. Is it at all feasible to organize control of international investment on an international level and, if so, how? Is it sufficient to develop rules of good behavior? Is it necessary to develop new international organizations? Are the existing international organizations sufficiently equipped to handle the problem? And how should it be handled?

The purpose of the conference is not to arrive at formal solutions to the problem, recommendations, or positions, but rather to promote an exchange of ideas that, hopefully, will add to preparation for the forthcoming meetings and conferences, both within governmental agencies and international agencies and with other vehicles of communication, that will direct themselves to these problems. We hope the conference will make a contribution to the preparation and handling of this problem in the future, rather than adding to the long list of demands, resolutions, and recommendations already on the table.

Let me come back briefly to the substantive matter of Panels I and II. For a European, a German in particular, there seem to be several aspects to the problem. On looking at the problem of the multinational corporation as one aspect of international investment, I find that we are interested in the problem both in relation to the

balance of payments question—or international monetary problems—
and in relation to the question of international control. By international
control I do not mean control over investment by an international
agency but internationalization of control arising from investment in
production facilities.

In the early 1960s Jean-Jacques Servan-Schreiber was one of
the first to raise the issue in a rather provocative way. At that time
the danger of falling under foreign control through international investment was very much on the minds of many Europeans. The tremendous
inflow of U.S. investment capital into Europe was increasingly sus-
pected as carrying with it more than the benefits of investment. Many
Europeans held the belief that the American flag would follow the
American dollar, and thus considerable foreign influence by way of
investment in Europe would have to be feared. In some of the more
celebrated cases, European countries, France and others, were trying
to forestall international investment, primarily U.S. investment, in
what were considered sensitive industries, such as electronics.

We have since learned that investment of this sort, even though
still disproportionate, is not a one-way street, and that there are
many ways of integrating foreign investment into the national economy.
But we also have learned that national economies as such are becoming more and more dependent on other national economies, and thus
are becoming more and more integrated in the international economic
area.

We notice this when we try to battle inflation. We find that our
national resources to regulate the national industries, the national
economies, are limited. We find that by economic integration we are
inviting the necessity of political integration. Therefore we have also
hinted at the connections between economic integration, economic
organizations for control, and parallel political integration. In Europe
this is a subject very much on all of our minds but we are fully aware,
as we were while drafting the conference proposals, that we cannot
discuss here, with any hope of relevance, the possibility of political
integration on an international basis extending beyond the limits of
the EEC.

In the developing countries, unlike the developed or industrialized
nations, the investment of foreign capital does not mean that trade in
industrial products is substituted for investment in industrial production. But here investment takes place in a country that previously
was not a very important partner in the international trade of industrial
products, although it may have been an important partner in the
international trade of raw materials. In the developed countries one
could state as a general rule that to some extent the flow of investment has been substituted for the flow of trade. The developing countries are looking for international investment to stimulate their own

economies on the one hand while on the other hand they have very few possibilities other than governmental or national control to balance the influences of international investment in their countries. They are aware that they must import know-how, technology, and money in order to develop their own industries. However, they find that in importing know-how, technology, and money from industrialized nations they are importing at least the possibility or risk of foreign dependence and control.

How to balance these two needs, to remain independent of foreign economic influence while obtaining technology, know-how, and capital, is an interesting question that Panel II might consider. And in this respect we are very fortunate to have some well-known and important representatives of the less developed countries at this conference.

The third panel on international organization for investment does not assume that international organization is imperative for investment. The intent is to discuss the question of whether international organization beyond that already in existence is really necessary. In other words, we do not want to restrict the discussion to various forms of international organization but hope that it will challenge the need for international organizations for investment.

It is not that I am or am not in favor of international organizations. At this point I must admit that personally I have no definite view one way or the other. Whether a new international organization is needed or required I do not know, and I hope to draw some wisdom from the panel discussions.

For the purpose of the conference is not to end up by formulating some resolution but to state positions that have been taken and that may be used as a starting point for new and further discussions, research, and action, and to identify relevant issues in the area of international investment control. If we can arrive at a definition of these issues, state some of the more important official and unofficial, academic and nonacademic positions—if we can accomplish this, then I think the conference will have been worthwhile.

3

REPORT ON THE CONFERENCE
Seymour Rubin

The conference theme was an inquiry into the desirability and feasibility of some sort of international governmental body that would affect the multinational operations of the international corporations.

This very cumbersome statement of the theme results from the very clear organization and purposes of the conference. The conference assumed that all possibilities were open for discussion; that perhaps there should be no regulation of the multinational enterprise (MNE) beyond that currently existing, and perhaps even present national regulatory laws, like the antitrust laws of the United States, should be mitigated in their application across national boundaries; or perhaps, on the other hand, that there should be some sort of regulatory or information-gathering and distributing mechanism. On this side, again, a multitude of alternatives were open: an international organization limited to informational activities; one that would seek to establish rules, presumably for both the MNE and the host (and sometimes home) states—the GATT for investment idea; or institutions that would seek to assist in the progressive disinvestment of foreign private capital.

Thus the conference focused on the broad idea of international action as well as the more specific manifestations of that idea, and it was split into two basic sessions. The first day of the meeting was devoted to a discussion of the substantive issues facing the MNE, its home state, and the nation in which it carries out its activities. That session was carried on in two simultaneous panels, one dealing with relations with the developed nations, the other with the less developed nations. On the second day the chairmen of these two panels made brief reports and the conference met in plenary session to consider what, if anything, should be done in respect to international organization, in the light of these prior discussions. The writer chaired the plenary session.

Despite the careful preparation of a substantial number of papers reflecting the thoughts of a wide spectrum of experienced observers, the proceedings themselves deserve special attention. In the nature of things, papers are written in solitude, reflecting individual thoughts. They can of course reflect study and careful composition. But statements made in an animated exchange of views take on the extra dimension of reaction to points made by others. And since the discussion at Düsseldorf reflected a wide variance of points of departure, the discussion was highly thought-provoking.

Given these divergent points of departure, what was perhaps most surprising was the considerable unanimity of opinion as to result: that a GATT for investment, much less a disinvestment agency, would be neither feasible nor desirable at present. This apparent consensus, modified by lukewarm approval for better compilation and availability of information via either existing or new agencies, was greeted with some relief by some industry representatives. There is some doubt, at least in the mind of the present writer, whether this sentiment is wholly justified. Lack of support for an international agency on the part of representatives of less well developed nations does not, in my opinion, reflect for the MNE in those areas a future of benevolent approval, or even benign neglect. Rather, the less developed nations would seem to fear that the international agency would seek to restrain their actions in regard to the foreign-based MNEs. And this attitude neatly balances the worry of business that any international agency would fetter rather than free the MNE. The suggestions of the numerous studies and reports that have emanated from developed nations and their economists—the well-publicized Canadian views, both of the Watkins and the Gray reports, the disinvestment proposals of Albert Hirschman, and the sharing-of-production suggestions of Jack Behrman, not to mention the massive studies conducted under the supervision of Raymond Vernon—would seem to furnish some foundation for this concern on the part of the business community.

For widely disparate reasons, then, there was consensus at the Düsseldorf Conference against any major attempt at an international organization to oversee the MNE. This does not mean that no new effort or extension of existing activities will be made.

On the side of gathering and exchange of information—presumably a safe enough subject—there was wide agreement that more ought to be done. The most incisive advocacy of an effort to "give small nations the knowledge necessary to deal with large corporations" came from a Nigerian economist, J. A. Oyelabi. The suggestion for a better way of collecting and exchanging information was endorsed by Luis Escobar of the International Bank for Reconstruction and Development (IBRD). Several speakers, the present writer included, pointed to ambiguities in the concept. What kind of information? How would it be disseminated? And how utilized? A possible although unstated difference may exist: Some seemed to be discussing the attainment of information as to how to "deal with" MNEs while others were discussing the kind of statistical information compiled by the U.S. Department of Commerce. There is a wide gap between that kind of information and information relating to more effective negotiating ability by less developed countries.

The existence of such a gap in fundamental attitudes underlay the comments of many of the principal speakers. The UN undersecretary for economic and social Affairs, Philippe de Seynes, discussed the developments at the last UN General Assembly and the increased activities of the UN in this field, emphasizing the basically political nature of many of the problems. Detlev Vagts, analyzing possibilities for an international control agency, arrived at the conclusion of impracticability. So also, from another point of view, did the U.S. assistant secretary of state for economic affairs, Willis Armstrong, who expressed the belief that increased consultation (which might eventually lead to some institutional structure) would be far better than any present attempt to set up a new international organization.

On the substantive side, suggestions and comments varied. The work of the Organization for Economic Cooperation and Development was discussed by Raymond Bertrand of the OECD. Anthony Solomon, former assistant secretary of state, suggested that a principal problem was not that of transfer-pricing or similar parent-subsidiary issues but that of the possible lessening of competition through assignment of territories to subsidiaries, and similar devices. He suggested, within the OECD framework, a semi-independent group to screen takeover proposals and transborder mergers. Jack Behrman, former assistant secretary of commerce, saw the problem as deeper and proposed what many considered the most far-reaching of regulatory organizations, with the objective of saving the MNE and preserving its unique benefits. On the whole, although there were notable contributions, as for example from John Petty, former treasury assistant secretary, the relations of MNEs in the developed world seemed to evoke few worries and very little in the way of organizational proposals. Considering that the vast MNE literature owes much to the worries eloquently expressed by Jean-Jacques Servan-Schreiber in his Le Défi Américain, this may indicate how much the focus of concern has shifted. Perhaps the fact is that countries like France are considered well able to take care of themselves; the effort toward international controls, guarantees, exchange of information, and so forth seems pretty well limited at present to MNE operations in the developing nations.

In an extremely interesting and brilliantly analytical statement, Ambassador Edwin Martin, chairman of the Development Assistance

Committee of the OECD, examined both the substantive and procedural aspects of various regulatory or similar proposals. He thought one great problem in assigning significant power to any organization, existing or to be formed, would be the nature of that organization. The IBRD was suggested by some, although its representative indicated his feeling that this would not be appropriate. The IBRD, dominated by Anglo-American votes and officers, is a "rich man's club." Other organizations—the GATT general assembly, as presently constituted, for example, or certainly UNCTAD (the United Nations Conference on Trade and Development)—would be unacceptable for opposite reasons.

In conclusion it is the writer's personal opinion that some movement toward a new international organization, or toward increasing the powers and role of existing organizations, is likely. It does not seem possible to put together a new information-gathering and distributing agency (a proposition almost universally endorsed) without facing the question of what kind of information this shall be, and in this way coming to substantive conclusions. If, for example, information is gathered with respect to takeovers and transnational mergers, some inferences could well be drawn with respect to enforcement, across national frontiers as well as domestically, of antitrust and restraint of competition legislation. If information is directed toward MNE profits, a decision with wide implications will have to be made: Does one take the normal accounting standards in calculating such profits or does one accept, in whole or part, the argument forcefully made by the secretary of the Andean Commission—that profits must be recalculated to take into account the fact that they have been drastically lowered in the less developed countries by unfair transfer prices?

Movement toward cooperation via existing or new international organizations will thus be difficult, even where seemingly noncontroversial issues are concerned. It therefore would seem that drafters might better seek a forum than a present definition of rules or perhaps even of functions. As Willis Armstrong has pointed out, better consultation may result in some progress toward agreement. But consultation at present is on a hit-or-miss basis. It tends not only to be spotty but to take place in an atmosphere of crisis. There is no forum in which problems, even those of a regional nature, are systematically examined.

It would seem sensible now to establish such a forum, or perhaps such forums, without attempting to formulate GATT-like rules. Within such a forum, with a disinterested secretariat and a regular program of discussion, there might be generated not the heat that often characterizes these matters but a considerable amount of light.

It remains to remind the reader that all participants in the Düsseldorf Conference were there in their personal capacities and not as representatives of organizations.

4

INTERNATIONAL CONTROL
OF INVESTMENT
IN THE TRADE SECTOR
Anthony M. Solomon

Increasingly we hear the view that the General Agreement on Tariffs and Trade (GATT) presupposes a model of international trade that has been substantially altered by the multinational corporation—that a large and increasing percentage of trade now is intracompany trade and not trade between independent exporters and importers. We usually hear this view in the context of a remarkably long list of widely varying concerns and anxieties expressed about the spread of the multinational companies. I will first deal with what the actual data can tell us about the accuracy of this view and then attempt to identify what should be the key areas of concern about multinational company activity in the trade area, along with the feasibility of international controls in the key areas of concern.

The most complete data are in two U.S. Department of Commerce surveys: one is for 1965, covering 330 U.S. corporations and their 3,579 foreign affiliates, published in the Survey of Current Business, May 1969, by Marie Bradshaw; the other and more complete is for 1966, covering 1,750 U.S. parents and their 13,400 affiliates, published in installments, the last in April 1972.

We also have some preliminary 1966 and 1970 data from the U.S. Department of Commerce on the giant U.S. multinationals (298 corporations with 5,200 affiliates), where we may look for some clues to trend.

U.S. Exports, 1966 (billions of dollars)

a. Total U.S. exports	28.6	
a.1 of which nonagricultural	22.0	
b. Total U.S. exports by U.S. parents	17.8	(62% of a)
c. of which, to affiliates	6.4	(22% of a, 36% of b)
d. of which, for further use by affiliates (as distinct from for resale)	2.7	(10% of a, 12% of a.1, 15% of b, 42% of c)

U.S. Exports, 1966 (billions of dollars)

e. of which, capital equipment for use by affiliates	0.6	(9% of c)
f. of the $2.7 billion exported to affiliates for further use by them (d above):		
affiliates manufacturing transportation equipment (autos largely)	0.9	($33\frac{1}{3}$% of d)
affiliates manufacturing nonelectrical machinery	0.4	
affiliates in chemicals	0.3	

The 1966 data given above show:

1. U.S. direct investors account for almost two-thirds of total U.S. exports.

2. However, the bulk of their exports are not intracompany: 64 percent is to nonaffiliates, 36 percent to affiliates.

3. Moreover, of the exports that parents sell to their affiliates, almost 60 percent is for resale (or lease) without any processing by the affiliate; the affiliate is essentially a sales office for these exports.

4. Only $2.7 billion of U.S. exports consists of intracompany transactions of the kind about which questions have been raised: e.g., transfer price, non-arms-length transactions, and so forth. This is about 10 percent of total U.S. exports.

5. Sales by parents of capital equipment to their affiliates is surprisingly small ($0.6 billion).

6. Of the $2.7 billion for use by affiliates, one-third went to affiliates in the transportation equipment (largely automobile) industry, which confirms the general view of the heavily specialized component production nature of the multinational companies in this industry but also shows how little that pattern is followed in the rest of the industrial sector, taken as one group.

7. The geographical distribution of shipments for resale by affiliates is interesting and unexpected. Goods for resale by affiliates were higher in trade with the developed countries (60 percent of exports to European affiliates but only 30 percent of the exports to Latin American affiliates). This means that the category of products for further use, reflecting intracorporate specialized production exchange, was relatively much smaller in trade with other industrialized countries than with developing countries.

The Marie Bradshaw 1965 sample survey is quite consistent with the 1966 results. It also shows that relatively few firms and affiliates account for a very large part of U.S. exports while a very large number of such firms and foreign affiliates account for a relatively small part. Of $8.5 billion of exports by 320 parent firms surveyed in 1965 (firms that accounted for one-third of U.S. exports), only $1.7 billion was to their affiliates for further use. Furthermore, of this $1.7 billion, well over half was purchased by only 25 individual affiliates; 5 of these affiliates were Canadian auto firms and they purchased almost one third of the $1.7 billion. More than 90 percent of the 3,500 affiliates made no purchases in the United States of goods for further processing or assembly abroad.

U.S. Imports, 1966 (billions of dollars)

a.	Total U.S. imports	25.6	
b.	U.S. imports from affiliates	5.9	(23% of a)
c.	U.S. imports from affiliates (intracompany)	4.6	(18% of a)
d.	of which:		
	from transportation equipment affiliates	0.9	
	from mining and smelting affiliates	0.5	
	from petroleum affiliates	1.2	

Sales of Affiliates of U.S. Parents, 1966 (billions of dollars)

(a)	Total sales	97.6
(b)	of which, local sales	73.7
(c)	Sales to U.S.	5.9
(d)	of which, intracompany	4.6
(e)	Sales to third countries	18.1
(f)	of which, intracompany	9.5

The 13,400 foreign affiliates of U.S. parents sell about three-fourths of their output in the host country and export about one-fourth. Of the amount they exported—$24 billion in 1966—$14.1 was intracompany. Of the $14.1 billion of intracompany sales, $4.6 billion was to the parent in the United States and $9.5 billion was to affiliates in other countries. The data do not show what share of the $9.5 billion of intra-affiliate trade was for use by the importing affiliate or for resale.

What seems clear from all this data is that the proportion of world trade that was intracompany—between parents and affiliates, and among affiliates—and particularly the proportion that was in non-arms-length transactions, was modest in 1966, at least for U.S. multinational enterprises. It is not the case that a large percentage of trade now is intracompany trade and not trade between independent exporters and importers, unless current data are very different from 1966.

However, the preliminary information from the Commerce Department study on 1970 compared to 1966 for 298 giant U.S.

multinationals shows no trend; about the same 10 percent of all U.S.
exports were possible non-arms-length transactions, that is, sales
by U.S. parents to affiliates for further use. (The only apparent trend
is in the proportion of total U.S. parent exports to affiliates represented
by capital equipment—and here there is a reduction from about 10 to
5 percent.)

In 1966 world exports were about $181 billion. Of that $181 billion,
$6.4 billion of exports from the United States and $14.1 billion of exports from other countries—$20.5 billion or 11 percent—were intra-
company transactions of U.S. multinationals. However it seems clear
from the previous data that a very substantial proportion of the $20.5
billion of intracompany trade was sale between parent and affiliate,
or between affiliate and affiliate for direct resale. It is reasonable
to suppose that exports to affiliates for direct resale are arms-length
transactions. It is likely that something on the order of 5 percent of
world trade could fall in the category open to the charge of non-arms-
length transactions.

What the data do not reveal should be borne in mind. Market
sharing between parent and subsidiaries or among subsidiaries producing similar products does not show up as intracompany trade, and
therefore the data do not tell us how much more U.S. parents and
affiliates might possibly have exported or imported if they had traded
as independent entities rather than as members of a multinational
family.

Perhaps the chief importance of the data is a negative one—that
the justification for international control over the multinationals does
not rest at the present time on their domination of international trade
or the drastically changed character of international trade due to a
large volume of non-arms-length intracorporate transactions.

The chief impact of the rapid growth of the multinational companies on international trade is not that the comparative cost advantage
theory of international trade is admittedly somewhat less relevant in
this kind of world. We have seen that non-arms-length transactions
among multinational companies characterize only a small percentage
of international trade. Furthermore, so long as parents compete,
does it matter that much whether subsidiaries source competitively
or not? The spread of the multinational company is undoubtedly lessening competition, but the key areas of concern in regard to multinational companies and competition are not in non-arms-length sourcing
within the multinational family.

The impact of multinational companies on competition has received much attention and warrants more. Despite the fact that in
some specific cases the net effect may be to increase competition—
as Charles Kindleberger has pointed out—there is a sufficient basis,
both from general information and from specific cases, for the widely

expressed concern that multinational company growth is lessening competition internationally. It is this area that should bear our primary concern as to the distorting impact on international trade from the spread of the multinational companies.

The forms through which competition may be lessened as a result of the growth of the multinational companies are well-known.

1. Takeovers of existing firms made possible not only by the easier access to capital but also, and perhaps more important, by the higher price-earnings ratios at which the parent company stock is valued compared to that of the smaller company being acquired.

2. Allocation of noncompetitive marketing areas among subsidiaries.

3. Limitation on use of technology.

4. International pricing behavior, particularly in the oligopoly-characterized industries where multinational companies tend to thrive.

If it is granted that there is a case for some form of international surveillance in the trade area over the multinational companies, primarily with respect to possible lessening of competition, in what form is it feasible? I am skeptical that a comprehensive GATT, or even an effectively suasive code of behavior that would cover the catchall called "restrictive business practices" can be negotiated. The Organization for Economic Cooperation and Development (OECD) is conducting a useful exercise in that it promotes reflection and discussion among the governments of the developed countries, but we should take a second look at the attempt to develop a general agreement on restrictive business practice that, because it attempts to cover the entire area, will almost assuredly lack sufficient clarity as well as investigative and enforcement authority. Given the complexity of the problem and the extent of our ignorance on many restrictive business practices, as well as the varying laws and practices of nation-states, a more successful approach would be to begin by marking out a narrow but clearly defined and understandable problem area that would command sufficient public interest to which democratic governments can therefore constructively respond—despite the natural resistence of some who would see themselves as disadvantaged.

I suggest that this area be the transnational takeover activities of multinational companies when they result, or threaten to result, in the lessening of competition. There is a commonalty of interest among the developed countries, as well as some diplomatic considerations, that make the chance of developing an effective surveillance agreement on takeovers greater than might at first be thought. The English-speaking Dominions, Japan, and the member countries of the European Economic Community (EEC) have all expressed varying degrees of concern regarding the takeover of domestic firms by foreign investors, largely American. In many instances the concern is primarily foreign control of the economy, but to some extent concern may involve competitive factors. In any case it is very likely that public opinion and government circles in the other developed countries would support international surveillance of takeovers.

What is in it for the United States, however, considering the predominance of U.S. multinationals in the takeovers? The United States gives a general warm welcome to investors from other countries, but this does not extend to takeovers thought to reduce competition within the national economy. British Petroleum found this out when it bought out the filling station network of Standard Oil of Ohio.

A second factor is that there is growing recognition in the United States that in the absence of some accepted rules on takeover policies, unilateral national actions in this area—such as Australia's newly announced screening of takeovers—are likely to proliferate and not be confined to the criterion that the takeover would lessen competition.

A realistic goal in this area might be an agreement setting minimum standards that would bar takeovers that would clearly reduce international competition in a given product. Thus a merger of Michelin and Dunlop-Pirelli on tires would presumably be prohibited whereas a merger of, say, Peugot and Volvo might be allowed to provide more competition to General Motors and the other automotive giants. Since any international agreement on takeovers would undoubtedly set minimum rather than maximum principles for competition, an individual country would still be free to take a more restrictive view toward takeovers within its jurisdiction.

The most important consideration is not the language on the minimum standards but the mechanism the agreement would create. Perhaps the least difficult approach would be to create a semi-independent takeover screening body linked to the OECD where it would have close links with the restrictive business practices committee of the OECD. However, unlike other OECD committees, the member countries should be prepared to give to the international takeover screening body or agency adequate investigatory and enforcement powers.

How much is adequate? In the investigatory area, it should have the right to request full information from the parties concerned and to hold hearings on particular cases at the request of a signatory government, or at its own initiative. In the enforcement area, it should at a minimum have the right to recommend, publicly and to signatory countries, that the parties abstain or be prevented from concluding or making permanent the takeover.

The proposed body should consist of a panel of independent and professionally qualified individuals, rather than representatives of signatory governments. Throughout I have used the term "signatory governments" rather than "member governments" since it is likely

20

that quite a few of the developing country governments might express a desire to adhere to the international takeover screening agreement—and it would be highly desirable to permit their inclusion.

If this body were to perform well with a simple and easily definable mandate on takeovers that lessen competition, it would then be practicable to expand its functions from time to time as the development of international consensus and agreement in other areas made it feasible. A very likely second function would be the surveillance of international cartels (an old-fashioned term usually not heard in recent discussions about multinationals). Defining this mandate and the criteria would be more complex than the takeover mandate and therefore should probably not be tackled simultaneously with takeovers.

I would envisage additional functions in regard to some other restrictive business practices as these even more difficult international agreements were reached. There are of course many other kinds of restrictive business practices, but those that are probably most important in multinational company impact on international trade, and also those on which it would be most feasible to develop international consensus, have to do with territorial export prohibitions resting on control of patents and licenses to affiliates or third parties, or on direct marketing allocations among affiliates. Multinational companies can more easily make collusive territorial market-sharing arrangements than national companies can. When and if the restrictive business practices committee of the OECD is able to reach agreement on standards in this area, the responsibility for their enforcement might also pass on to the semi-independent body screening takeovers and surveilling international cartels.

Ultimately, and theoretically, it might be possible to tackle the most difficult area of restrictive business practices—ad hoc agreements between companies on oligopolistic markets. However, unlike the three kinds of restrictive business practices described above, the feasibility of this coming to pass is extremely low for reasons clearly to those familiar with the problems of oligopoly in large national markets such as the United States.

The character of the international agreements that may be reached on transnational takeover surveillance, international cartels, and other restrictive business practices such as territorial export prohibitions would necessarily be general in language on standards of permissible behavior, with the emphasis on the mechanism and its working on a case-by-case procedure.

An additional trade-distorting factor worth commenting on arises not from multinational companies' activity but from their superior ability to take advantage of competition among developed country governments in subsidizing investment—usually but not always in depressed areas. Western European countries generally, Canada, and a number of state governments in the United States follow a wide range of incentive policies that in some cases—frequently involving a multi-national company—reach absurd extremes. The excessive subsidization for aluminum smelters that locate in Great Britain and Germany is a case in point. A large part of the net economic benefit can be lost to the host country, and where the excessive subsidization diverts investment from the developing countries it is particularly ironic and unfortunate that the greater wealth of the rich countries should be used in this manner.

In this area we probably need not only a mechanism—that is, a forum for complaints, inquiry, and public recommendation—but an agreed upon set of reasonable limits on competitive subsidization. The member governments of the OECD should give this a high priority. Its enforcement might also be best handled by the kind of semi-independent body proposed first for screening takeovers and then for the additional functions mentioned.

Perhaps I should explicitly comment on the reasons for omitting here two problem areas frequently mentioned: the extraterritorial issue arising from various U.S. trading-with-the-enemy controls and the transfer price problem. An international agreement on the extra-territorial trade controls issue is probably feasible but should prove unnecessary within the next few years—and the attempts to negotiate an international agreement might actually delay the evolution of U.S. policy along sensible lines. The second problem, transfer pricing abuses, does not fall primarily in the trade area—this problem is significant enough in some industries to justify international action but is best handled by tax collection authorities with a set of investigative procedures and follow-up actions different from those appropriate to the trade area. Finally, I have omitted the GATT in Geneva as the forum or mechanism for handling the key concerns in international trade related to the spread of multinational companies because of the antitrust nature of these key concerns. Certainly a GATT to enforce intracorporate arms-length transactions (which conceivably would be more relevant to Geneva) is neither desirable nor feasible.

A final comment on the perspective of what might be gained by international action. Even if a reasonably effective international mechanism can be put in place to deal with the problem of market domination or the lessening of competition by the multinational companies through takeovers, cartels, and export prohibitions, we have lost the battle (not that it was ever waged internationally) against giant company size. In the U.S. national economy it was waged and lost at the turn of the century. International trade economists have never been as concerned with the problem of market domination as with the international free movement of capital and technology for integrating the world economy and narrowing (more effectively than trade) the differences in factor prices. In terms of economic growth, they have almost certainly been right.

The most that can be hoped for from a GATT mechanism on international investment as far as trade is concerned is that some of the worst distortions of trade patterns and resource allocations can be curbed or prevented—that earlier competition by new entrants into the product cycle Raymond Vernon has described as typical of much multinational company activity will be more feasible—and that there will be a significantly larger number of oligopolistic multinational companies than otherwise. These would be considerable achievements.

$$* \quad * \quad * \quad * \quad *$$

COMMENT
Willis C. Armstrong

As is sometimes said in Washington, let me make one thing perfectly clear, and that is that I am not speaking for the U.S. government. My comments are entirely personal, which I believe is in the spirit of this conference. My observations will seek to stimulate thought and reaction. It is suggested that multinational corporations have substantially altered trade patterns and have rendered the GATT outmoded, thereby transferring the center of the stage to the question of investment, which leads one to suggest that there ought to be some form of GATT for investment.

I have very considerable doubt as to the validity of this proposition. As Anthony Solomon has indicated, the bulk of international trade is arm's length and between nonaffiliated units. This has continued, so far as the data indicate, during a period of enormous expansion in world trade. The great expansion in world trade that has occurred in our own generation has also been accompanied by enormous expansion in capital flows and organizational activities by multinational corporations. The net result is a very substantial increase in levels of living, particularly in the developed countries. Whether it is the world trade expansion that stimulated the multinational corporations or vice versa, or what causal relationship there may be between these two, one obviously cannot establish.

The composition of international trade has of course altered as technology has changed and developed. International trade has become more sophisticated in that more things move across national boundaries at different stages of processing. The final product frequently involves raw materials from a great many places and processing in a great many other places, and the final product therefore has a great variety of national components.

This has frightened some in the AFL-CIO in the United States. When you say exports are important in terms of American employment, it seems a fair proposition and a fairly simple one, but I find that persons in the AFL-CIO are increasingly saying, "How do we know that what we are exporting are American goods anymore? They are probably made in Japan or Taiwan or some other place, because the multinational corporation does this variety of sourcing and they don't make anything here anymore." This sort of allegation is quite familiar.

But at any rate, world trade has become increasingly sophisticated because of technology and variations in costs and because it is possible for multinational corporations to organize it this way. This leads me to the next rather obvious observation that the multinational corporation is a highly flexible and useful instrument that can cope with economic and technical change a great deal better than a government can. After a government, the most rigid kind of institution tends to be the international organization, which is less able to deal with change than government, itself less able to deal with change than the multinational corporation.

In recent years governments have tended to become more control-minded, which is understandable because they are under pressure from constituents who want certain things that are not necessarily economically identifiable and usually cost money or require some kind of government activity.

For example, in the United States the AFL-CIO is staunchly supporting the Burke-Hartke Bill which would limit investment, limit trade, limit economic growth and probably everything else you could think of. The reason is that the AFL-CIO does not see any other answer to the kind of problem which expresses itself to them in a rate of change faster than they can stand. This is a natural social reaction all around the world. If a rate of change at first adversely affects some individuals, they at once do not like that faster rate of change. Therefore, appeals to their government to impede change are made, and governments respond to what people in their constituencies say.

Furthermore, in the past, in an era of less affluence, capital was a very scarce commodity and payrolls were smaller and less numerous and any business looked pretty good. Therefore, there was more reluctance to impose controls over capital or over entrepreneurs. Now capital markets are bigger; capital is still scarce but there is a lot more of it and people feel that it can be, shall we say, pushed around a little more.

Offhand, one might entertain the proposition that rather than multinational corporations having affected the patterns of trade to the point where the efficacy of GATT is under question, governments have done far more in this direction under pressure from their constituents, as have groups of governments organized together in such institutions as the European Economic Community. Potentially the interest in modifying the terms of trade and business, and therefore having a distorting effect that was not anticipated in GATT, is most likely to come from governments, and probably more likely to come from governments than from multinational corporations. The multinational corporations being really quite genuinely economic creatures, and governments not being such, the multinational corporations tend to figure out ways to frustrate governmental or intergovernmental plans by asserting the primacy of economic principles that tend to laugh at locksmiths.

I would venture the thought that there is more consistency between the principles of GATT in trade and the actions of the multinational corporations than there is between the principles of GATT and the actions and intentions of governments or international organizations or groups of governments.

I therefore come to the conclusion that the proposal for a GATT for investment is a reflection of the failure of governments and groups of governments to succeed in controlling trade as fully as they would like to along national or community lines. This expresses a wish to get beyond trade into the enterprise itself, which is itself performing more or less in accordance with GATT principles.

I take a good deal of comfort from Anthony Solomon's recommendations. I think that what we really should do in considering what might be done about multinational corporations is to encourage the principle of competition, as he suggested. Those who suggest a system for control of investment probably do not have this in mind, but I do think this is worth emphasizing because it is consistent with the principles of GATT. If we emphasize competition, we are giving effect to the GATT ideas.

Finally, with respect to any possible negotiation of a control system, an organization or guidelines, let me say that when I was with the International Chamber of Commerce I had a certain amount of experience with a proposed code for investment. It contained some very fine language. It also had the defect or difficulty inherent in teaching the Ten Commandments: They do give people ideas.

I do believe in consultation, and increasing consultation between governments to see if they can develop a common view on some of these matters. The OECD is a good forum for this purpose of consultation. I think that consultation on substantive problems is far better than an effort to do a lot of detailed drafting because after a while the general public loses interest in the detailed drafting, but the general public does live with the consequences of actual happenings.

* * * * *

COMMENT
John Evans

I found a good deal of comfort in the wisdom of our first observer, appropriately named Solomon—his wisdom in refusing to be lured down roads that are almost certain to turn out to be dead ends. Dead ends, either because the problem to be solved has not yet taken on shape and substance or even because it is not possible to say with certainty that there is a problem. I admired his good sense in avoiding the trap of trying to conjure up a problem to fit some existing or imaginary organization.

He was also on the right track when he narrowed the field to what, is, at least potentially, a real danger—that multinationals may interfere unduly with the free play of competition. But on this point I suggest that he may have narrowed the field too much, and in doing so may have reduced the chance that his proposed solution would obtain international acceptance. That may sound paradoxical, but I will explain what I mean a bit later.

First let me address myself to the question posed in the program for this conference. Its implications, I think, are not quite those that have been assumed in some previous remarks. It is true that GATT, as drafted, presupposed a model of international trade that is being substantially altered by the multinational corporation. But this does not necessarily mean that the activities of multinationals must frustrate the purpose of the GATT. It is true that GATT was based on the expectation that economic motivations, if permitted sufficiently free play, would work out in a particular way and that, because of the multinationals, the reality that is emerging is somewhat different. It is therefore easy to conclude that GATT has been rendered an inadequate instrument for the accomplishment of the objectives for which it was set up.

I do not think that conclusion is justified by the facts we now have. The basic objective of the GATT—the underlying assumption on which it was based—was that, left to themselves, private enterprises, in competition, would bring about a more effective and economic utilization of world resources than is possible if governments interfere with the role of the market place. Consistent with that supposition, the GATT does not require that governments supervise or monitor the activities of private enterprise. The one apparent exception is not an exception in fact. It is true that the GATT contains provisions concerning dumping. This is relevant to our subject because the detection of dumping is made difficult when international transactions are not conducted at arms length, and this situation is increasingly likely to occur with the growth of multinationals. But this does not increase the likelihood of violations of the GATT. Dumping is not prohibited; the agreement simply provides the importing country with a remedy against the practice, namely, the imposition of a countervailing duty.

There are, however, two ways in which, at least in theory, the expansion of multinational enterprises could have a decisive impact on the GATT, even though they do not violate its substantive rules. One, which appears highly unrealistic, is the possibility that, as a result of the proliferation of the multinational organization of private enterprise, factors of production would obtain such perfect international mobility that freedom of movement of goods would become relatively unimportant. The direct effect of such a development would be to reinforce the GATT objective of optimum allocation of resources. But if you can imagine this taking place, you can conceive of the corporations taking over the role that governments have played efficiently throughout the ages—that of interfering with the free flow of trade. Then the GATT, which was created to regulate the acts of governments, would be relegated to the position of a policeman who hands out tickets for parking violations while the robbers are holding up the bank down the street.

I think that approach tremendously underestimates the continued ability of governments and combinations of governments to interfere with competition and trade. Even if factor mobility were to become much more perfect than it is, it would still be necessary to find some means of restricting the full freedom of action of governments to frustrate international trade in goods.

The other theoretical possibility—and this one is a bit more realistic—is that the multinationals can frustrate the GATT objective of improved allocation of resources by engaging in price-fixing agreements, market allocation, and other restrictive business practices. Thus, there is the possibility that the beneficial influence of multinationals in improving the allocation of resources could be nullified by their exercise of excessive power over the marketplace. This brings me back to Anthony Solomon's suggestion for the establishment of an international agency to screen takeovers, for the purpose of preventing an undue concentration of market power. My difficulty is that it would attack only a part—and, I suspect, a relatively small part—of the problem of restrictive business practices. And, paradoxically, it might be more difficult to create an agency with such limited objectives than one to deal with the whole problem of restrictive practices. Most sovereign governments today have the power to prevent or regulate takeovers in their territories. They may find it economically disadvantageous to do so, but they have the sovereign power. If the OECD countries were to propose a takeover screening agency, the prospective host governments would be pretty suspicious of their motives; they would assume that the OECD governments were acting on behalf of the enterprises based in their own jurisdictions. There could be similar suspicions even as between OECD countries. If the United States were to suggest an international agency to screen the takeover bids of U.S.-based companies in Canada, wouldn't the Canadian government decide in favor of doing its own screening? If, on the other hand, we were to broaden the terms of reference of the proposed agency to cover restrictive business practices in general, most governments would see the possibility of controlling predatory practices over which they do not now have jurisdiction, acting alone. They might now be willing to give such a proposal more favorable consideration than they did at the time the charter of the International Trade Organization was drafted.

Any agreement to establish such an organization would certainly have to provide it with sounder teeth than did the restrictive business practices chapter of the Havana charter. That instrument, after setting out elaborately all the collusive business practices to be deplored and creating a mechanism for bringing specific cases to the attention of the organization, then empowered the International Trade Organization to make recommendations to the members, who were required to give those recommendations their most serious consideration.

Well, those provisions, if they had been implemented, would not have eradicated restrictive business practices. But it is possible that the alarm that has now been created by the growth of the multinationals may have produced a greater sense of urgency than existed in 1948. If so, it might now be possible to fill this gap, with which the GATT does not deal at all.

If that were to be the case, I would suggest that such an organization have universal or potentially universal membership. It might be appropriate to use the GATT. Or it might be appropriate to set up a separate organization for the purpose. But because of the very close relationship between these objectives and those of the GATT, I think the first try should be made in Geneva.

*   *   *   *   *

COMMENT
Philippe de Seynes

I want to address myself to the question raised by Anthony Solomon of control or surveillance of takeovers or other restrictive business practices. I think one can do that in the context of the remark made by Kurt Biedenkopf that we should try to be a little more positive and see in what way the activities of international corporations can be inserted in a more general scheme of cooperation. I think in a real sense the existence of a degree of surveillance would serve this positive approach in that it would help in meeting the populist feelings against multinational corporations that are so vivid around the world, even before such surveillance is effective in a functional sense.

I think this might be to some extent a process similar to the one that took place at the turn of the century in the United States when the corporations started to go national and the fear of their bigness led to antitrust legislation, which had a psychological effect before having its real functional effect. I think this is valid for the international field as well.

I would also challenge Mr. Solomon when he restricts the surveillance function to the takeover bids and I would just like to add one argument. I think if that was the case this might very well lead to an increase in the other forms of restrictive business practices because there evidently is more than one option open to international corporations and they use a lot of inventiveness to find the best means to achieve their ends. I doubt that it would be wise to have separate compartments. I also doubt whether the criterion of lessening competition is going to be the most easily accepted. This is difficult to judge. I just do not know the answer myself. It is possible that a more elaborate notion of the harmful effects of collusion, or of bigness, might provide a criterion that would be more easily acceptable. I was glad that John Evans referred to the Havana charter. I had been under the impression that this Chapter Five had been completely forgotten, but after all, as far back as 1947 it was felt necessary to establish some degree of antitrust surveillance and one could hardly say that the Havana charter was a futuristic document; so the long silence over this is, to me, a strange phenomenon of the international world.

Perhaps it is not well known that on the basis of Chapter Five of the Havana charter, the United Nations did draft a convention in 1951 and 1952, and the text of this convention exists. It is there in full even though it has gathered dust in the archives; it was shelved because of political changes in an important country at the time when its drafting had been completed. It is interesting in that it provided for a procedure of compulsory consultation between the parties concerned, and investigation in an international body. It did not visualize any enforcement measures, only recommendations, but it still had the sanction of publicity for its findings, which perhaps at an early stage, at least, is the most that can be hoped for and is not entirely negligible.

Finally, I would very much support John Evans' observations in terms of arriving at those institutional arrangements on as wide a basis as possible. I have very grave doubts about international agreements that are supposed to be widely applicable but are arrived at in a restricted circle of countries, and I am still talking personally rather than in my official capacity when I say this.

29

5

INTERNATIONAL CONTROL
OF INVESTMENT IN
THE MONETARY SECTOR

John R. Petty

Controls on investment are characteristic of the post-World War II period. National restrictions have existed in various forms in most developed countries since the commencement of reconstruction. Indeed, they were condoned if not codified in the Bretton Woods system. They will remain with us in the future although their details will be altered from time to time in response to changes in the economic environment and to the capital needs of corporations and countries. The Eurodollar system is a byproduct of controls and regulations in other markets, and their continuation assures its continuation.

Investment is comprised of many forms of capital flows: direct investment, portfolio investment, medium- and long-term borrowings, short-term investment, export financing, and development assistance. I will direct my attention to the privately sponsored first four, although it should be borne in mind that officially financed investments are very important. As development finance becomes more and more related to industrial projects, the value of categorizing it separately will diminish. However, for the present and for my purposes here, private capital flows to the less developed countries are not a basic issue with regard to investment controls. Export financing is a category of official capital flows that is also free of controls, even though the amounts involved may be large and these flows may work directly counter to other aspects of a government's domestic economic policy. For example, surplus developed countries—especially their official agencies—buy major capital equipment on low-interest, long-term loans at the same time their treasuries are fighting off revaluation pressures.

Other official flows also have been counterproductive. A couple of years ago central banks switched their short-term investments from New York to London in order to maximize their earnings—a not uncommon but inadequately recognized central bank motive. This additional money brought to London was borrowed by large European companies that then bought their local currency, raising the foreign exchange reserves of the central banks. These dollars were again placed in London, and the cycle was repeated. The practice was stopped, but only after a foreseeable major capital influx into Germany that lead to the Deutschmark transitional float of 1971. I use this illustration to argue that official and private investment flows are closely related. Capital controls, intended to facilitate balance of payments adjustment or to insulate the domestic economy, concentrate their restrictive efforts on the private sector while large and contrary official flows frequently move unrestricted. Controls on the private sector may be only good political cosmetics, but there remains a strong case for increased international cooperation to coordinate official capital flows to have a consistent overall policy.

Another arbitrary distinction taken for granted when dealing with controls is the view that investment capital flows are distinct and distinguishable from trade and other current account payments. Theoretical differences over whether this distinction can be made underlie differences that will emerge in monetary negotiations between those who look upon capital controls as a natural and even desirable aspect of a viable balance of payments adjustment mechanism and those who would characterize as unsatisfactory a system that requires the use of capital controls for its viability.

In understanding the monetary reform negotiations now under way, one should keep in mind this basic difference which lies back of many attitudes. However, this basic difference in approach which causes some to segregate capital flows from other payments will be clouded behind another and primarily political consideration: the United States is concerned that in pursuing its objectives with respect to removing now old, no longer useful controls, it might be misread by others. Some negotiating partners would say this is premature and the controls should not be undone until the work of the Committee of 20 is over and ratified or until the United States is in equilibrium. No one believes that U.S. direct investment controls mean a great deal any more. They are a symbol of self-restraint, but the volume of foreign investment has not been noticeably affected. Of course the manner in which this investment was financed has altered, as was intended. I suppose that since most developed countries control private investment outflows to some extent, it is easier—in domestic political terms—if they can point to the major deficit country as imposing similar restrictions. This is cosmetics maintained for reasons of political imagery.

THE EURODOLLAR SYSTEM TODAY AND
TOMORROW

The Eurodollar system has become the marketplace through which foreign currency holdings of various countries are banked. These foreign currency deposits (foreign to a particular domestic economy) and their lending were not subject to the same degree of restraint placed upon domestic deposits. It was only natural that these funds were fed into the Eurodollar system. Regulations distinguished them from domestic deposits; relative freedom from regulations permitted them to be employed via London.

Regulations over domestic deposits had two origins: (1) to serve balance of payments objectives by restraining the purchase of foreign currency by residents and (2) to help control domestic credit expansion and channel resources in given directions. Considerations of this type will continue. Therefore, in considering international investment controls, I shall assume that most financial authorities consider direct controls on credit and capital flows to be necessary weapons in the arsenal available to manage the domestic economy of the various industrialized nations. There are ample examples of those who have resorted to these weapons.

Yet regulations on domestic deposits have not been sufficient. Leaving aside the likelihood that this "insufficiency" might be traced to other causes, it became clear that the large European companies that qualified as borrowers had an advantage over small companies in obtaining financing abroad. It is also clear that the local currency proceeds of the foreign borrowings tended to upset the money supply pattern intended by the central bank. For the most part the developed countries have a very limited capacity to engage in open market operations to counter unintended movements in their money supply. In a sense an underdeveloped capital market offered few alternatives (given the exchange rate assumptions) to extending controls to foreign currency transactions. The objective of a reasonably independent monetary policy forced the classic choice of extending controls or looking for a new exchange rate. Only Canada elected the second course.

Will controls on foreign currency capital transactions of industrialized nations be a characteristic of the new monetary system? The answer is yes, and the issue will probably be resolved in the context of the degree of exchange rate flexibility involved in the new monetary arrangements. A country may accept wider bands if it has the security of controls ready at hand. Of course others would argue that relatively rigid rates and independence in monetary policy must have available the crutch of controls. Both arguments will be heard.

It seems likely that greater flexibility will be achieved in the new exchange rate regime only by permitting industrialized countries to have their controls at the ready. However, employment of the controls should require some presumptive rules. That is, by qualifying under agreed international rules, a country would be eligible to employ capital controls for balance of payments reasons. The rules would not permit the controls to be in effect indefinitely; rather, they would provide for a phasing out. And of course there will be debate on such questions as whether capital controls should be employed while contrary or no measures are taken in the trade area. If we are to have a monetary system with somewhat more exchange rate flexibility than provided for in the past, it is logical that balance of payments controls be used sparingly and for a limited duration. It is true that the complexities of managing modern economies are such that officials are not prepared to forswear the use of controls on the international transactions of their residents. They have been used as a balance of payments protection device in the past, and they will be used again. This need not be inconsistent with introducing somewhat more flexibility into the exchange rate system. In fact, these controls are probably necessary to achieve a political willingness to accept more flexibility.

There are several nonfinancial reasons to expect this. A not unimportant reason is the ability these controls (even only in the "ready" position) give the government to influence various sectors of the economy. This is viewed as a substantial benefit to officials who believe the state should play an active role in guiding the allocation of resources. Some officials feel influencing the locale of foreign direct investment is a particularly useful benefit. Politically, there is no domestic cost in playing this role with the foreign investor, and frequently there is considerable political benefit.

Finally, there is an important political reason for me to forecast that investment controls will linger. This concerns the continued trend toward political unity in the European Economic Community (EEC). Monetary union now carries the full momentum of the unity movement. The technical complications of achieving substantial progress in the financial area will have to be assisted through a reinforcing control network. Moreover, if such controls accelerate achievement of the objective, then in the long run we may have arrived at a situation where these investment controls will go off sooner and stay off longer than if they were abandoned in the short run.

U.S. INVESTMENT CONTROLS

Another interesting aspect of the question of investment controls is whether the United States should be included among the developed countries that should now employ investment controls.

U.S. investment controls commenced in 1963 with the interest equalization tax (IET). There are three noteworthy elements of the approach the United States took in the IET: (1) by employing the tax mechanism through a statute, no governmental bureaucratic review of individual transactions was intended or desired; (2) the technique was basically market-oriented in that a price was announced in advance for those who wished to pay it; and (3) short-term capital flows were not covered by the tax.

In 1965 the controls were extended to bank loans, and direct investment was limited through voluntary restraints. These programs were tightened progressively until 1969; there have been modest liberalizations since then.

Public borrowings in the United States by developed countries came to a halt under the IET, except for exempted Canadian borrowings which rose substantially. Direct investment restraints had the intended effect of influencing the method by which the investment was financed, but the gross volume of plant and equipment expenditures abroad continued to increase after February 1965.

What was happening in the other developed countries?

The pattern was mixed. Up until late 1967 restrictions were being eased on both domestic and foreign currency transactions. Dating from the November 1967 sterling devaluation, capital controls began to increase. Measures to guard against the exodus of domestic capital were reimposed, followed by restrictions imposed through the banking systems to insulate the effect on the domestic economy of transactions undertaken in foreign currencies. Basically, mechanisms that administered prior day exchange controls were reemployed.

At present, investment controls are used to help insulate the economy from external influences on the domestic money supply caused by investment transactions in foreign currencies. They are also used in some cases to prevent a flight of domestic capital. The important characteristics to keep in mind are that the patterns vary from country to country and from time to time. At one time the main burden of the controls is to prevent a capital outflow. At another time they are concerned with moderating capital inflows. Japan throughout has remained highly selective in the administration of its comprehensive control network.

During this period, of course, the United States did not limit investment flows to Canada or to the less developed countries (LDCs). These exclusions remove over one-third of the controlled long-term flows from regulation.

The most pronounced effect of U.S. investment controls has been upon the Eurodollar market. Causing sophisticated prime U.S. borrowers to turn to the Eurodollar market created a demand for credit in London at rates advantageous to the lenders. Comparable

risks in New York got lower yields. This demand created by investment control put the financial community to work. Borrowing opportunities were brought home to U.S. corporations. New depositors
were educated to the wonders of The City. Growing supplies of Middle
East money, burgeoning reserves of central banks, including very
substantial deposits of LDC central banks, fueled the expansion of a
broad marketplace for which foreign currency deposits of various
countries could be employed advantageously.

Incidentally, the growth of the Eurodollar market for the six to
seven years prior to 1963 must be attributed to the structural limitations and regulations of the U.S. banking system. With currency
convertibility expanding trade and investment, there was bound to be
a more productive use of foreign dollar holdings than that which New
York offered, e.g., a time deposit controlled by Regulation Q and a
bankers' acceptance rate always a clear margin below the prime
lending rate. Indeed, the rate implications of the fundamental structural differences between the U.S. banking system and that of others—
for example, overdrafts versus loans and compensating balances—
assure a rate differential that will attract the foreign currency holder
to London.

The U.S. investment controls were part of a combination of
measures that permitted the United States to postpone until August 15,
1971, the type of adjustment the postwar economic order had come to
require. Earlier the world financial community had not been any
more ready than the United States to accept all the ramifications of
an adjustment of the dollar in the monetary system. One of the benefits of this succession of events is that the Eurodollar market developed more rapidly and became more broadly based than evolutionary
forces alone would have permitted. Its growth has educated bankers,
borrowers, and depositors alike to the advantages that can be obtained
through having access to this market. These advantages are also
clear to industrialized countries. For one thing, this development
permits their multinational corporations to benefit from the Eurodollar
market. The country itself—through its various agencies or through
its banking system—benefits from having access to these monies,
and the Eurodollar market is an important income source providing
yields higher than could be obtained for various currencies if funds
were deposited directly in the country of issue.

While the international capital market has been consolidated
this past decade, the rationale behind the U.S. controls disappeared.
They were designed to buy the time necessary to improve the U.S.
comparative advantage and avoid a dollar devaluation. The controls
helped delay matters, and this was an important contribution.

TRANSITIONAL INVESTMENT CONTROLS

These thoughts lead to some interesting conclusions:
* Regardless of the presence or absence of U.S. controls, Euro-dollar funds will always be at the command of creditworthy international companies in sufficient volume to cause other industrial countries to want to be able to occasionally exercise restraints on inflows during at least the medium-term period ahead. While I am sympathetic with the view that exchange rate flexibility is an alternative to the use of controls to suppress capital movements, I recognize that this is not a practical approach today, not least because non-economic objectives influence governmental behavior. Therefore, I imagine that controls will be complementary to exchange rate flexibility in the years immediately ahead.
* The Eurodollar system is not a function of the U.S. balance of payments deficit as Professor Fritz Machlup ably demonstrates. Moreover, there is a case for arguing that without U.S. investment controls, the growth of the Eurodollar market may even be retarded.
* The objectives of the industrialized nations with respect to investment flows are so varied and so varying that no design of U.S. controls could possibly be responsive to the varied and changing needs of others. Moreover, effective U.S. investment controls would ignore the inducements offered by industrial countries to attract investment into selected areas of their economies.

Today, seven to nine years after their introduction, the U.S. controls have doubtful value. They create distortions in the marketplace. They cover only a segment of U.S. flows. And, judging from the industrial countries to which U.S. capital flows, I suspect that import credits create greater capital inflows to some industrialized countries than do direct investments. Analysis may show that import credits and direct investments attracted by various national subsidies constitute the majority of long-term inflows that many countries experience with nonresidents. Thus, U.S. controls have no influence over what are probably the most significant movements of capital affecting the economy of other developed countries.

This leads to the conclusion that if certain industrialized nations find that their own domestic economic objectives are best served for the time being through controls, those controls should be their own. Only in this manner may the many varying purposes of controls be served.

The investment control atmosphere we will see in the years immediately ahead is probably a series of national controls, coordinated to the extent possible. U.S. cooperation and coordination in financial and monetary areas must continue and be intensified, but this is in no way dependent upon the United States employing a similar set of controls. Indeed, I believe the purposes of others would be best served if the United States did not continue its regulations.

The political aspect of U.S. controls is more important than the economic aspect. The initial "benefits," as measured statistically, cannot be repeated each year. I have already argued that the philosophical attitude of the United States toward controls should prevent it from accepting a monetary system that expects it to employ investment controls. I would expect, however, that some other industrial countries may get a sense of security if they have controls in being or in reserve. This may permit them to accept a system with more flexibility than they would otherwise tolerate. In these terms a monetary agreement that transitionally permits the use of investment controls under agreed conditions is an adequate tradeoff if a significantly greater degree of exchange rate flexibility is thereby obtained.

Perhaps transitional controls would do something more in the context of the EEC as well. Controls, national but closely coordinated, will be necessary to keep the exchange rate within the limits of a wider band, a major preliminary to monetary union. Given the political directions, speeding along this process is very much in the U.S. financial interests. This is true because the preoccupation the EEC has with advancing rapidly toward monetary union causes its members to appraise events primarily in terms of how they will serve themselves and the cause of monetary union. The best chance we have of getting the EEC to expand its frame of reference to the world system is to make notable progress toward EEC monetary union. With respect to investment controls, I imagine the EEC members will judge that their national investment controls are necessary for at least the transition period.

It will be a job to coordinate the regulations of the EEC members. The full range of techniques and objectives in managing capital exists among these nations. Commencing with consultations on common economic policies is only the first step on a long staircase of issues of ascending difficulty. As national circumstances differ, so will the controls differ. As situations become more uniform, the opportunity will emerge to employ, external to the EEC, reasonably similar investment controls. Dealings in the Eurodollar market will of course be regulated as foreign currency transactions.

Frankly, I view the problems of designing and then achieving common EEC attitudes and practices toward the host of issues involved as problems of unbelievable difficulty and complexity. Direct tax harmonization, for example, is involved. So is the common agricultural policy. Consequently, money managers and their counsel should anticipate more or less related investment controls in Europe for a considerable period ahead.

CHARACTERISTICS OF TRANSITIONAL CONTROLS

Increased international investment controls among developed countries will still be basically national programs. Progressively, these programs will be conformed in the EC. Japan will continue to have its autonomous controls.

- It is doubtful that direct investment will be singled out as an investment to be controlled any more than it has in the past. That is, it will continue to receive political criticism in general and economic stimulants in particular. Screening and approval of new investments will certainly continue. If I were an optimist, I would say wholesale criticisms of "takeovers" will give way to a more balanced consideration of the pros and cons. In its search to find things to agree about, it is not unlikely that the EEC could develop a common position in one area: acquisition of EEC companies by non-EEC companies. This could increase the difficulty of consummating a takeover. Official authorities look upon takeovers as adding nothing to a nation's economy and characteristic of a trend toward bigness and ugliness. Discussions in official circles simply do not recognize that a "raid" is rare and the seller usually wants out, that benefits may also exist, or that there are not infrequent occasions when vitality is being introduced into an otherwise lost or moribund enterprise.

- Short-term flows will be no easier to come to grips with in the future than in the past. Specifically, the various devices of reserve requirements, dual currency rates, interest limitations, wider bands, and governing the net foreign currency position of banks, will be practiced.

- Medium- and long-term borrowings will continue to be concentrated in London. First, the lender is well satisfied with the absence of a political or transfer risk on foreign currency funds booked via London. Second, regardless of the U.S. balance of payments position, the Middle East oil funds will continue to be employed via London, but of course not exclusively. Third, the dollar will remain the preferred vehicle and investment currency for the same reason it has in the past: No suitable alternative has yet been found.

- Regional financial capitals will get increasing attention. One of the characteristics of the evolving world financial markets is the growth of regional financial capitals. Not only is this the natural feature of a world in which commerce and tourism grows steadily, but it is also an objective of national policies. There are countless seminars going on in central banks and monetary funds of the world designed to show countries how to gather savings and redistribute these funds to various sectors of their economies. This revolution is currently under way. The increased numbers of financial centers will provide much broader alternatives to financial officers, but they

will also expose them to the jurisdiction of additional political authorities.

CONCLUSION

We have seen that controls—not static but changing controls—
have been a feature of the world's international capital markets for
years. Indeed, their existence created the Eurodollar system. While
controls may have become more extensive since the Smithsonian
Agreement of December 1971, they have not hampered the Eurodollar
system. Indeed, it has continued to grow, always adjusting to the continuing parade of political and economic developments reflected in
the investors' expectations.

For the most part, this has been a lenders' market, with the
borrowers having relatively little leverage to establish the terms of
the financing. However, the pendulum seems to have swung—it certainly has in the short term. I would expect the present "borrowers'
market" to continue well into the future. This trend is reinforced as
the funds available to be placed continue to grow and as investment
controls on foreign currency transactions of European borrowers continue.

In 1973 tighter monetary policy in the industrial world will place
a special call on the short-term funds on the Eurodollar market.
These borrowings will be permitted to the extent they are necessary
for commercial bank liquidity, but they will be discouraged when they
appear to be an escape from domestic monetary policy.

Currency stability—or the lack thereof—is a more important
variable to the market than increased investment controls. The preference for particular currencies shifts, and the deposit rates also
change, but these changing elements do not cripple the market or constrain its operations. Rather, these currency market changes, as
well as increased controls, are simply part of the array of new factors
that bankers make a living adjusting to. If controls and excessive
inflation on the Continent cause European authorities to limit the
number of corporations that would be candidates for Eurodollar loans,
then the bankers search out qualified borrowers in the developing
world. This may mean a bit fewer 15-year bond offerings, but it will
increase the volume of 5- to 10-year Eurodollar credits.

The market, in its impersonal way, has distributed its benefits
broadly. Its breadth and flexibility simply mean that the providers
and users of international capital may have to modify the method of
business somewhat, but not basically. But the market is a friend to
everybody, even though a country may from time to time use controls
to take a vacation from the benefits it provides.

*   *   *   *   *

39

COMMENT
Franz Ballman

I want to underline one point made by John Petty: It would seem to me as a matter of principle that what is more required now and in the future is a better coordination of policies on a national level in order to achieve a better national equilibrium, rather than a growth in a network of controls on the flow of funds whether in the capital or the money markets.

Nevertheless, realities somewhat lagging behind requirements, I feel we have to face the fact that as long as the present imbalances exist—and I am afraid they will exist for some time—capital controls may linger on or might even be increased. I am grateful to Mr. Petty for having outlined in so realistic and sober a way what the past developments were and what the likely trend for the future will be.

I find myself in agreement with his analysis as to these developments. In particular I would like to second the plea for increased international cooperation to coordinate matters, to avoid controls where possible, or to agree internationally on controls if and where they should be found necessary.

I also fully agree that where controls become necessary in the future they should be allowed only under certain presumptive rules such as balance of payments considerations, whether in connection with deficits or strong surpluses, and they should be imposed only on a temporary basis. There should be an international understanding that controls will have to be phased out as soon as possible. In other words, they should not develop into a permanent feature of the international economic scene which, unfortunately, controls have a strong tendency to do.

In some nuances I differ somewhat from Mr. Petty. First, I am not fully convinced that U.S. controls originally were responsible for the creation or the strong growth of the Eurodollar market. I believe the development of the Eurodollar market was caused by a number of complex issues, of which the original one was the establishment of external convertibility of the European currencies at the beginning of 1959. The external convertibility made it technically possible, and in substance often desirable, for commercial corporations and financial institutions to hold foreign currencies temporarily, instead of first converting them into domestic currency while buying them back at a later time. The international liquidity thus created was used for lendings and borrowings, as the case might be, and the Eurodollar market originated from this fact.

I agree with Mr. Petty that the restrictive practices subsequently imposed in the United States for balance of payments reasons contributed as one of several elements to the growth of the Eurodollar market. But I think there are additional reasons as well. For instance, the time difference. London, the main center of Eurocurrency trading, is in Europe. New York is five or six hours behind and this makes it more convenient for Europeans and Asians to do business in London rather than New York. It is even more difficult of course for San Francisco. Therefore American banks found it increasingly attractive to be represented in London, not just for the domestic British business but for the European business or the global international business.

Second, I believe that in earlier years New York may not have been suitable to the same extent as London for conducting international money or foreign exchange business because the New York market then was and to a large extent still is basically a domestic market. New York is a dollar market. The American banker in New York, particularly also the New York money trader, did not have the rich international experience that his European counterpart already had ten years ago. The European banker was used to dealing in foreign currencies; he was familiar with swaps and forwards and he knew his way around with currencies like the Italian lira or the Danish kronor. I doubt whether all these details were equally well known in New York ten years ago. Thus, I think the expertise in Europe, plus several other factors, contributed to the growth of the Eurodollar market.

As a third and very strong, element I think it is possible to connect the extreme growth of the Eurodollar market, particularly during recent years, with the rapidly increasing deficit in the U.S. balance of payments. I believe that without the U.S. balance of payments deficit there could not have been such enormous growth in the Eurodollar market, whose total volume is now most likely somewhere between $70 and $80 billion.

And there is another area where I see the problems slightly differently from Mr. Petty. I personally believe that a premature removal of the present U.S. restrictions on capital movements could aggravate international imbalances, although I do not want to go into detail on whether this would fully apply to all elements of these capital restrictions, such as Regulation Q, the Office of Foreign Direct Investment (OFDI) requirements, or the reserve requirements on Eurodollar borrowings. But in general I should think that a premature removal could not be beneficial to the system under present circumstances given the fact that confidence, not only in the present international monetary system but also in various currencies, is still shaky.

I would like now to stress a few additional points. In dealing with controls basically involving money market operations, we are talking about an entirely different problem than when we talk about capital controls, restrictions concerning direct investment, or take-overs. Except for the intermediation that banks provide, there is hardly any link between those two categories.

Perhaps one can already recognize this difference from the division of labor in public authorities. It would seem to me that this is more a subject that concerns central banks, treasuries, and perhaps the International Monetary Fund (IMF). The problems of development aid are entirely different, and direct investments concern the economics or trade ministries but not primarily central banks.

Money market operations are closely related to credit and monetary policy. If we accept this, we can perhaps reach some conclusions that may not necessarily be the same as the ones we might adopt tomorrow with regard to capital controls as a whole. Disregarding in this connection the liberalization code for capital movements of the Organization for Economic Cooperation and Development (OECD), its counterpart in the EEC, and the special programs for the flow of funds between developed and less developed countries, we could say that here is an area that has not been explored fully enough by a coordinated international approach, that is to say, central banks and governments on the one hand and existing international institutions on the other. By existing international institutions I mean particularly the OECD and the IMF. Some additional useful role could perhaps be played by the United Nations or the Bank for International Settlements (BIS).

It would seem that in this field there is no clear need for a new international organization in whatever form. Existing forums could deal with these matters either based on their present statutes and responsibilities or based on enlarged or changed authorities in their statutes as a result of the forthcoming international monetary reform. But should this also apply to money market problems?

These days it is asked not only whether there should be controls but also what kind of controls there should be, how long the controls should last, who should supervise them, and so forth. I do not believe that a network of international control handing over national sovereignty to international organizations could cope with the everchanging needs of international money markets. This is not to deny that international organizations could play a useful coordinating role.

Just as a central bank must cope with and quickly adapt to varying circumstances whenever domestic monetary conditions change in a national sector, so I feel the same must apply to the international sector.

It is an essential task of national governments and central banks to provide for balanced growth under conditions of external and internal stability. This is also the principle listed in Article 1 of the International Monetary Fund and governs its operations. In a system based on fixed exchange rates and external convertibility, there is no possibility for domestic credit policy to operate independently without protection of what the Germans have called the external flank. The alternative to temporary controls would seem to be fluctuating rates as chosen by Canada, dual rates as chosen by Belgium and France, or exchange rate adjustments regarded by the markets as sufficiently drastic to restore equilibrium and set in motion a counterflow of funds. Unfortunately, in order to convince markets, such exchange rate adjustments sometimes have to be drastic enough to produce an overkill that might easily harm the economy as a whole. Exchange rate adjustments are a very heavy and blunt weapon.

The German problem recently has been that a greater degree of revaluation might have been possible vis-à-vis the U.S. economy but would not have been possible vis-à-vis the other European countries, not to mention the Japanese economy. In this complex situation I believe that capital controls, as they presently exist, can serve a useful purpose.

The European capital restrictions are designed to prevent the inflow of foreign funds. The U.S. controls are the opposite side of the coin, designed to prevent funds from flowing out. We already have here an example of international coordination, which perhaps did not come about deliberately but because circumstances forced the hands of the authorities.

Perhaps it is the most we can hope for under present circumstances that governments and central banks exchange views and try to better understand each other's problems—that they take action in the interest of international stability as might be necessary, or would move into the right direction.

I agree with Mr. Petty that such action ought to be basically on a national level, although hopefully coordinated internationally. I do not believe, on the other hand, in a system that, for instance, would control the Euromarkets as such. I would see much harm if the hands of the authorities, particularly the British authorities, were forced into action in order to put the Eurodollar market into more orderly conditions.

First of all, I believe that in such a case the Eurodollar market might shift to other places. It is a tendency of markets to shift to places where the attitude is more liberal, provided telecommunications are good. If local authorities or an international organization tried to restrict transactions in the Euromarkets, the markets would simply move. I want to mention Singapore in this context because the Asia dollar market has already developed there to a present volume of approximately $4 billion. This market is based on the same principles on which the Eurodollar market operates.

In summary, in my opinion international money markets have developed not predominantly for reasons of restrictions or controls but for a whole set of complex reasons. They are here to stay and it is largely irrelevant where they are centered because they are reaching around the globe. Restrictions to curtail these markets cannot be in the interest of the world because the markets serve a useful purpose. In times of international monetary crises they are heavily used for hedging activities and produce a change in terms of payment by commercial corporations. The banks operating in the Eurodollar market have their normal dealer positions in money and foreign exchange, but I would venture to say that these dealer positions are much smaller than many people might expect.

The American banks in particular seem rather conservative in their approach to money and foreign exchange positions compared with their European counterparts. Consequently, while there is need to coordinate matters better in the future, and possibly to strengthen the authority of the OECD and the IMF in this field, I am not convinced that there is a need for a new international organization, or a need that existing international organizations take over full responsibility in these matters which ought to remain within the sphere of national sovereignty.

*   *   *   *   *

COMMENT
Yves-André Istel

I too find myself in broad agreement with John Petty's thesis, which I understand to be that we are going to have continuing but transitional controls. They will be mostly national in character, and they will be used in a kind of balance with the degree of exchange rate flexibility that is either allowed or that the national in question wishes to pursue.

Everyone seems to want to keep the benefits of the international capital market as it has existed, while trying to regulate it in various ways. I would like to expand on a few aspects of this market and perhaps draw a conclusion or two that might be slightly different from other viewpoints.

First of all, I think it is important to remember that an incredible web of controls already exists. The general notion of the international capital market is that there is an unregulated Eurodollar market and an unregulated Eurobond market. In fact the only place where there is a relative lack of regulation is in situ—at the point where the funds are collected and the decision is made as to how to reemploy them, or the point where the decision is made as to when to issue a bond issue.

Here, interestingly, there are figures that are published every year, and there are billions of dollars of Eurobond issues, and much larger amounts of Eurodollar credits, and in the meantime, of course,

44

every single country tends to have regulations that affect the access of its citizens and its funds to those markets. Some are inward capital flow restrictions; some are outward capital flow restrictions. And there are very different types of not strictly financial restrictions that can completely change the pattern of capital flows. Simply what constitutes a public issue, what securities and exchange commission type of disclosure treatment is required, and what public access is actually given, are examples.

Then it is necessary to keep in mind the different types of controls. A sovereignty question that blocks a direct takeover in an industry is quite different from the type of regulation that tells an insurance company how much of its assets can be invested, say, in shares or bonds not listed on that country's stock exchange. So there are different patterns of regulation affecting different types of areas.

It is particularly interesting that with an increasing pattern of regulation in the last year or so, particularly as regards capital inflows, there has been an amazing growth in the market. In other words, this rapid growth in the market has come despite a regulatory pattern of an extremely complex kind, and despite a tendency for certain of these controls to be expanded.

The reason, I believe, is in large part attributable to the lack of regulation at the source, of which I spoke earlier, and to the flexibility and the initiative and ingenuity that this has permitted.

There are few added pieces in the puzzle that I would like to present. One is that I think it is a truism in today's economic world that once an economic benefit is gained, nobody is really willing to offset it. By that I mean that once there has been growth in the Eurodollar market, that is a largely irreversible growth. Although people tend to think of this as hot money sloshing from one place to another (and there have been those aspects), the real fact is that that money would not be there unless it was lent to somebody for some economic purpose. In other words, the Eurodollar deposits are not just being transferred between eager speculators; some bank somewhere in the chain has actually lent that to someone to carry inventory, or to carry accounts receivable, or, perhaps not too wisely, to build a factory.

Now that this money has entered the economic system, it has contributed to employment and to existing gross national product of the country involved, and it is not going to be washed away. The same is largely true, by the way, on a national money supply level; if a country has too great an increase in its money supply, we have yet to see a major country actually go into a period of declining money supply. What it may decide to do is have a much smaller increase in the money supply in the following year. I think it would be a mistake to draw the conclusion that defining the constituent parts necessarily means you can take different approaches to all of them, although in some limited cases one may be able to. Knowing the chemical parts or the ingredients that go into a recipe does not necessarily mean you can duplicate the dish.

And even in those aspects where there has been the most success in defining terms—very short-term capital movements as opposed to all other kinds of capital movements—the fact is that these segments are very closely related. For example, Italy in the last year or so has had a very significant outflow of flight capital. That money in turn has been converted in many cases to dollars, and the Italian government agencies and entities have in turn contracted medium- to long-term Eurodollar credits in a major way to offset the private capital outflow. Now to say that the two are unrelated would probably not be very accurate. In addition, the main disequilibrating flows were attributable at least in part to the consistent overvaluation of the U.S. dollar, and no system can long hold the line against fundamental change. And now that that problem has reached a more stable area, for the moment at least, one can look at a large part of the capital movements and find that they have been equilibrating—in other words, that money is coming out of surplus areas and being rerouted to deficit areas through this market mechanism which, I think, is also very important to keep in mind.

Further, because of this flexibility at the source, and in view of the regulations that have been placed in Europe, the market has been redirecting itself in a very important way toward new areas. Although good statistics are hard to come by, analysis of the growth figures in the Eurodollar market brings a clear conclusion that there has been only modest growth in that market, in either sources or uses, from either the United States or Europe, and that the great bulk of the growth has come from other parts of the world that so far had not been brought into these international flows.

Certain surplus areas have invested money; even areas, say in the Far East, which were not in regional or national surplus, where the people had surplus savings but had not been willing to trust them to the money economy or the international money economy, have now done so, thanks to this system.

These funds, in turn, may have been relent to the same governments via the Eurodollar market, where it would have never been lent to them on a straight loan basis in the first place.

These observations describe a market that has existed and grown in the face of national regulations and by and large has tended to act in an equilibrating fashion. That is not a rationalization; it is a simple fact that you do business by borrowing money from those who have it and lending to those who need it. Disequilibrating flows have occurred when there has been really major disequilibrium in exchange rate parities, and additional regulation certainly would not have prevented that. Also, regulations to keep money from flowing out are notably less successful than regulations to keep money from flowing in.

At the meetings of the Committee of Twenty on monetary reform, the major positions, as advanced so far, all basically propose that each nation adjust more rapidly to evidences of balance of payments disequilibrium. A country with a surplus should do something, either change its exchange rate or take other measures; the same with a deficit. Under any of these concepts, we cannot suppose that this would allow an increasing web of regulations on long-term capital flows that would prevent the more fundamental kinds of adjustment from taking place. So I think there will be some sort of general basic agreement in a liberalizing direction, and I think that what we could best do, perhaps, is to urge that that continue.

Perhaps one will find that as there is less national regulation of the type we now have, and gradually this will decline, that the international capital market and its so-called unregulated aspects will tend to wither away a bit anyway.

There are excessive anomalies in today's situation that exist because of these regulations, where non-German companies can borrow long-term German marks at two percent less than the German companies can, and where non-French companies can borrow French francs at one percent less than French companies can. Now French and German companies in theory could have access to the Euro-deutsche-mark or Euro-franc markets, but in Germany the "Bardepot" effectively prevents this and the French treasury does not give permission to French nationals to borrow abroad.

So it is obvious that one logical way in which these anomalies would tend to disappear would be for there to be very large French issues that were allowed to be sold everywhere, rather than a compartmentalized Euro-franc market separate from the domestic French-franc market. I am not suggesting that this is going to happen tomorrow; all I am suggesting is that the worst mistake that one could make, which would remove the benefits without giving any new advantages, would be to press for some new kind of regulation at the source of decision, when there are already effective national regulations that should be reduced—there will be a tendency to reduce them anyway, but they can be kept in reserve in case of need.

Another aspect I would tend to urge, again perhaps making an exception for very short-term capital movements, is that any general discussion on trade matters should include capital flows. A priority does exist in the IMF and, as the existence of the General Agreement on Tariffs and Trade proves, in the mind of governments, for trade liberalization versus capital liberalization. I think that with the kind of direct investment flows we have been experiencing, it is going to be very hard to separate long-term capital flows from trade flows much longer, and there will have to be a sort of dual approach.

So that in concluding I would urge (1) that there should be no new organizations, (2) that there should be a nonsectoral and nonsegmented approach to overall trade and capital flows (again with the possible exception of very short-term capital flows), and (3) that we should simply move forward as regards regulations of financial flows from the existing OECD stand, with gradual progress along the lines of removing many of the existing exceptions of direct investment.

The more complicated kind of sovereignty notions obviously lend themselves to a different treatment as they have significant non-financial aspects. I only wanted to relate the financial flows that we have been seeing to the kind to regulatory attitude we might take toward overall direct investment.

6

INTERNATIONAL CONTROL
FROM THE STANDPOINT
OF THE EUROPEAN
ECONOMIC COMMUNITY
Fernand Braun

I doubt that more knowledge can be added to the impressive results of academic research undertaken during recent years. As a matter of fact, wherever we lack inside knowledge, we are aware of the missing links due to the absence of a lot of statistical data or other relevant information. Only a policy decision could bring about a change in this field. But the amount of research realized and above all the recognition of the political sensitivity of the phenomenon of investment by multinational companies are sufficient to initiate a discussion on the policies pursued and possible changes of policy.

At this point I would like to stress that most of the ideas I am going to venture reflect only my personal point of view or to some extent the ideas of a limited number of colleagues in my own department, and that they should in no way be construed as an official opinion of the Commission of the European Economic Community (EEC) or its staff. This is more than the traditional disclaimer put forward by national or international officials, which nobody takes at face value. In fact, the specific issues I will consider have never been the subject of any organized discussion inside the EEC Commission or Council of Ministers.

It would of course be wrong to assume that there have been no discussions with respect to foreign direct investment and multi-national companies. As early as January 1965 the EEC Commission ordered the gathering of a working group to establish, under my guidance, a comprehensive analysis of the facts related to American investment in the countries of the EEC. This piece of work was never made public, but somehow it became the starting point for more searching and/or more politically orientated studies such as those subsequently undertaken in the EEC by Rainer Hellman and Jean-Jacques Servan-Schreiber. Follow-ups were realized in the Commission from more specific points of consideration from time to

time. In 1965 the Commission made only two procedural proposals
to the Council of Ministers, one providing for the ways and means to
assure information on capital movements for the benefit of investment, the other organizing a yearly exchange of views in the Council
on the economic results of foreign investments made the year before.

A decision of the Council is still pending.

More recently, in March 1970, in a memorandum on industrial
policy, the Commission defined in relatively precise terms the way
it looks upon foreign investment. The Commission noted that on
several occasions in the past it has emphasized the vital contribution
of foreign investments to the economy of the EEC countries.

These investments frequently represent a sizable contribution
to the productivity, technology, and financial resources of EEC industry and are among the most effective means of achieving international division of labor.

The Commission is convinced that the right response to this
competition that the industry of the nine member countries must face
from within the EEC itself does not lie in a restrictive attitude but in
the strengthening of the structure and vigor of European undertakings.

To establish "protectionism" for the benefit of firms can only
place them in an artificial environment that would scarcely be favorable to their expansion inside or outside the EEC. However, in certain sectors the very rapid growth of foreign investments in the EEC
during the last ten years may present difficult political and economic
problems, as demonstrated by the attitude displayed by one or more
member states in the course of specific operations.

These problems are posed in different terms depending on
whether the operation is a new investment or the acquisition of a
minority or majority holding in companies in the EEC.

In the first case, the net increase in the means of production
undoubtedly leads to fiercer competition but necessitates the creation
of new jobs and resources to new technologies. Such new investments
have not usually caused member states to take different attitudes.
It can be said that the general desire of member countries to attract
new investments has led to strong competition in the granting of state
aid so that sometimes foreign firms have been placed in a better
investment position than their competitors within the EEC.

Harmonization of aid is essential to reconcile the necessities
of regional development with fair conditions of competition.

When it comes to takeovers or the acquisition of minority holdings in EEC firms by firms from third countries, member states
have adopted attitudes that often are at variance. This may be explained by different views on the relative importance of the various
sectors and differences in policy. This divergence of national policies
is undoubtedly a serious problem for the governments of member

states in certain cases of intercommunity grouping. Indeed the creation of multinational groups in the EEC presupposes the adoption of a common policy by the member states with regard to them.

An essential component of this common policy is the adoption by member states of a common attitude to the takeover of firms in certain sectors by companies from third countries. Member states have been studying the far-reaching changes that the acquisition of such interests produces in the structure of a given sector of industry; much more than the establishment of new firms with foreign capital, such acquisitions distort the balance of the forces at work.

This problem is particularly marked in sectors where, as a result of the present weakness of European industry, such takeovers are likely to create an obstacle for some time to come to the birth and development of transnational European industries. The consequences, not only as regards competition between products but also for the future of the sector in question—balance of financial and technological forces at work in the sector, possibility of keeping up activity in the sector at national or EEC level, in short the need to amend the entire strategy in the sector concerned—illustrate the interdependence of industrial structure policy and the attitude on the acquisition of holdings by outside companies. An EEC industrial structure policy would indeed be very difficult to put into practice if a common attitude to such operations were not defined.

The Commission does not think by any means that a concerted attitude in this matter should be reflected in a restrictive policy in regard to takeovers or the acquisition of holdings by firms from third countries. But in cases where such operations run counter to the objectives pursued by governments—which need not necessarily be purely economic but may also be bound up with security considerations and for the sake of which the public authorities have made considerable financial and economic sacrifices—the Commission considers that a concerted attitude is essential. It does indeed appear necessary for member states henceforth to take action at the EEC level of the kind they have thus far been taking at the national level, which is no longer satisfactory precisely because the national framework is too small. This concerting of their action should make it possible to adopt a common policy in regard to the few sectors in which large-scale takeovers would imperil the legitimate aims pursued by member states or defined by the EEC. It would rest with the frame of industrial policy to work out an EEC scale the alternative solutions that may prove necessary.

When this memorandum was submitted to the Council of Ministers and discussions began on its more controversial aspects, the issue of how to discuss and possibly to channel foreign investments became a major topic for dissent. It was not that any participant in

the discussion wanted to ignore the problem or avoid the discussion.
In a way, the division was more on philosophical than pragmatic lines,
at least as far as the more important member countries were concerned. Indeed, a consensus might well be possible on specific problems if and when they arise, as indicated in the Commission's memorandum. However, any formulation of policy that might, if only
slightly, indicate a will to restrict foreign investments has been opposed above all by those countries that depend on foreign investments
for their industrial development, for fear of either the psychological
effect on would-be investors or the precedent that could be followed
in presently unforeseeable occasions.

Tentatively I would suggest that the EEC member states agree
that foreign direct investments are, on balance, beneficial to the host
and the source countries. I hasten to add that this is true for the
time being, under prevalent circumstances; a changing international
economic climate could well entail more ambiguous appraisals and
possibly hardening attitudes.

All I have said up to this point concerns essentially the problem
of foreign, that is to say third-country, investments in the EEC.
Since 1958 investments across the borders of the member states have
created trouble only in exceptional circumstances and there are no
serious restrictions, psychological or administrative, to overcome.
However, an important impediment to intra-EEC investments is still
to be found in the legal and fiscal niceties and disharmonies between
the member states if and when the investment is supposed to realize
a merger.

At this point I must bring up the more specific problem of the
multinational company. No attempt is made here to define exactly
what a multinational company is. A precise definition would in any
case be of little interest when it comes to the problems the EEC
faces and the solutions that could be considered. In practice, the
"multinational" character of a given company can generally be recognized at first sight. But the fact that it is or is not multinational
is of secondary importance. What counts is whether it causes a
problem or several problems—or perhaps no problem at all. In most
cases, there are also visible problems and unwanted effects with
companies that could not be considered truly multinational. The case
of the multinational company is simply due to the fact that such a
company can produce, in a concentrated form, a variety of problems
that are encountered only rarely or in any case less often in regard
to other companies. Multinational companies can speculate, evade
taxation, or abuse their dominant market position. In many cases,
nonmultinational companies can do so as well or almost as well.

From my point of view, the EEC should therefore avoid adopting
an attitude or policies against multinational companies simply because

they are multinational. What it should do is to examine the various problems and their effects and adopt the appropriate solutions, regardless of whether or not they are linked with the multinational character of the companies. But obviously most problems are due to the fact that the companies in question operate on an international basis, are large and rich, may be conglomerates, are relatively mobile, are often active in high technology fields, and so forth.

The major problems that may worry European public authorities and possibly call for policy proposals and measures at the EEC level, or in some cases on a broader international level, may be briefly summarized as follows:

1. Balance of payments problems: In the short term, investment abroad has a negative impact on the balance of payment of the investor's country and a positive one on that of the host country. In the long term, it is the reverse. Up to now the net impact of foreign investments on balances of payment has in general not exceeded 3 to 4 percent. But a systematic and enduring imbalance in investment flows between two countries would in the end tend to create difficulties.

2. Foreign trade: The share of international companies in the foreign trade of the host country is generally larger than their share in domestic production. In many host countries, foreign companies account for a very sizable proportion of total exports. In most cases, sister companies are not entirely free to develop their exports as they wish, for example toward the national market of their mother company or toward communist countries. This may not be in line with the economic or political interest of the host country.

3. Capital market: International companies finance their investments in host countries by self-investment to a great extent and for the rest mainly from funds provided by the mother company. The remaining capital is obtained either from local aids or from the local capital market in forms other than shares. Possibilities for local investors to become shareholders of the sister company are thus practically nil. In the case of U.S. foreign investment, only 15 percent is American money; the rest comes from foreign capital markets and from the sister companies' cash flow. But in the very large majority of cases, the 15 percent of U.S. investment gives 100 percent control over the sister companies' capital. This process, when applied to takeover operations of existing local firms, may go as far as acquiring ownership without spending a penny and without giving any right on the mother company's capital. To many this appears excessive since local money can be used by foreigners to obtain control over local industry.

4. Employment: Most countries welcome investments by multinational companies largely because they create additional employment. However, some observers fear that, in case of business depression,

multinational companies might be less preoccupied by job reductions in the host country than national companies would be. Others contend that in practice multinational companies have exerted a stabilizing effect on the labor market.

5. Wages and industrial relations: In general, multinational companies tend to pay slightly higher wages than others, but establish a closer link between wage level and productivity. It also seems that strikes are less frequent in multinational companies than in national ones. Policies such as "hire and fire" and lock-outs, which some of them practiced before, have become rare. However, trade unions fear that multinational companies might take advantage of the trade unions' lack of cohesion at the international level.

6. Regional policy: Most governments now show considerable concern regarding balanced economic growth in the various regions. They try to orient investment flows toward the less developed regions and to this end they seek the support of industrial circles. Some observers fear that multinational companies might be less inclined than national ones to comply with the orientations given by public authorities of the host country. But multinational companies regard themselves as the ideal means of ensuring a rational division of labor at the international level and consider that their action tends to even out social and economic disparities.

7. Research and technology: Up to now it has not been possible to ascertain with accuracy whether multinational companies exert a positive or negative influence on the technological level of the host country. In many countries, people fear that local talent will serve to bring about discoveries that might be patented in the country of the mother company or elsewhere, as best suits the interests of the multinational company.

8. Management: Criticism concerns the fact that most multinational companies give local personnel insufficient opportunity to reach top management posts. This is not as true of personnel and research manager posts but does apply to general managers, controllers, and members of the board. As far as management methods are concerned, it is generally agreed that multinational companies exert a beneficial effect.

9. Tax behavior: It is practically beyond question that multinational companies manipulate internal price relations so as to locate their profits either in the country of the mother company or in countries where taxes are lowest. This behavior entails tax losses for host countries. In particular, when a tax haven company is geared into the process, it brings about unfair competition for national companies.

10. Competition: Not all, but a sizable number of multinational companies enjoy dominant positions for certain products, practically at world level. In many countries, antitrust laws are nonexistent or

rudimentary. Besides, no coordination exists at the international level. Abuses of dominant positions thus may not be ruled out. Furthermore, when a multinational company is a conglomerate, the risk that it might indulge in unfair competition in a given sector becomes even greater.

11. Monetary problems: Short-term capital movements and internal booking procedures of multinational companies without doubt contribute to monetary instability. The extent to which they do so has not yet been quantified. However, it must be borne in mind that multinational companies are far from alone in doing so. Apart from pure speculators, private banks and national firms also seek to avoid losses due to modification of exchange rates.

12. Safety of supplies: The fear exists that for some commodities, energy sources, or high technology materials, in case of economic or political crisis or world shortage, multinational companies will give priority to servicing the home market of the mother company to the detriment of the host country.

Most of these problems call for action by the EEC. Some will be greatly alleviated by the achievement of economic and monetary union and by tax harmonization. The solution to other problems clearly implies the setting up of adequate countervailing powers to multinational companies. It prompts public authorities and trade unions on the path to multinationality. Finally, other problems call for new regulations or agreements such as codes of good behavior between public authorities and multinational companies. The EEC Commission cannot evade the task of examining adequate solutions to this specific problem and hopefully will submit proposals to the Council of Ministers shortly.

The lines the Commission's services are exploring at present are the following ones, with the understanding that each investigation may not lead to specific proposals for action:

1. To provide channels of appropriate information on multinational companies to whoever needs it. In fact, even the home countries of multinational companies hold only one piece of the puzzle and in some cases that piece is very small. There is already cooperation between fiscal authorities of various countries that have concluded tax treaties, and these countries exchange information enabling fiscal authorities to check the truthfulness of their residents' income statements. To control multinational companies, such bilateral exchanges of information are not enough. What is needed is a pooling of information on these companies on a multinational basis, information relevant not only to taxes but also to foreign exchange transactions and marketing agreements, to name but a few topics.

2. To adapt company law to multinationals, in particular in order to avoid, as much as possible, the prospect that a mother

company located outside the EEC could evade the commitments and debts of a sister company registered in EEC toward shareholders, workers, and third parties.

3. To organize tax control at the EEC level in order to channel transfer pricing and licensing into acceptable paths.

4. To control short-term capital movements, which would be made easier by a proper working of tax controls.

5. To control the origin of funds to be invested to assure that the funds come from self-financing or from regular issues on normal capital markets.

6. To bring the Eurobond market within bounds. This could be achieved, at least to a certain extent, by making all banks operating in the EEC, regardless of the nationality of their mother company, subject to certain rules of good behavior.

7. To adopt a community regulation regarding general purchasing offers to bar wild takeovers.

8. To make sure, through the application of Art. 86 of the EEC treaty, that the creation of a dominant position, and not only the abuse of it, can be barred; that the conglomerate aspect can be drawn into consideration for clearance. (One may wonder if the EEC should not set up a stock exchange commission or at least organize a cooperation of existing national bodies in order to stop sweeping maneuvers before they result in the creation of dominant market positions and to stop or delay due time takeovers without any kind of economic justification. One may also wonder whether a stronger competition policy will not require a revision of the treaty stipulations on dominant positions and mergers.)

9. To organize worker protection. This implies the adoption of a community regulation on collective firing and a community "mergers code" to find appropriate answers to social consequences.

10. To stimulate the creation and to help the expansion of European-based multinational companies within the limits indicated above. This can be done by eliminating fiscal and legal obstacles to transnational mergers within the EEC and by devising incentives such as the marriage bureau, community development contracts, community guarantee schemes for investments abroad, and so forth.

There remain two important problems that the Commission's services have pondered without yet finding appropriate answers. The first is that of ensuring EEC subjects a fair chance to reach top posts in non-EEC-based multinational companies. The second is to avoid a situation where European money is used by multinational companies to acquire European industry without sharing control with European shareholders.

These two questions are particularly awkward. But Europe is certainly not inclined to adopt solutions in the style now fashionable in developing countries and Latin America.

In conclusion I will consider whether an international effort, if only informal, might not be more feasible than the immediate efforts of the EEC and the Organization for Economic Cooperation and Development (OECD).

I have indicated before, at least implicitly, that I do consider international measures negotiated through channels still to be defined—by the EEC, the United States, and others—as an important element, among others, in bringing about a situation where objective criteria regulate the flow of investments and the situation of multinationals with no specific regard to their home states.

The EEC indicated at a recent OECD meeting that it would welcome further work on the phenomenon of the multinational company specifically and foreign investment generally within this organization. OECD's working procedures, in a way, are highly informal. No decision, no negotiation with binding obligations can take place in the Château de la Muette. Nor can recommendations, if I understand the wording correctly, be self-executing. The OECD may help where a question suggests something to be done outside in a less formal approach. For governments, I an afraid, the formula cannot and should not be less formal.

As a matter of fact, the OECD is not the place for a GATT for investment if GATT means obligations entrenched in rules that cannot be infringed upon without, at least in principle, paying a due price for infringements.

If this is so, are we all ready for a GATT-type negotiation, and is such a negotiation the most opportune way for some international regulation of investment?

To the first part of my question, I venture to say, maybe yes, for instance when it comes to defining multilaterally the tax treatment of multinationals. But I must say that I do not consider the EEC yet in a position to negotiate within this assumption. The EEC as such lacks today the policies to be negotiated, as no policy has yet emerged among the nine. I was therefore sketching possible policy outlines only, not even an emerging policy, and of course the problems that exist and require solution.

7

COUNTERVAILING POWERS TO
THE MULTINATIONAL CORPORATION
Rainer Hellman

There is widespread fear that some 200 or 300 gigantic multi-national corporations (MNCs) will control more than half the world's industrial production in 10 or 15 years, that they will make decisions without much respect for regional or national interests. George S. Ball considers the MNC the greatest challenge to the nation-state in the Western world since the decline of the temporal power of the Catholic church in the fifteenth century.

I will not try to minimize these apprehensions. But I intend to attract attention to some countervailing powers to the MNC, developing at the same speedy pace as the MNC itself.

According to Jack N. Behrman, a multinational company needs three conditions for ideal functioning: (1) central control by the parent company, (2) a common strategy for the entire enterprise, and (3) integrated operations between affiliates and between affiliates and the parent company.

Central control, a common strategy, and integrated operations presuppose that the multinational corporation controls its affiliates. It means that wholly- or majority-owned foreign investment is author-ized in the host countries. Yet today multinationals are free to choose the form of ownership and operation they deem best for the company's purposes only in the United States, Canada, and Western Europe. Even in the North Atlantic area, sectoral or qualitative restrictions on foreign investment are not completely unknown, although they are the exception and not the rule.

Japan is embarking on a policy of liberalization of foreign direct investments, but it has banned 100 percent foreign direct investment in more than 600 out of 850 sectors of its economy.

In Latin America, the Andean Group members have officially embarked on a policy of admitting only new foreign participations of up to 49 percent and of transforming wholly-owned foreign subsidiaries of non-Latin American origin into mixed companies with a 51 percent local participation. In other Latin American countries, preferential treatment is given to foreign capital invested in joint ventures over wholly-owned foreign subsidiaries.

In Eastern Europe, multinationals can only operate as such in three countries: Yugoslavia, Romania, and Hungary. But also in these countries only 49 percent foreign direct investment is possible. The multinationals are thus forced into the position of a minority partner. They have no determining influence on the run of affairs, even if they are often contributing the technological know-how.

Investment conditions for foreign capital vary in the developing countries, but generally multinationals cannot acquire more than 50 percent participation, above all in mining and primary production but often even in manufacturing.

This rapid and certainly superficial world tour on foreign investment cannot make me overoptimistic about the future of the multinational company if it tries to operate as such. Certainly multinationals can participate in many countries in joint ventures and so-called "accords de coopération." But how long can a multinational operate in a cohesive manner if it participates in a large set of operations that it can no longer command and in which it is only the minority partner? A large share of the advantages of multinational operations is lost if central control of these operations can no longer be guaranteed because there is a foreign majority or a 50:50 partner.

My doubts on the unlimited and uninhibited growth and prosperity of the multinationals also have quite another source. In addition to the obstacles to further expansion posed by the desire of nation-states and regional organizations to preserve their entire sovereignty unimpaired by multinationals, a countervailing power to the multinational corporation is slowly but vigorously developing in the international labor movement.

For many years the labor movement was slow to organize itself in the same international structures as the multinational corporations. But there is clear evidence that the unions are rapidly catching up and are already a remarkable countervailing power. Labor unions are becoming a real match for the multinationals in two different ways. The first is the formation of transnational federations of trade unions, such as the European Metal Workers or the International Chemical Workers. The second and complementary way is the formation of liaison groups between the workers of different affiliates of one MNC. In many MNCs such liaison groups have already been formed and have been successful. The best known are those of the St. Gobain workers and the AKZO trade unions. The latter forced the Dutch-German company to completely modify a restructuring plan and to abandon the project of closing down an artificial fiber plant at Breda in Holland.

Common action of trade unions is a factor effectively limiting the MNC in the free disposition of its plants. Ford felt this very hard when even parts for the assembling of the American Ford Pinto in Detroit were lacking due to strikes in the British Ford plants. If the unions effectively exercise their countervailing power, the MNC can no longer decide autonomously about the locations or closing down of its plants. Even the planning of production can be seriously disturbed by multinational labor action.

Another new factor influencing the MNC is the increasing flexibility of the international monetary system. A greater flexibility is doubtlessly favoring MNCs in relation to companies operating only inside their national boundaries. A MNC has more access to information about changing monetary conditions. It has above all greater possibilities for hedging against parity losses than a company operating in its home country and exporting from there. Such a company must insure at high costs the parity risk of the export credits granted to its clients. The MNC can try to mix its risks inside its own group so that it need not rely on expensive banking reassurance against parity losses. But this advantage has its price and its negative side. The goodwill of the MNCs has suffered badly by the recent monetary crisis. I shall not go into the detail of the contested question, whether multinationals themselves create or at least contribute to international monetary trouble. I do not think anybody is able to tell exactly how far MNCs and multinational banks were involved in the monetary crises of the last years. What is evident is the fact that the recent crisis has given new vigor to the worldwide plea for an international control of MNCs. More and more, people find that the worldwide activity of the MNC can be a threat for the monetary order, a menace that needs to be brought under some kind of control.

Yet the chances are small that a mighty international organization will mushroom out of the United Nations framework in order to control the MNC. This is true not only because the MNCs do not languish waiting to be controlled but also because those in whose favor the control would be organized do not want it and prefer their newly acquired 100 percent sovereignty to any real international control. This of course leaves the unsolved problem of the supervision of the MNC, which can create or amplify monetary crisis.

In fact, in the postwar period we have tried the Bretton Woods system of fixed exchange rates. It served us well, as long as the economic policies of the main industrial countries were well aligned. As soon as the inflation rates began to diverge too much at the end of the 1960s, it failed. Neither the countries with big surpluses nor those with big deficits in their balance of payments wanted to change their parities. So we came to the crisis of 1971.

In reaction to the excesses of a too rigid system, we are now trying a flexible policy with parity adjustments whenever there seems to be a disequilibrium in the balance of payments. Theoretically the increased flexibility should allow free movement of capital and liberal international exchange. In practice we have rarely lived in a period in which more capital export and import controls, negative interest rates, and restrictions of all kinds have been introduced, even by "liberal" countries like Switzerland and Germany.

The parity adjustments and the new flexibility also were deemed to attract more European investments to the United States and to discourage American investors from increasing their investments abroad. But investors pay more attention to possible new parity changes than to those already registered. If parity changes can be expected, they accelerate or delay foreign direct investments technically planned for the next years. Therefore, in periods of high flexibility and monetary instability we risk "leads and lags" in international investments, just as in international trade. In international direct investment, the implementation of the projects themselves, not only the payments, may be delayed or accelerated. The mushrooming of capital controls and the lack of stability for direct investment in a system of high flexibility lead us to the recognition that the new dogma of flexibility, which certainly has shown some positive results, is not yet the definite answer to our problems.

I venture to say that we are in the middle of a dialectical process. In the first stage, the thesis consisted of very rigid, almost invariable parities. It failed in 1971. We are now going through the second stage, the antithesis of high flexibility. We are going through it in the naive belief that it must bring better results because it is the opposite of rigidity. The synthesis we must attain, in my opinion, is the recognition by the important industrialized countries of the Western world, accounting for some 90 percent of international investment by MNCs, that neither rigidity nor flexibility can replace a solid economic policy. The synthesis is the recognition that the United States, Europe, and Japan must harmonize up to a certain extent their economic policies and their monetary policies on interest rates. It is the recognition that their economic interdependence is already much more important than they realize. It is perhaps also the bitter recognition that in a world economy that can hardly survive without multinationals operating beyond national borders, a national independent economic policy is impossible and unrealistic even for countries of the importance of the United States.

Unless at least Europe and the United States harmonize their economic and monetary policies in a way that assures sufficient stability of their exchange rates within the broader band of tolerated flexibility, they will never find the way back to a practicable monetary order and to free trade and capital movements in the Western world.

To summarize, the countervailing power to the growing activity of the MNC will not be an international organization. The real and effective countervailing powers are already in operation. They are:

● National regulations on foreign direct investments, which make majority-owned investments of multinationals more and more difficult, above all in less developed countries.

● Regional organizations, like the European Economic Community (EEC) or the Andean Pact, that are strong enough to exercise supervision over foreign and multinational investment.

● The labor movement, which is starting its multinational counterorganization.

● The recognition of the interdependence between the most important industrialized countries in the task of favoring a harmonized anti-inflationary policy oriented to real growth and not just to inflationary nominal growth rates that serve no one but speculators.

This last point may seem unrealistic because an independent economic policy is considered absolutely primordial by the United States with its economy of $1,000 billion, of which only four percent is due to exports. Nevertheless, I have the feeling that recognition of growing economic interdependence is making progress on both sides of the Atlantic through the various crises in which we are living in the Western world, not only in monetary affairs but also in regard to energy.

Europe and North America are two continents strong enough to allow free foreign investment on a two-way street. If the EEC and the U.S. government agreed on a permanent system of consultation on mutual problems of direct investments by multinationals, on questions of interest rates, fiscality, transfer pricing, and antitrust surveillance, they could easily assure against economic and political domination by multinationals. They can make sure that multinationals contribute to the exchange of technology and to the increase of well-being on both sides of the Atlantic.

*　*　*　*　*

COMMENT
Charles Kindleberger

Concern over foreign investment is not new. Last year in Europe I spent some time studying the problem historically. The example I found took place not far from Düsseldorf: At an 1852 stockholders meeting of an Essen coal company, Gustav von Mevissen complained about the entry of French, Belgian, and British investors into the coal industry of the Ruhr. That was 121 years ago. Further German worry about Ueberfremdung was expressed in the 1890s when the electrical companies from the United States undertook investment in Germany, and a further wave of resentment was expressed over investment during the 1923 inflation, plus more resentment at the end of the 1920s. Similar expressions of antipathy to American investment were recorded in Britain in 1900, in France in 1929, and, to make matters symmetrical, over German investment in Italy in 1915.

On the other hand, the scale is new. Transnational investment today is on a far larger scale than in the previous 100 years because of the decline in the cost of transport and communication. This decline has enlarged the optimum economic area of a corporation but has not changed the optimum cultural area of society. It is cozy to limit cultural areas to regions—like New England, Wales, Flanders, or Friesland. When cultural standards become homogenized—like wall-to-wall international hotels, without local color or Gemütlichkeit—we may lose in cultural terms what we gain economically.

The problem is thus largely the clash between culture and politics on the one hand and economics on the other. Unhappily I suspect that economics will dominate in the long run.

My second point is that interference with direct investment— departure from laissez faire—is justified only on noneconomic grounds or second-best reasoning. Noneconomic grounds are those like national defense or the preservation of cultural autonomy. Second-best rules are justified when the first-best do not perform effectively. If the market does not function, it is a mistake to use it. A classic example of interference with laissez faire on this ground was the moratorium on foreign investment in Germany imposed by the occupying powers in 1945, before the settlement of reparations or monetary reform. This policy was readily agreed to by the U.S. officials: Secretary James Francis Byrnes, Director of Economic Stabilization, from South Carolina, General Lucius DuBingnon Clay, Administrator of U.S. Occupied Germany, from Georgia, and Undersecretary of State for Economic Affairs William L. Clayton from Texas. One only had to say one word to them: carpetbaggers.

If markets do not function well, it is a mistake to rely on them. The first-best policy, of course, is to improve the functioning of the market. A second-best policy of interfering with the international corporation is justified only when first-best policies cannot be used or will not work.

An interesting example against which to test this precept arises in connection with Italy and capital markets. Italian capital markets function badly, largely because Italian capitalists are fearful and put their funds abroad. When an Italian company gets into trouble, it would normally raise more capital to tide it over its difficulties. Today that is impossible. The question is whether to let the company go under or to save it, and in saving it whether to let foreign capital buy it up or use governmental agencies such as the Institute for Industrial Reconstruction (IRI), Ente Nazionale Idrocarburi (ENI), the International Marketing Institute (IMI), and the Study Group on International Productivity (GEPI). In the ordinary case, governments do not buy up private firms, and thus British Leyland, Philips, Hoover of England, and many American firms are buying up Italian companies in difficulties. The first-best policy is to restore confidence in the Italian capital market. Failing this, there is the awkward question of whether or not to permit foreign purchase of companies caught in liquidity squeezes.

My third point touches one form of market failure: the distortions that come from the existence of different tax systems in different national jurisdictions. Markets do not allocate resources in accord with fundamental scarcities when private capitalists respond to proximate tax incentives. From the viewpoint of economic efficiency, taxes should be neutral. In the real world, without harmonization of tax systems, they are distortionary. Tax havens continue to distort resource allocations despite the limitations on them in the 1962 Revenue act in the United States and the Swiss-German double taxation agreement. In the long run, the Netherlands Antilles, Lichtenstein, Luxembourg, Andorra, San Marino, Zug, and Appenzell are going to have to stop trying to entice tax evaders. It is not attractive for the big countries to push around the little entities, but it is strongly dysfunctional to continue them. Like Delaware and Hoboken in the United States, in the long run they will have to give up exploiting gaps in the system.

Let me now raise a question posed by Fernand Braun about the best way to make progress in eliminating the conditions that make for restrictions in international investment on second-best grounds, or distort it because of non-neutrality. The question is whether rules about international corporations should be postponed until Europe succeeds in working out its own rules for European corporations.

There is a strong antithesis in European integration between integration achieved entirely within Europe and integration that relies on outside factors. Up to now, the latter has dominated. Such integration as has been achieved in the labor market has come largely from the mobility of southern or Mediterranean labor from one Common Market country to another. Capital markets have been joined not directly but through the Eurodollar market. And the most truly European corporations—in the sense that they are prepared to move about the EEC—have been American corporations. There have been a number of European transnational mergers—Agfa-Gaevert, Dunlop-Pirelli, and the like—and many European takeovers, but much of integration has rested on external actors.

The same problem is confronted in the monetary field. Should monetary reform be held up until Europe constructs its own currency, or should the separate countries of Europe participate in a world monetary reform?

The same issue arises between Canada and the United States. Should the direct investment issues be settled bilaterally or within the wider context of a world system? When the Watkins report was being written I suggested an international solution, and my students and friends, Stephen Hymer and Melvin Watkins, regarded that as a cop-out, saying that Canada is always avoiding the necessity for a national foreign policy by opting for a global solution.

I do not regard a European solution to the problems of international regulation of the corporation as a completely negative one. It evidently has positive features for European integration. But it has grave risks of postponing for too long an international meeting of minds on the problem of international regulation of the multinational enterprise, and reducing it, when it takes place, to a European-U.S. confrontation and stalemate.

Let me say one word more: I am troubled that if we move rapidly to the national or European level, and a country or integrated region tries to take care of its national or regional interest with no thought for the international interest, we can quickly find the world in trouble. The fallacy of composition sometimes ensures that the whole is a great deal less than the sum of its parts. When Canada and Norway are content on the national level that Alcoa buy up the last Norwegian smelter to cut prices in aluminum, the world loses. Canada and Britain may be willing to let Massey-Ferguson in Britain punish any dealer who sells farm machinery that would get to Canada and break the monopoly price structure in that market, but the world should not be. There are national interests, but there is also an international interest. It may be necessary to construct international machinery to safeguard it.

8

THE REALISTIC PROSPECTS FOR GREATER POLITICAL INTEGRATION AND ORGANIZATION OF DEVELOPED COUNTRIES RELATED TO INVESTMENT

Nicholas deB. Katzenbach

The prospects for formal agreement as to investment among the developed countries are not very great. I think there are several reasons for this.

There is much confusion and ambivalence in the attitudes of developed countries toward direct foreign investment. There are many reasons to welcome foreign investment, for any investment, foreign or domestic, contributes to the national productivity, creates jobs, and increases the general welfare. Insofar as foreign investment is made within a country, there is really very little difference between it and domestic investment. If anything, it is preferable since it represents an input of savings generated elsewhere. Therefore, as a general matter, countries welcome foreign investment within their territory.

Often the foreign investment represents not only an input of savings from other economies into investment within the nation but also an input of technology and other skills. To the extent this is true, it is again preferable to domestic investment of comparable size.

Another plus is the prospect that such investment will contribute to the country's balance of payments position, since in most cases the goods produced locally by the direct investment would otherwise be imported at least to a degree. It may also contribute in a net way in the sense that part of the goods produced locally through the foreign investment may be exported.

Most of the foregoing is true even if the foreign investment occurs merely to get in behind tariff walls and produce largely or exclusively for the local market.

For the foregoing reasons, in the past thirty years countries have traditionally been more concerned with an outflow of capital than with an inflow. In general, countries have welcomed any foreign investment but are more concerned about the possibility of capital flow into other countries. Concern with capital flowing into a country is a relatively new phenomenon on the international scene.

Furthermore, concern with direct capital inflow is directly related to political rather than economic considerations. Political concerns have been largely related to big multinational corporations. These concerns have been of a political nature because the countries in which such foreign corporations have made direct investments fear that the multinational corporation is less subject to political control than a wholly domestic corporation would be. The corporation doing business largely or exclusively within a country is bound to be extremely sensitive to the political desires of the government. This is not merely a matter of complying with local regulation and local laws; obviously all corporations doing business within a country are subject to local laws with respect to local business and local production. But to the extent that governments wish to control various forms of investment, channel into particular areas, coopt a part of production for national defense purposes, and so forth, there is a feeling that the multinational corporation is less sensitive to some forms of regulation than a purely local corporation would be. It is in a better position to transfer investment to a more favorable climate if it so desires; by its multinational character it enjoys more latitude in the transfer of funds through intercompany loans, payments, and transactions; perhaps it is believed to have political loyalty to a foreign government, and therefore to be less responsive to appeals to patriotism, national defense, and so forth; some believe that merely because of its multinational character it may be not only less responsive to local needs and demands but also responsive to those of another country, its home base, and that in general it can and may constitute some kind of threat to the various forms of economic nationalism that are ever with us.

Very recently, especially in the United States, there has been a throwback to the older forms of prohibition on capital outflow. Largely as a result of union pressure, there is a movement in the United States to seek to restrict capital outflow, on the theory that it is a form of exploiting cheap labor abroad—of exporting U.S. jobs into foreign countries. This is accompanied by a form of neo-isolationism. In a sense this is the opposite side of the coin of the fears that other countries have—that U.S. investment means U.S. domination of their economies. There is some sentiment presently in the United States that tends to accept the argument of the developing countries in this regard and sees U.S. investment as a way toward U.S. political involvement in various matters abroad in which the United States should not interfere. By and large I believe this is an argument based on investment in developing countries, and primarily in those industries where the size of the investment as measured by the local economy is very large indeed, and therefore is bound to raise suspicions with respect to political involvement. It is not an argument that makes much sense with respect to development.

Until relatively recently, the multinational corporation has meant, in a large number of cases, American corporations. Although there are long-standing and large exceptions, I believe that normally the identification with multinational has been American. Because until recently the United States has played such a major, verging on dominant, role in the international economy, it is natural that politicians seeking to emerge from what they conceive to be U.S. dominance would aim their attacks at American multinational corporations. The U.S. government has probably inadvertently encouraged this view, not only by the normal American ebullience but also by the effort to make extraterritorial application of some American policies. Primarily these policies are those identified with American concepts of national security, and I think to a lesser degree, by the extraterritorial application of the seldom understood and often misunderstood antitrust laws. Efforts by the U.S. government to regulate American corporations in their foreign business have been offensive to many foreign nations, and have caused them to reexamine the political consequences of direct foreign investment by foreign corporations.

However the changing economy on the international scene probably now serves as a damper on efforts to restrict foreign investment. More and more larger European companies are now seeing the values—albeit hazardous—of investment in the large American economy. The same appears to be true of Japanese companies, even though Japan has had an extremely restrictive view with respect to foreign investment. At the same time, as discussed above, the United States is far more in a frame of mind to encourage American corporations to invest abroad. To the extent this trend continues, as it probably will, it will be increasingly difficult for any developed country to restrict foreign investment within its borders for fear of reprisals against investment by its corporations in foreign countries.

The current outlook, as I see it is this: As the developed countries become more and more interested in expanding their own direct investment into other markets—and the economies of an international business become more and more obvious to all—the conditions for agreement as to the conditions of foreign investment will improve. I think we are embarking on such a situation today, but we are not far enough along to create the environment that could lead to international standards with respect to such investment.

There are no international organizations really equipped or ready to deal with regulating direct foreign investment. Organizations that include developing countries such as those associated with the United Nations, have far too broad a spectrum of problems to hope for any common agreement. If there is to be agreement, it will have to be among the developed countries, and on the basis that each government is as anxious to have its business enterprises invest abroad as it is willing or reluctant to have foreign enterprises invest within its borders. This is not a condition that will occur within the developing countries for many years to come.

I think it is very difficult at this time for governments to explore the common rules that might govern such investment. The only presently existing organization that could possibly deal with such problems is the Organization for Economic Cooperation and Development (OECD). But the OECD is not now a strong organization, governments are unsure of what their positions are, and I doubt that in the next three or four years the OECD would be willing to embark on serious studies aimed at setting up a serious agreement for the developed countries. There are just too many problems. There is too much dispute, too much dissension, too much uncertainty.

The areas worth exploring seem to me to be the following:

● Taxes, with the hope of securing some further harmonization of tax systems as they affect corporations doing business in a number of countries.

● Efforts to apply national laws to foreign subsidiaries of national corporations. Apart from occasional reach of tax laws and requirements to remit funds for balance of payments reasons, most of the problems in this area center around national security provisions and laws affecting competition. Whether it would be possible to arrive at agreement on substantive matters within these areas is perhaps questionable. It might, for example be extremely difficult to deal with forms of subsidy such as occasionally occur either by way of direct governmental contribution to certain corporations or by discrimination against foreign-dominated corporations by local governments in their purchasing. It would, for example, be extremely difficult to cope with the relationships between the Japanese government and Japanese industry in international agreements.

● Perhaps further exploration of balance of payments and intercompany transfers. Again, this is a technically complex area and while from time to time governments have expressed fears that runs on currencies can take place because of intercorporate transfers, I doubt very much that this is the reality. Certainly it is a subject that can be legitimately explored, and on which rules might be possible to achieve.

It is quite possible to take the position that as far as developed countries are concerned there is relatively little need to develop rules governing direct investment. Many of these have been evolving with some success, and there presently appears to be no great need for further regulation from the point of view of either the public or the multinational corporation. But it seems to me that those needs may evolve, and in any event are almost certain to be causes of some friction with respect to the less developed world. Agreement with developed countries would, at a minimum, be a starting point for negotiations and discussions with developing countries with respect to the same problems. The rules would not need to be the same, although presumptively they might well be, but in any event this would give a common starting point for the developed countries in any such discussions.

The panel analyzed the functioning of multinational corporations, very much in a European-American context. There was by and large a consensus, unstated but there nevertheless, that the functioning of such corporations was proceeding fairly well in the absence of explicit international controls or new control mechanisms. Of course there were shades of opinion, but the farthest left represented at this conference believe that what might be necessary is a suborgan or appendix of an existing organization like the Organization for Economic Cooperation and Development, perhaps to monitor and from time to time admonish activities of multinational corporations that seem to be leading to abusive practices. That was the far left in our meeting.

The general agreement was that regulation is not necessary, that existing organs should be better used or more used, that the Commission of the European Economic Community (EEC) had within itself the ability and mechanism to cope and compete with American multinationals, to develop methods of competition that would be salutary both to the multinationals and to the EEC members generally.

The term "developing country" was rarely used, and I wonder why that was so, quite aside from the fact that our focus was "developed" as opposed to "developing" countries. There was no consideration really given to the relationship between multinationals and developing countries.

The underlying assumption was a feeling that multinationals and developing countries would deal between themselves on an ad hoc basis to the mutual advantage of both, from a position of open bargaining. That issue certainly was not considered as relevant to the present economics and functioning of the multinationals.

PANEL II:
PROBLEMS OF
DEVELOPING COUNTRIES

Most discussion in recent years of multilateral control of international investment has focused on relations among the more advanced industrialized nations, essentially the members of the Organization for Economic Cooperation and Development (OECD). For two decades, investments in other advanced countries have apparently been the leading edge of the growth thrust of multinational enterprises. Moreover, as companies based in Europe and Japan assumed a larger role alongside their American-based counterparts, it became possible to envisage a future of mutual corporate interpenetration in which all the participating nations would be both corporate bases and corporate hosts. The concerns of all these governments would then be sufficiently similar to facilitate the development of multilateral regulation and multilateral adjustment of disputes, since all would share in any advantages from such regulation.

In the case of the less developed countries (LDCs), no such symmetry exists or can be anticipated, except for a few countries that may in due course "graduate" into the group of industrially advanced nations. In this case, moreover, the terrain of tension between host country government and international corporation is far more politicized than among industrialized countries. It resounds with charges of neocolonialism and economic imperialism, capitalist exploitation and "giveaways" of irreplaceable national assets. Poverty, insecurity, and recency on the international scene have a natural reflex in assertive nationalism, along with an understandable sensitivity to real or imagined threats to sovereignty. In the unstable politics of most of the less developed world, it is easy for the actions—or even the presence—of large and highly visible foreign-based corporations to be made into key issues by rival contenders for power. And substantial political elements throughout the less developed world oppose all private enterprise, domestic as well as foreign, so that nationalist hostility to the multinational corporation (MNC) is re-enforced by socialist ideology.

Largely because of this politicization, the post-World War II efforts to achieve consensus among corporate home base and LDC host governments on rules of the game for international investment have been dismal failures. The first and greatest of those efforts was the draft Havana Charter of 1948 for an International Trade Organization. In that effort, LDC insistence on reservations to protect national sovereignty produced clauses that most of the investing community considered worse than no agreement at all. Even the tepid experiment of the World Bank-sponsored International Commission for the Settlement of Investment Disputes encountered universal opposition in Latin America and the Middle East, and it has been almost nonoperative even in the less hostile regions of Africa and Asia. So it is no surprise that more recent proposals for an investment GATT or "GAME" (General Agreement on Multinational Enterprises) have been confined to the industrialized countries, with a lukewarm expression of hope that LDCs might affiliate at a later stage. Since the former group shows no great sense of urgency in this matter, that later stage may be very distant indeed.

Yet the problem of relations between multinational corporations and LDCs may properly be considered more important, as well as more difficult, than among the advanced countries. That is certainly the case from the viewpoint of LDC governments. Except for the unique case of Canada, the proportion of national economic activity conducted or affected by foreign-based companies—especially in the modern industrial sector—is generally much higher in LDCs than in industrialized countries. Such companies account for a larger share of tax revenues and employment in both manufacturing and extractive industries. The companies have a greater impact on foreign trade and the balance of payments. Since their home bases are in industrialized countries, their cultural impact, ways of doing business, and obtrusive "foreignness" are bound to contrast more sharply with domestic patterns. And in the case of less sophisticated governments, there is an understandable fear of being overwhelmed by the battery of managerial, technological, financial, and legal talent at the service of huge multinational enterprises, to say nothing of concern that association with them may expose their countries to political pressures from powerful governments of the home nations.

At the same time, the LDCs have a greater need than the industrialized countries for the capacities of the multinational corporations. Their goal of rapid development implies major structural economic transformation: the generation of entirely new fields of production, the introduction of new types of skills and technology, and connections with new markets. Capital in the purely financial

sense is also of consequence, especially in extractive industries requiring huge outlays on inherently risky ventures, but in most cases
its importance is outranked by management, technology, and market
access.

Hence the typical love-hate relationship between multinational
corporations and LDCs. The corporations are both more needed and
more feared than in the advanced countries.

As to the viewpoint of the companies, their advanced country
investments now greatly exceed those in the LDC—in the case of
American based companies at a ratio of 2.5 to 1 at the end of 1971.
The "headache ratio" of problems with LDC operations, however, is
probably much more equal. In any event, the character of the tensions
is different. As and if the advanced country relationships come increasingly to resemble the model of symmetrical interpenetration,
company operations can approximate more closely the global supranational ideal, in which resource allocation, the location of production,
and the flow of raw materials, components, and finished products re-
sponds to market forces independent of national frontiers. Governments often express a vague uneasiness about the loss of "economic
sovereignty" to MNCs, but the practical scope of intergovernmental
concern with these operations is mainly a matter of tidying up marginal areas: preventing both tax evasion and tax duplication, avoiding
intrusive extraterritorial interventions, harmonizing antitrust measures, controlling short-term speculative capital movements, and resolving disputes on alleged discriminatory treatment.

In the LDCs, however, the issues are more fundamental. They
concern whether, and under what conditions, multinational corporations
may function at all in their territories. Overt or disguised expropriation and abrupt alterations in the rules of the game are commonplace
in the LDCs. Moreover, since some form of directive, and not merely
indicative, economic planning is almost universal in the LDCs, with
any major investment in extractive or manufacturing industry subject
to ad hoc governmental licensing and negotiation, a substantial political
element is built into multinational corporation operations from their
inception.

Since LDCs are not bases for companies operating in the advanced
countries, there can be no tradeoff for them in reciprocal symmetrical
treatment. Their interest in MNC activities is focused on what good
or harm the MNC will do to their national development plans and
aspirations. (I omit the special and dwindling number of cases of
corrupt alliances between companies and politicians unconcerned
with their own national welfare.) Corporate operations under these
conditions must inevitably depart more radically from the global
transnational ideal. Unless the companies are prepared to fit into
national development needs, even at some cost to global integration,

they are unlikely to survive. Working out the terms of such a fit, however, may still be good corporate strategy.

It is evidently a premise of these considerations, and of my observations as a whole, that there does in fact exist a substantial area of potential mutuality of interest between host nations and multinational corporations operating in LDCs. That view is by no means universally accepted. Apart from ideological opponents of all private enterprise (whose objections to MNCs today seem strained in the face of Russian and other Eastern European efforts to make "coproduction" arrangements with the companies), there is virtually blanket opposition to MNCs from many political elements in the LDCs and from respectable academic sources.

If it were not so widely disseminated, I would pass over the objection based on simplistic balance of payments calculations that count inward transfers of capital on the plus side and capital repatriations, interest and dividends, and patent royalties and similar fees on the minus side, without making any allowance for the trade effects (import replacement or export earning) of the enterprise. That calculation will always show "injury" to the capital-importing country's balance of payments over a period of years, but it is simply bad economics.

More serious are arguments that direct foreign investment, especially with 100 percent equity control, may be a relatively costly way of importing capital, technology, and management; that in some cases foreign companies may hinder the development of domestic national entrepreneurship; that the technology favored by the foreign enterprise may not be suited to the needs of a capital-scarce, labor-abundant society; and that foreign companies in import-replacing manufacturing are likely to concentrate their marketing efforts on a small upper- and middle-class segment of the LDC society. Real-life examples can be found to support all of these points. But examples can also be found to refute them.* As blanket indictments they are as unrealistic as the old-fashioned orthodoxy which saw nothing but good in any international investment that could turn a profit: "What's good for General Enterprise is good for Ruritania."

In a well-developed market economy, there is a fair presumption in favor of any investment whose promoter is willing to risk his own capital. But where development requires major structural transformation, and where capital and foreign exchange are tight constraints

---

*With respect specifically to Albert Hirschman's claim that MNC operations suppress local entrepreneurship, I believe that the evidence in many countries, notably including Mexico and Brazil, is strongly to the contrary.

on rates of growth, large investments characteristic of multinational corporations should indeed be tested for conformity to national developmental goals. Against this test, the conclusions are likely to be eclectic; some will be good, some will be bad, and most will be good or bad depending on the terms. Neither blanket indictments nor blanket endorsements are warranted.

There are at least some indications that the pragmatic consequences of such an eclectic conclusion are increasingly being reflected in the attitudes of LDC governments and of company managements. The Andean country governments, for example, are showing considerable resiliency in bending the apparently rigid terms of their investment code. And on the company side there has been a radical departure from the theology of 100 percent equity control, with great ingenuity applied to the design of majority and minority joint ventures, profit-sharing management contracts, payment in kind for equity transfers, and other ways of seeking areas of common interest.

The record of U.S. direct foreign investment is summarized in Table 10.1. The figures confirm the relative surge in the proportion in industrialized countries (especially Western Europe). The LDCs now account for less than 30 percent of total book value as compared with 50 percent two decades ago. The table also brings out the relative strength of manufacturing and service investments in the last decade, as compared with extractive industry, where there is a sharp reversal in relative proportions from the 1950s. In absolute terms, however, the LDC figures are very substantial, again with special emphasis on the nonextractive areas.

Corresponding data are not available for foreign investments based in other industrialized countries, but it is plausible to assume that they would add very considerably to the LDC totals. Japanese company activity in Asia, and more recently Latin America and Africa, would be an important and rapidly growing component in any worldwide compilation.

It would be rash to predict with confidence the role of multinational corporations in the LDCs in coming years, but my own expectation is for considerable expansion. The prospects in extractive and nonextractive areas must be considered separately.

In the resource industries, there is a sizable school of thought that sees no future for MNCs. Copper expropriations and the Organization of Petroleum Exporting Companies (OPEC) drive for oil participation are seen by that school as the beginning of the end, with state operation as much the future rule in those industries as it has become for railroads and electric power. Nationalist sentiment opposes foreign ownership of depletable national assets. Extractive technology is said to be relatively simple, and in any event available on the world market without necessary ties to equity investment. OPEC is seen

TABLE 10.1

Direct U.S. Investment Abroad, 1951-71
(book value at year's end; in millions of dollars)

	1951		1961		1971		Percent Increase	
	amount	percent	amount	percent	amount	percent	1951-61	1961-71
All areas	13,089	–	34,684	–	86,001	–	165	148
Allocated by area	13,089	100.0	33,221	100.0	81,683	100.0	153	146
Industrialized countries	6,440	49.2	21,087	63.5	58,346	71.4	228	177
Extractive	n.a.	–	7,129	21.5	17,014	20.8	n.a.	139
Nonextractive	n.a.	–	13,958	42.0	41,332	50.6	n.a.	196
LDCs	6,649	50.8	12,132	36.5	23,337	28.6	83	92
Extractive	n.a.	–	7,214	21.7	11,823	14.5	n.a.	64
Nonextractive	n.a.	–	4,918	14.8	11,514	14.1	n.a.	134
International unallocated	–	–	1,463	–	4,418	–	n.a.	195
Extractive (all areas)	5,020	38.4	15,212	43.9	30,978	36.0	203	104
Nonextractive (all areas)	8,069	61.6	19,472	56.1	55,023	64.0	141	183

Source: U.S. Department of Commerce, Survey of Current Business, January 1953, August 1962, November 1972.

as a precedent for other producer cartels among the LDCs, with the growing raw material import dependence of the industrialized world—at last including the once resource-rich United States—assuring sellers' markets.

In my judgment, this sort of sweeping generalization is much too facile. It is correct to expect growing world trade in raw materials, and LDCs will probably supply an increasing share of the total since for most items they possess larger high-grade reserves. Nationalist sentiment, reenforced by greater LDC sophistication and by the force of example elsewhere, will certainly rule out the old-fashioned form of long-term concession where the MNC functions as a foreign enclave in national territory. But for many LDCs, and most extractive industries, association in some form with MNCs will continue to be the most beneficial way of exploiting natural resources. The risks at the exploration stage can be placed entirely on the companies, as can the heavy capital requirements for initial exploitation and subsequent major expansion. Technology is certainly more readily available than in pharmaceuticals or computers, but considerable technological dynamism still exists in mineral beneficiation, offshore operations, and the working up of lower-grade ores.

The most important considerations from the viewpoint of the LDCs, however, are market access and markets security. The bland assumption of sellers' markets for most raw materials does not withstand close scrutiny. For the bulk materials, there is a wide dispersion of lower-grade sources that could be exploited at some additional cost. Substitution is generally possible at the margins of consumption. In the major case of aluminum, the technology of economical extraction from omnipresent clays is probably not very far down the pike. For a number of nonferrous metals, deepsea mining of manganese nodules may soon come to rival land-based sources. Moreover, the importing markets are not models of pure competition to be set up against LDC selling monopolies. A large share of consumption is in captive processing facilities often controlled by the same MNCs that engage in mining and bulk transportation. It is plausible to expect a continuing mixture of buyers' and sellers' markets, with substantial price fluctuations, rather than the steady upward price pressure observed for petroleum. There is good reason to believe that OPEC is sui generis rather than a workable model for other raw materials. The efforts of the International Council of Copper Exporting Countries (CIPEC) to control copper markets will be an interesting test, but I would not bet on its success.

In these circumstances, an LDC government may find great advantage in MNC participation in its extractive industry, provided that the terms distribute the benefits fairly among the parties involved. There are other ways of assuring markets, notably long-term sales contracts to reliable purchasers. Again depending on the particular terms, however, alliance with an MNC may provide an attractive package in which capital, management, future as well as present technology, and assured markets are all combined. For these reasons, I foresee a major continuing extractive industry role for the MNCs, although not on traditional concession terms.

The prospects in manufacturing industry are even brighter. As Table 10.1 shows, the growth rate of U.S. investment in LDC non-extractive areas during the last decade has been very impressive. The increase of 233 percent compares with a trebling for nonextractive investment in industrialized countries. Even though the absolute volume in the LDCs is much smaller, the growth rate is almost as high. Here any prognosis must be related to forecasts for general LDC development and for the evolving role of the LDCs in world trade. If growth rate targets of the kind called for in resolutions of the United Nations and UN Conference on Trade and Development—6 to 8 percent per year overall—have any hope of realization, manufacturing must expand at much higher rates. If the minimal foreign exchange requirements of the LDCs are to be earned, they will require large increases in exports of manufactured goods, not only to one another but mainly to the markets of the advanced countries. The developmental "success stories" of recent times—such cases as Taiwan, South Korea, Singapore, and Brazil—have demonstrated these trends.

As the number of MNCs with operating experience in all regions of the world grows, they become a major potential instrument for the redistribution of manufacturing activity. Unless thwarted by political restriction in home base or host countries, the logic of MNC organization—with almost total mobility of capital, technology, management, and even supervisory labor—is toward an accelerated shift of labor-intensive industry to relatively low-wage LDCs. Greater absorptive capacity for pollutants, even under similar air and water quality standards, may be an additional factor favoring industrial location in LDCs. The Vernon product cycle theory states that new products will first be manufactured in the richer countries which constitute their main markets, but if the new products are developed by established MNCs and involve significant labor costs, it is hard to understand why even their initial production might not be in LDCs.

The question of home base country political restraints, symbolized by the Burke-Hartke bill in the U.S. Congress, lies outside the scope of these observations. In host countries, there are typically three sources of tension: distribution of benefits (similar to the case of extractive industries), conformity to national development plans or aspirations, and fear of excessive foreign control over the modern sectors of the economy. It was to minimize such tensions that the concept of preplanned "fade-out" of foreign investments was developed, and seized upon by the authors of the Andean Code.

In my view, the terms of that code are excessively rigid. They fail to recognize the interest of the member countries in a spectrum of possible arrangements with MNCs reflecting differences in potential advantage to the host countries. In some cases, the technology, capital, and management accompanying the original investment may be the main foreign contribution, and subsequent transfer of full ownership to domestic hands may be quite appropriate. In other cases, however, the technology may be a continuing stream rather than a one-shot affair, and long-term association with the MNC may be the only way of sharing in that stream. An even stronger reason for long-term association is access to the MNC's worldwide marketing network in any case where sales are envisaged beyond the domestic market. Such an association may have more than direct economic value; it can also help reduce the danger of import restrictions in the home base country.

For service industries, the outlook is less favorable because most are inherently limited to the domestic market. The balance of payments costs of remittances are not offset by gains on trade account. At a given phase in development, foreign banks, insurance companies, retailers, hoteliers, and engineering and management consultants all have important roles, and some may become permanent parts of the LDC economy. Long-term survival, however, is likely only where the service is directly related to the country's other international economic transactions.

It may be charged that the above analysis is so eclectic that it defies any generalization and leaves no room for the development of international law. If investments may be good, bad, or indifferent, depending on the terms, and if the terms in each case are to be determined by ad hoc negotiation, is there any scope for rules, codes, orderly procedures, or useful intervention by international institutions? Spokesmen for the MNCs keep calling for stable rules of the game and sometimes say that they do not care what those rules may be as long as they are stable. When codes are drafted, however, they show a great interest in the content of the rules, and then usually conclude that "ad hockery" is preferable.

Given the diversity in LDC degrees of development, governmental sophistication, attitudes toward foreign investment, and developmental priorities, it would be fanciful to expect any meaningful general code on treatment of MNCs to be agreed upon among LDCs as a whole or any substantial number of them. The obstacle does not lie only in real differences in economic situations and interests; it is rooted in the politics of foreign investment in the LDCs. In that framework, theoretical concerns for sovereignty loom much larger than the pros and cons of specific terms for particular MNC operations. As a result, when broad principles and formal draft codes are under review in international discussions, even the more pragmatically minded governments find themselves compelled by the pressures of internal politics to support extreme positions for maximum conservation and protection of national sovereignty. Given this inherent thrust toward least common denominators, it follows that the only kinds of international codes that could be agreed to formally by LDC governments would be their very nature be unacceptable to the investors.

Most individual governments do make the effort to establish codes, at least for extractive industry and increasingly for manufacturing industry as well. International organizations such as the appropriate United Nations agencies can contribute through technical assistance a great deal toward the rationalization—and therefore the stabilization—of such national codes.

At the international level, the realistic alternative to formal intergovernmental codes is the evolution of a kind of case law: the gradual building of international doctrine and practice that may ultimately lead to generally accepted principles concerning international investment in LDCs. On the institutional side, it would be futile to create new agencies for this purpose. Reliance should rather be placed on the existing relevant agencies of the United Nations, but especially on the financial institutions—the World Bank and the regional development banks—that often participate in private international investment projects through direct financing or guarantees.

The first task for such institutions would be to assist LDC governments in strengthening their bargaining power in negotiations with MNCs. In this connection it is important to bear in mind the heterogeneity of LDC governments. In such cases as Brazil, Mexico, Taiwan, or Singapore, there is a high degree of sophistication and no particular need for outside technical assistance. The oil producing country governments assembled in OPEC have amply demonstrated that their bargaining power is in no need of "equalization." But there are perhaps 70 or 80 LDCs with very little governmental sophistication in international economic bargaining. For them, outside technical assistance might make a crucial difference.

As a corollary, it would be enormously helpful to establish an international registry or clearinghouse maintaining current information, not only on the content of pertinent national laws and regulations but also on the specific terms of all MNC investments of substantial size in all LDCs. That implies a uniform requirement of disclosure. Such a requirement may at first blush seem objectionable to some governments and some companies. In my belief, however, it would be advantageous to both in the long run. Disclosure and publicity would help protect companies against charges of corruption or "special deals" with a particular regime after a successor government had come to power, either through election or some less orderly procedure. (The political history of the LDCs in recent decades has been marked by countless coups d'état, and there is little reason to suppose that such abrupt changes of regime are a thing of the past.) For similar reasons, disclosure and publicity is an important protection to the officials of governments in power at any particular time, lessening the danger of subsequent recriminations against "secret deals." The information compiled in an international registry would, of course, be important raw material for technical assistance and for the gradual development of a system of case law.

Beyond these two preliminary tasks of technical assistance and publicity, there is a need for explicit appraisal of investment benefits and their allocation among the parties concerned. The parties will always include host nation and foreign corporation, and may also include domestic private participants and the home base nation. The international institutions could develop a systematic format and objective analytical techniques for making such appraisals. They go to the heart of two sources of tension: charges of "inequity" in benefit distribution and charges of unequal bargaining power between large international corporations and the governments of small countries.

There is no simple objective standard of equity in these matters. Assuming a non-zero/sum game in which the investment can be of benefit to both principal parties, there is a zone for bargaining that has the basically indeterminate solution of any bilateral monopoly transaction. International institutions, however, can narrow that zone in three ways. First, by promoting explicit appraisal of the size and allocation of benefits, they can assure that each party receives some share of the total benefits. Second, as already suggested, they can provide technical assistance to less sophisticated governments to help equalize bargaining skill, to bring to bear knowledge of comparable arrangements in other countries, and to reduce the fear of being "taken in" by high-powered corporate managers and lawyers. Third, especially where they are themselves directly involved in part of the financing, they can provide a neutral third-party judgment on the fairness of the terms, as well as good offices or mediating services to help resolve specific disputes. However, I would not expect them to act as formal arbitrators.

A deliberate policy and procedure of this type on the part of the World Bank and regional banks might gradually develop a kind of case law on fair terms for MNC operations in LDCs, conformity to which would tend to forestall uncompensated expropriation or drastic changes in the rules of the game. It would obviously not cover cases of extreme revolutionary ideology. In more moderate situations, however, the "certificate of good corporate behavior" implied, say, by World Bank participation, coupled with the LDCs' continuing interest in ongoing financing from the Bank, should tend to depoliticize and stabilize the relationship. This is an onerous burden to recommend to the international institutions, but it could have enormous leverage in facilitating the developmental role of private investment. Over the long run, it might become a more successful indirect route to the acceptance of third-party arbitration of disputes than the direct efforts of recent years.

The extractive industries are especially difficult, not only because of the nationalist emotions associated with depletable resources but also because of the dramatic shift in evaluation of interests and in bargaining power that follows successful exploration and the first large fixed investment in mines, wells, or refineries. The typical history has involved overgenerous concessions to induce exploration and initial investment, followed by demands for renegotiation (or expropriation) once the reserves are located and the heavy investments completed. Many companies have learned the bitter lesson that stability of relationships requires the conviction of continuing mutuality of interest. Gratitude for past risk-taking is an evanescent commodity once the gamble has been won.

Since this bargaining power shift is perfectly predictable, it would be desirable to anticipate it in the terms of the original bargain. Risky exploration should be paid off very rapidly, including a premium for the risk as well as actual costs incurred, with exploitation then based on long-term sharing of benefits. Here again the international institutions might have a role in devising more stable forms of phased concession terms, including regular renegotiation at intervals of five to ten years.

In manufacturing also, there may be shifts of interest in particular cases, especially with low-technology products. With all its admitted drawbacks, some form of joint venture is likely to outlast wholly-owned MNC subsidiaries. The trend toward joint ventures is a welcome sign of the adaptability of most MNCs.

That adaptability is also relevant to some of the current complaints against the social consequences of MNC operations in LDCs, such as their alleged focus on luxury goods or inappropriate technologies. Industrialization through a policy of highly protected substitution for imported consumer goods does indeed have these tendencies, but the fault lies with LDC policy rather than the MNCs which take advantage of those policies. If the national developmental goal favors goods for mass consumption or income redistribution, and if the proper relative prices of labor and capital are allowed to govern, or if the thrust is toward exports able to compete on world markets, the appropriate policies can make those opportunities attractive to MNCs. Much of the literature in this field conveys an image of all-powerful international corporations bending weak governments to their will. But as skill is developed in the use of sovereign powers, a more accurate image would picture MNCs as liquid bundles of resources ready to adapt their terms and organization to flow into the molds formed for them by the sovereigns, as long as those molds are sufficiently profitable. There is ample room for ad hoc bargaining, with the ultimate sanctions of exclusion on the government side and nonentry or withdrawal on the MNC side.

The discussion above focused on the principal parties: LDC governments and MNCs. The essential character of the proposed contribution of the international community, which represents both industrialized and less developed country governments, is to assist in expanding the zone of rationality and equalizing the bargaining power in that central relationship, with the hope of developing a consensual case law on norms of equity in the distribution of benefits.

The Williams Commission has suggested a complementary device with similar objectives, in the form of "a well-organized, regular forum for reasoned discussion in which high-level representatives of the private sectors of developed and developing countries meet together with government officials to examine issues and formulate policies for encouraging investment and resolving disputes."* The United Nations Secretariat and the regional banks have sponsored several such meetings, and their institutionalization would be a useful step.

What of the home base government? Should they refrain from assistance to MNCs through investment guarantees and diplomatic support in their relations with LDCs, as Raymond Vernon has urged? Political realism and the nature of industrialized country interests make it very difficult to accept this notion. As raw material import dependence grows, touching on the economic survival of the industrialized nations, their governments are likely to become more closely associated with MNCs in the extractive fields, as the Japanese example demonstrates. In the United States, the idea that government should simply ignore uncompensated expropriations of American corporate subsidiaries disregards the structure of congressional politics.

A more modest goal would be the multilateralization of investment guarantees and a harmonization of investment incentives among homebase countries, coupled with reliance on international institution judgment of fairness of treatment in disputed cases. Even though the LDCs were not parties to third-party arbitration, diplomatic action or economic retaliation against alleged maltreatment of corporate subsidiaries would have greater international moral standing if the industrialized country governments accepted the guidance of the kind of "certificate of corporate good behavior" suggested above.

---

*Commission on International Trade and Investment Policy, United States International Economic Policy in an Interdependent World (Washington, D.C.: Government Printing Office, 1971), p. 249.

There is also the possibility of organized confrontation between advanced and less developed country governments as groups—a not wholly unrealistic destination of the road down which OPEC sometimes appears to be leading the international oil economy. Such an outcome would not be conducive to LDC development or to the emergence of a rule of law for international economic interdependence. It should be considered only as a very undesirable last resort. Harmonization of rules by LDC regional groups seeking market integration, on the other hand, is highly desirable.

It will be evident that the concept of supranational incorporation and MNC responsibility to a global control body is wholly unfeasible for the foreseeable future, at least with respect to LDCs. More limited functional controls are possible, and some or all LDCs might participate in some of them. Some form of global regime for deepsea bed minerals will be indispensable in the immediate future. Any arrangements on which industrialized countries might agree for tax basis allocation, review of intracorporate pricing, antitrust policy harmonization, or reciprocal limits on extraterritorial jurisdiction should be welcomed by the LDCs. But on the more central issues of whether MNCs should operate at all in LDCs, in what areas, and on what terms and conditions, the paramount concern for structural transformation to promote national development, to say nothing of the force of political nationalism, rules out the kinds of surrenders of sovereignty implied by world incorporation.

* * * * *

COMMENT
Milic Kybal

Lincoln Gordon reaches very realistic conclusions with which I find myself in agreement as a whole. We can only hope that the main findings of this conference and those of similar forums will contribute to the creation of a modest but growing institutional framework that will give greater confidence to the parties involved in private international investment.

Mr. Gordon raises the question of whether the traditional distinction between industrialized and less developed countries may not result in some limitations in the analysis of the problem and lead to some simplifications in the solutions. For instance, the difference in per capita income between the richest and the poorest country of one region with which I am fairly familiar, Latin America, is 10.5

times, while it is only 2.3 times in the enlarged European Economic
Community (EEC).*

The temptation to divide the world (outside the group of centrally
planned economies) into two neat parts is all the greater since numerous statistical sources are presented this way. This is also the case
of the U.S. Department of Commerce data on U.S. direct investment
abroad included in Gordon's observations. The question is whether
conclusions drawn from this dichotomy are as generally valid as a
more detailed subdivision that would take more into account the factual
situation in specific countries.

It is pointed out that among the more advanced industrialized
nations—essentially the members of the OECD—there is a symmetry
in the sense that it is possible to envisage a future in which all these
countries would be both corporate bases and corporate hosts, while
no such symmetry exists among the developing countries. Under
these circumstances, it is thought that there can be no tradeoff for
the less developed countries in reciprocal symmetrical treatment.

It is unlikely that reciprocity of the roles of capital exporter
and importer, whether actual and potential, has a major influence on
the conduct of most industrial countries. Their attitude toward private foreign investment is largely only one aspect of the role they
assign to private enterprise in their own economy, without distinguish-
ing much whether it is domestic or foreign. This role is not much
influenced by considerations of the policies of other industrialized
countries or the position of their own investors in such countries.
This is the reason they never have any overall foreign investment
codes.

Considering actual governmental action in the developing countries regarding private foreign investment, it appears that in many
of them such action, regardless of various formal requirements, does
not differ very much from that undertaken in the industrialized countries. The only general way of assessing actual practice is by its results, on the basis of statistics on changes in such investments in
specific areas and specific fields. For purposes of a more detailed
illustration, the case of Latin America is shown in Table 10.2.

The remarkable thing is that U.S. direct investment in Latin
America in manufacturing—which constitutes the most important
field in this region—increased by 184 percent in 1961-71 and is quite

----

*Per capita GNP (at market prices) in 1970 in Argentina was
US$1,160 and in Haiti $110; in the enlarged EEC the two extremes
are Denmark with $3,190 and Ireland with $1,360. See International
Bank for Reconstruction and Development, World Bank Atlas: Population, Per Capita Product and Growth Rates (1972).

TABLE 10.2

U.S. Direct Investments in the World and in the Latin American Republics, 1961–71
(book value at year's end; in millions of dollars)

	World			Developed Countries			Latin America		
	1961	1971	percent increase	1961	1971	percent increase	1961	1971	percent increase
Total	32,778	86,001	162	21,087	58,346	177	8,166	12,978	59
Mining[a]	3,061	6,720	120	1,514	4,060	168	1,105	1,356	23
Petroleum	12,151	24,258	100	4,972	12,954	161	3,248	3,303	2
Manufacturing	11,936	35,475	197	10,036	29,483	194	1,655	4,708	184
Other	7,536	19,549	159	4,565	11,848	160	2,159	3,611	67

	Argentina			Brazil			Mexico			Venezuela		
	1961	1971	percent increase	1961	1971	percent increase	1961	1971	percent increase	1961	1971	percent increase
Total	635	1,350	113	1,000	2,045	105	822	1,840	124	3,017	2,698	-11
Extractive[b]	—	—	—	106	264	149	178	156	-12	2,371	1,634	-31
Manufacturing	283	813	187	543	1,409	159	414	1,272	207	196	516	163
Other[b]	352	537	53	451	372	-18	230	412	79	440	548	25

[a] Includes smelting.
[b] For Argentina investments in the extractive industries have been included in other industries; for Venezuela investments in mining and smelting have been included in other industries.

Sources: U.S. Department of Commerce, Survey of Current Business, August 1962 and November 1972.

close to the 194 percent increase achieved in the developed countries. The great majority (nearly 87 percent) of investment in manufacturing in the region is concentrated in the four countries—Brazil, Mexico, Argentina, and Venezuela—with the largest GNP and presumably the largest domestic markets. Thus, assuming a reasonably receptive governmental policy, it seems that the growth of private foreign investment in manufacturing is determined by the size of the domestic market, and that many types of industrial production cannot be attracted to very small markets. This can change, should several enterprises direct an increasing part of their output to a regional market or to the world at large. Hence the major potential role of regional economic integration schemes. Thus it is possible that a basic economic con-sideration—the size of the market—might be more significant than the classification of a host country in the developed or developing cate-gory.

I share Mr. Gordon's confidence that private investment and especially the multinational corporations have a great role to perform in promoting industrial development. They are by far the greatest source of new technology, risk capital, and managerial know-how, and therefore their participation is being sought in various ways in most countries of the world, including those of the socialist group.

In the extractive industries, U.S. direct investments almost stagnated in Latin America as a whole in 1961-71 while they have about doubled in the world. In the mining and smelting industry, there are considerable differences in government policies, with Brazil and Chile standing at opposite poles. In petroleum there is a retrenchment in Venezuela but an expansion, in different forms, in Ecuador and Peru. From a worldwide standpoint it is notable that in extractive industries the greatest expansion has taken place in oil in the Middle East or in two developed countries, namely, Canada and Australia. The long-term trend seems to be toward costlier and technically more sophisticated extractive industries calling for a major role by the multinationals. The recent discussions concerning foreign investment in natural gas exploitation in the Soviet Union for export to the United States and Japan supports this belief.

The group of "other" industries is too varied to permit a gener-alization except for the fact that U.S. investment has grown much less in Latin America than in the developed countries. Many such activi-ties are linked with the production and movement of goods, and their slow growth perhaps explains in part the region's lag of exports and service receipts.

Possibly some major conclusions can be drawn from the Latin American case, which are likely to find some corroboration in other areas:

1. The policies the developing countries are willing to follow toward private foreign investment will vary considerably, depending in a large measure on the size of their economies, their relative degrees of development, and the dynamism of their own private sectors. Of course, in some instances, ideological and other noneconomic considerations can be overriding. Probably three subgroups could be usefully distinguished among developing countries:

a. Countries with a relatively large domestic market, sufficient institutional stability, and a dynamic private domestic sector. Such countries usually follow a rather confident policy and are willing and able to attract a large volume of private foreign investment.

b. Countries with medium-size markets. Particularly when such countries are heavily dependent on extractive industries for their exports, their attitude may be restrictive and, as a recent case shows, even entirely negative.

c. Countries with small domestic markets. Such countries feel a greater need to attract private foreign investment but, unless they have significant petroleum or mineral resources, their ability to do so is rather limited.

2. Another major distinction is along fields of investment. Receptivity seems most widespread in manufacturing and least in petroleum.

3. The multinational corporations have shown a great deal of flexibility and adaptability. There is every reason to believe that they are capable of adapting their activities to a great variety of conditions but not always with the same effectiveness in terms of transfers of capital, technology, marketing, and other aspects.

4. The differences in size and economic development among the developing countries make it desirable that a network of direct investment be stimulated among them. Argentine, Brazilian, and Mexican investments in neighboring countries should be considered as only the beginning of a trend, leading to a free movement of capital among members of the same economic group.

5. Foreign direct investment will find a more receptive and potentially fruitful climate if it works together with an expanding domestic private sector. Unfortunately, the role of the international financial agencies for the strengthening of the latter has been rather marginal. These agencies could have a major impact if they directed more resources to the strengthening of the capital market institutions in the developing countries. The latent possibility of invigorating such institutions has been recently shown in a dramatic way in Brazil.

Finally, I agree with Mr. Gordon's assessment as to the modest scale on which international controls on multinational corporations are desirable and feasible, stressing instead the harmonization of incentives among capital-exporting countries and the multilateralization of investment guarantees. Any institutional arrangement that might finally emerge will progress mainly because of the services it can usefully offer to the parties concerned. In this sense, the international financial institutions that are daily engaged in the practical issues of economic development and try to see the problem in its many facets could be of considerable help.

At the Inter-American Development Bank the role of private foreign investment in economic development is being given careful consideration. Its President, Antonio Ortiz Mena, on the basis of his long experience as finance minister of Mexico, attaches great importance to the elimination of double taxation, based on the principle that income should be taxed only in the country where it originates.

Mr. Gordon points out the usefulness of a regular forum for exchanges of views. The Inter-American Development Bank, together with the Organization of American States, has already arranged for three off-the-record round tables on private foreign investment in Latin America with the participation of a group of government officials and businessmen of the region and a good representation from multi-national corporations.

* * * * *

COMMENT
Edgar Cruft

I want to point out that although I am an Englishman, my comments are based primarily on the natural affiliation of spending most of my professional career in the United States and Canada. So I tend to speak as an Anglo-American with a lot of African and other overseas experience.

I feel somewhat at a disadvantage at a conference at which perhaps I am the only scientist or technologist. But perhaps I have one advantage in that, as the president of a small but very multinational corporation, I am involved on a day-to-day basis in sitting down with government representatives and members of the civil service of developing countries in various parts of the world, and thrashing out the very questions that are being discussed here.

Being a geologist gives me one other advantage, and that is a very strong awareness of the value of the deposits in the ground in the developing countries. This kind of knowledge is particularly lacking in less developed countries. Unfortunately, the people often do not have sufficient understanding of the value of their own resources; a better understanding and inventory of domestic resources, whether made by some international organization or consultant group, is a prime requirement for an LDC.

This applies to an astounding number of less developed countries, not only to relatively small African countries that might understandably have no geologists or engineers but also to a country ranking right on top of the LDC list, such as Brazil, for although Brazil has excellent professionals, they are relatively inexperienced. Of equal importance is the organization of professional expertise, in the form of mineral surveys, and this is often as sorely lacking as professional training, particularly in Latin America, which has no recent colonial history.

Thus there is a considerable lack of professional and experienced experts who can speak confidently on behalf of the LDC. This lack of expertise in most professional areas means the plane loads of executives, attorneys, engineers, and accountants from MNCs who go to negotiate agreements are, without question, markedly intimidating to the LDCs.

Someone who is intimidated tends to put up a very strong front for fear of losing face and respect among peers, and the LDCs also are afraid of giving away what might be a real mineral bonanza. In actual fact, true bonanzas are quite rare and more commonly the MNC is faced with a very strong front that must be broken down, hopefully by persuasion and common sense. The alternative for the MNC is simply to walk away because it is impossible to reach agreement with a particular country.

Our company tries not to take the approach of going in with a large number of people. We attempt to work on a much more personal level, and in my experience it has paid off. I think I might suggest that this would be a good approach for the major industrial corporations to follow.

Many MNCs do this of course, but often some of the international positions are occupied by people who could have a little more sensitivity and training at the international level. But regardless of whether the MNCs change their approach in dealing with LDCs, I reiterate that LDCs must gain their own professional expertise or use an international agency on a consultant or other basis with personnel who are realistic enough to see the technical and business aspects from both sides. Such an agency does not yet exist, but it should be set up.

I would like to congratulate Lincoln Gordon on his excellent observations and say that I am astounded that he has never worked for a major corporation involved in day-to-day negotiations because the points he made cover the entire spectrum. He missed very few points, and he brought to light many of the issues that consistently hang up agreements and business.

I will focus my observations on natural resources aspects because this is my area of expertise, and also because it is a vitally important aspect in the development of an LDC. Some figures were previously presented in Table 10.2 regarding mining investment in Latin America by U.S. corporations; these figures show a very small increase, or in fact often a decrease. Perhaps they are not overly representative figures but they do show a very strong corporate reaction over recent years to events in much of Latin America. Major mining companies (and here I am talking about the mining industry although similar figures might hold for the petroleum industry) have decided as a basic corporate philosophy that Latin America is not a healthy place to be over the last few years. Much of the risk investment is now going into Africa, Australia, Canada, and other areas.

What is of great concern for the LDCs and the world community as a whole is that more and more investment is going into larger LDCs or even developed countries, relative to investment in smaller LDCs. Certainly the latter need investment in their natural resource industries more than any other form of investment (see Table 10.2). Latin America is losing out, certainly by choice, and I would stress that the Latin American model is not a good model for the LDCs to follow. There are other and better routes for LDCs to obtain fair, fast development of their natural resources and earn the return they desire and the respect of the international community. Nationalization of developed resources—although I would be the first to admit it has not always been unwarranted—and changes in the ground rules are not the way to play the game. Countries tend to suffer guilt by association and this is obviously very true of Latin America. One cannot equate all of the countries: One cannot equate Brazil, with a liberal mineral rights law but severe capital movement and repatriation problems, with Chile and its present climate severely restricting foreign ownership, or with Mexico, a booming economy that, perhaps rightly for itself, seems to believe that the last place for foreign investment is in its natural resources. It is important that the confrontations of U.S. MNCs with Latin American governments not dominate our thinking or dealings on the question of MNC-LDC relations.

I return to the question of expertise, but it is important to recognize that in many cases the question of development of natural resources is the first time the government of a small LDC really sits down face to face with the multinational corporation. LDCs do not generally start industrialization with the entrance of a computer or electronics company. The first MNC-LDC confrontation in many cases is precisely in the area of mining and oil, and specifically at a time when the LDC is perhaps less equipped to handle some of the problems. Therefore the establishment of some agency or group to disseminate information or provide help to the LDC at this very critical period should be very much appreciated by the LDC.

95

The area of natural resources also involves strong emotional problems that can be used politically. To build a computer factory requires just a few acres sitting outside town. To do effective mineral or oil exploration requires hundreds of square miles of concession rights. Mr. Gordon made the statement that perhaps the concession area type of exploration is on the way out; I think this is unfortunate if true, and I will have some further comments on this later.

Mr. Gordon has made the premise—and I totally agree with him— that multinational operations in less developed countries are essential. In fact, I would have made the point even more strongly, for to have exploration and exploitation of natural resources in LDCs without the private investment sector would certainly be very difficult.

The basic reasons are, as Mr. Gordon pointed out, the risk capital question, the question of technology, and the question of markets. Mr. Gordon gave considerable attention to the relative importance of markets but this, while of particular importance in the nonextractive industries, is generally of lesser importance in the major extractive industries.

The two very important areas are, of course, considerations of risk capital and technology. The degree of technology necessary to explore for or develop a mineral deposit is often considered less than that required for building a nuclear reactor or designing and making a computer. Without doubt, however, the application of these principles is as difficult or even more difficult in the natural resources industry where profits must be won from what are often marginally economic ores. How much of a profit is made, if any, is totally dependent upon the technology. This may seem a trite statement but it is fundamental, and the wag who said that "more money has been put into mines than has even been taken out" was nearly right. The difference is in the application of technology. This is being demonstrated in some countries where nationalization has occurred.

There is a lot of technological claptrap at the present time, somewhat overstating the idea that it is quite simple to do mineral exploration or mineral resource inventories using, for example, satellites and high-flying aircraft.

The argument made is that now all an LDC need do to perform its own mineral survey is to buy or loan expertise to look at photographs from satellites. This is far from the case, and I bring it up here because I see some LDCs being trapped by over reliance on this approach.

LDCs should bear in mind that the technology is not as easy as it sounds. Many of the claims made for natural resource inventories from satellites are made by agencies or individuals who have vested interests in particular satellites and/or programs. In point of fact, at the present time a satellites or high-flying aircraft flown over all the known bodies of minerals in the world would probably pick up less than one-tenth of one percent of these bodies, even if observers knew where the bodies were and hence where to look for the signals. This technology can be of great assistance, but only as part of a properly conducted mineral survey. Quick and easy technology is not the answer. The answer is getting on the ground and spending risk money, often in lengthy programs, and using expertise the multinational corporation can best supply.

An important form of aid for LDCs to make mineral resource surveys is that of the experienced crews supplied by foreign governments and the United Nations. However, it should be recognized that these are preliminary surveys.

The Canadian, German, U.S., and British governments as well as the United Nations programs can provide basic mineral resource inventories of inestimable value to a less developed country trying to develop its mineral resources. An LDC that develops basic geological information on its own or with outside help so mineral exploration targets can be identified will have many points of leverage in negotiating mineral concession rights with an MNC.

A few comments on the risk capital required are important because of the general feeling that there is a lot of capital around for exploitation and exploration of natural resources but there is not too much know-how or technology. Thus, it is felt, the MNC is more required for the technology than the capital.

I do not agree because I know that the type of capital required for exploration carries a very high degree of risk. Preproduction capital is more readily available on a "bankable" basis. Risk capital is very difficult to obtain, other than from the multinational corporations or the purely private sector.

As an example, one country that has statistics on domestic exploration costs is Canada. In fact, it may be the only country that has any statistics, and even those are difficult to dig out. But statistics for a foreign MNC that is in my estimation one of the better exploration groups show that over a 22-year period its true exploration cost in finding and preliminary development of a mine was $43 million per property.

Now this amount of capital (whether we talk about a lower estimate of $15 million or we talk about an upper estimate of $50 million), mostly pure risk, unsecured, and, if you like, "roll of the dice" type capital, which might result in a mineral deposit and might go totally down the drain, is, I submit, really only available from the multinational corporation or private sector. The MNC have an essential and necessary role to fill in exploring and developing the mineral resources of the less developed world, and they have to be attracted to take these considerable risks.

It might be interesting also to note that in Canada (and I keep coming back to Canada because it has such an admirable record and is a very good model of the way a less developed country can go) a tremendous amount of basic technological work is done by government and provincial surveys to attract industry. These surveys reduce by as much as 20 to 50 percent the amount of money needed to be spent on basic exploration by a multinational corporation exploring in Canada. A comparison of Canada and Brazil (which is of similar size but with no basic information) illustrates this point: the chances are significantly better in Canada because one knows where to look. It might be fair to state that $1 million spent in this particular area of basic resource study can generate perhaps $10 million to $20 million of exploration funds supplied by a multinational corporation. There is also a substantial psychological advantage for the LDC that has its own information when negotiating with a multinational corporation. I fully recognize, however, that even this approach, which might apply for the larger and richer LDCs, is too sophisticated at this time for other LDCs. In that case assistance in formulating mining laws or negotiating with an MNC must be supplied directly.

Mr. Gordon makes the point that the traditional concession area type of exploration should be abandoned. There are a lot of problems with using the concession area type of exploration, not least that it infringes on the territorial rights of the less developed country. However, I do not know how one is going to do effective exploration by eliminating the concession area or some sort of advance mineral rights. A corporation that is willing to come in and do exploration must be sure of having exclusive rights to land and the rights to exploit the mineral deposits found on that land.

Perhaps some changes that could be made are that the governments could be a little stricter on how the company should act on its concession, how long it should hold the concession for exploration, and how much money should be spent on the concession. I believe unquestionably that it is to the advantage of LDCs to be much tougher in getting pertinent information out of those concessions.

At the moment, in many countries, concession area exploration by a multinational corporation requires written reports to the LDC. These are often some kind of token report every six months or once a year, and they can be a pretty poor representation of the real situation inside the concession. LDCs should have outside assistance to police or evaluate activities within concession areas. I do not think it would hurt the multinational corporations to be far freer in disseminating information to LDC governments. It would certainly create a freer, more trustworthy attitude on both sides. On the LDC side, however, such information should not be used to change the ground rules of the concession grant. A consulting body or agency should be set up to enable governments to have technical, financial, and legal assistance when and where they need it. Control by international legislation is not needed, but help is.

I also agree that there should be a center for dissemination of information. In dealing with the government of a less developed country, I find intense interest and concern for how these problems are being handled elsewhere. The Latin American confrontations get an excessive share of the limelight, but the African and Asian countries in particular are evolving their own formulas, which are as relevant.

On the whole it is very difficult for LDCs to get information on the approaches taken in specific LDC-MNC relations elsewhere. Agreements between multinational corporations and LDCs could be put into a central clearinghouse where they would be available to all.

I also think the LDCs and MNCs should take a much stronger role in training nationals to occupy positions in the corporations set up in their countries. The nationals could be trained for professional operating levels. The benefits of highly trained local personnel to the MNC are enormous, as are the obvious benefits to the LDC. There seems to be a tendency today for many LDCs to get hung up on the idea of 51 percent ownership. It all sounds very fine and it says, "well, we've really got control of our natural resources because we own 51 percent," but I am sure there are numerous cases where a multinational corporation is operating in a less developed country with the LDC owning 51 percent but with real control in the hands of the MNC. Token positions on the board of directors are less important to the LDC in the long run than skilled operators, professionals, and managers who are nationals. The training of such personnel, is really what the LDC should be pushing for. In the ultimate development of a country's industry, this will have far more impact than 51 percent ownership and a few token directors of a specific property. I think if is very important that the MNC and the LDC get together and supply extensive training for persons who can eventually be placed in senior positions.

Financial incentives that are necessary for the MNCs to be attracted to invest, and that are fair to both parties, include the following:

● Exploration costs must be given a very rapid writeoff, and the LDC must permit exploration costs within a whole country to be written off.

● Rapid writeoff of development capital also is needed.

● Any equity sharing by LDC and MNC should come after all exploration and development capital is written off and then should be related to the tax rate, with increased LDC equity offset by tax concessions.

I certainly do not agree with Mr. Gordon that the concession should be renegotiated every five to ten years as this can lead to serious trouble. Once you have an agreement, you should try to stick to it. A formula could be agreed upon, however, so that after rapid writeoffs, and after a reasonable amount of profit has been made and dividends repatriated (and I think they should be spelled out by amounts in relation to capital employed rather than by time), there should be very definite opportunities for the LDC to come into the venture on a basis of equity participation or increased profit-sharing.

It is always possible, and perhaps more common than not, that at the beginning of a mining venture you can see reserves for ten years, but you often end up with reserves for twenty years. Those last ten years can provide the "bonanza" aspects of the mining investment, and I think there is no question that the LDC should have a bigger and bigger share of the overall profits and dividends by a pre-arranged formula.

11

THE DEVELOPING COUNTRIES'
POINT OF VIEW: I

J. Ade Oyelabi

What do the initiatives from the developing countries—such as the Andean Code, UN Conference on Trade and Development (UNCTAD), investment laws and planning—tell us about the political possibilities in developing countries and their willingness to submit to an international regime with respect to investment?

If taken in the narrow sense, the answer to this question must involve some prediction of political reaction in the less developed countries (LDCs). Obviously, such an exercise is fraught with hazards. Alternatively, one can interpret the question in the broad sense so as to evoke a discussion of the main issues involved in relations between foreign investor and host country. This broader view will be taken here.

I will begin with a general discussion of the emergence of multinational enterprises. Then I will review the Nigerian experience; it can be claimed that in many respects this experience is shared by most LDCs. The third section is devoted to a discussion of the main issues or complaints that arise from the operations of foreign investors in LDCs. The fourth section reviews the search for solutions to some of the problems raised, and my observations end with a few final comments.

EMERGENCE OF THE MULTINATIONALS

In the context of world economic history, the multinational corporation is a very recent phenomenon. It started to seriously impinge on our consciousness only from the decade of the 1950s. Prior to that time, what existed among the industrial countries was, for the most part, portfolio investment. As for the LDCs, there was direct

101

investment from the appropriate metropolitan countries. However, colonial relationships were such that the direct investment was hardly regarded as "foreign." Today, a national of an LDC would define a multinational corporation as a foreign business enterprise that owns and/or controls economic production facilities in two or more independent nations.

Most conventional international trade theories advocate and welcome the growth of multinational corporations. For one thing, the operation of these corporations leads to the attainment of a more efficient allocation of capital and allied scarce factors of production. For another, it allows for easier transfer of technology from the industrial countries to the LDCs. The emergence of the multinationals can therefore be said to be a vindication of "the strategic view that business should find the best markets, employ the best technology," and be financed "through the best channels, irrespective of geography "*
In this search for the best we have reached the stage where a few hundred multinational corporations (originating mainly in North America, Europe, and Japan) dominate the world economic scene. One authority (A. Barber, "Emerging New Power: The World Corporation," War/Peace Report, October 1968) predicts that within the next generation about 400 to 500 of these corporations will own about two-thirds of the fixed assets of the world.

The magnitude of private investment flow from the industrial countries to the LDCs for the period 1959-68 is given in Table 11.1. The net flow in 1959 was $2.8 billion. It fell to $2.4 billion in 1962 but rose to $5.7 billion by 1968. As one would expect, the major sources of private capital in 1968 (as indeed in many of the preceding years) were, in order of importance, the United States, West Germany, France, Italy, the United Kingdom, Japan, and Switzerland. Every year during this period, the United States was by far the largest supplier. And it is assumed that the multinational corporations (MNCs) have been responsible for most of the private investment flow.

The main problems that the operations of the MNCs pose for the LDCs will be discussed later. But it is appropriate to mention at this point that although the problem of the multinationals is world-wide, there is one feature that is particularly resented in the LDCs: It is a one-way problem. While most industrial countries of Europe are, in varying degrees, both exporters and importers of direct investment, the LDCs are (almost by definition) just recipients of direct foreign investment. The effects of this and other characteristics of foreign investment in the less developed countries generally will be discussed after a brief presentation of the Nigerian experience.

---

*Raymond Vernon, "Economic Sovereignty at Bay," Foreign Affairs, October 1968.

TABLE 11.1

Net Flow of Private Capital to Less Developed Countries and Multilateral Agencies, 1959-68

(in millions of dollars)

	1959	1960	1961	1962	1963	1964	1965	1966	1967	1968
Australia	—	—	—	—	—	14.8	15.0	20.0	25.0	30.4
Austria	-8.3	5.8	18.0	17.2	3.8	6.7	15.8	16.1	21.3	45.8
Belgium	88.8	81.2	71.8	48.4	95.0	93.0	119.3	96.9	65.6	150.0
Canada	22.3	69.5	25.5	55.2	32.5	14.1	45.0	55.0	58.9	93.6
Denmark	(8.2)*	32.4	25.2	7.3	(0.8)*	21.2	2.3	(-4.8)*	(-3.2)*	45.0
France	336.7	476.8	462.8	418.2	391.3	529.2	547.2	574.9	515.8	627.7
Germany	483.3	276.3	228.9	143.0	185.9	283.5	252.7	296.5	593.8	1,068.3
Italy	65.2	192.9	177.2	279.3	242.6	196.6	172.5	516.6	131.4	400.9
Japan	(98.6)	102.6	160.0	118.0	93.9	79.1	132.1	127.1	170.1	240.5
Netherlands	168.7	203.3	144.4	49.2	96.6	69.2	169.2	160.2	114.7	141.7
Norway	1.9	0.1	17.9	-0.1	0.9	5.9	26.6	4.0	14.7	34.6
Portugal	—	—	—	—	—	—	9.3	15.4	31.8	13.3
Sweden	27.0	39.9	43.5	18.8	30.5	34.4	34.6	51.1	60.8	57.4
Switzerland	115.8	153.3	187.2	156.2	196.6	100.9	187.8	107.0	130.1	222.9
United Kingdom	466.6	473.8	442.2	322.9	306.3	425.5	547.1	413.3	343.4	341.0
United States	954.1	1,042.2	1,101.7	819.0	880.0	1,326.0	1,897.5	1,359.9	1,922.4	2,204.0
Total	2,828.9	3,150.1	3,106.3	2,452.6	2,556.7	3,200.1	4,174.0	3,809.2	4,196.6	5,717.1

*Multilateral only.

Source: Development Assistance Review, 1969 (Paris: Organization for Economic Cooperation and Development), p. 299, Table 4.

FOREIGN INVESTMENT IN NIGERIA

Systematic comprehensive information on the magnitude, structure and time trend of direct foreign private investment (DFPI) in Nigeria is still fragmentary. Some of the available statistics are presented as Table 11.2.

Table 11.2 provides information on the distribution of total DFPI both by source and by type of economic activity. The first notable thing is the sharp decline in net flow of DFPI between 1964 and 1968, from £N63.0 to £N37.7. (During that period one Nigerian pound (£N) was officially equivalent to U.S. $2.80. The current official rate is U.S. $3.02 to one £N.) It is clear that the low level of DFPI in 1968 was not just a reaction to the political crisis that began in the country in 1967 since the progressive decline was uninterrupted even before the crisis.

The second point to note is the dominance of the United Kingdom as source of DFPI. This is not surprising since Nigeria was a British colony until 1960. Nevertheless, a significant trend is observable. Among the main sources of DFPI, the share originating from the United Kingdom fell gradually from 56.1 to 51.1 percent during the period. (This relates to cumulative investment rather than the net annual flow figures given in Table 11.2.) That of Western Europe also fell from 23.5 to 21.6 percent. In contrast, the United States increased its share from 12.4 to 20.3 percent during the same period. These three sources continue to account for over 90 percent of DFPI in Nigeria.

When we look at the distribution of DFPI by type of economic activity, we get a typically African and perhaps typically LDC picture. Foreign investment flows, in order of importance, into mining, commerce, and manufacturing. During the period under review, mining accounted for between 40 and 50 percent of cumulative foreign private investment. Commerce, consisting of trading and business services, accounted for between 23 and 31 percent, and manufacturing absorbed between 17 and 21 percent. These three activities normally attracted over 90 percent of DFPI.

THE MAIN COMPLAINTS OF LDCs

The benefits and costs of DFPI have been discussed extensively in general terms in many journal articles. But few of these commentaries reflect the politicosocial realities of the world of the under-developed countries. In this respect, I think it is always helpful to keep in mind three distinctive features of DFPI in most LDCs as opposed to, say, American investment in West Germany or British

TABLE 11.2

Distribution of Cumulative Foreign Private Investment in Nigeria
(in percentages)

	1964	1965	1966	1967	1968
By region					
United Kingdom	56.1	53.3	53.3	50.8	51.1
United States	12.4	15.5	15.4	19.8	20.3
Western Europe	23.5	22.9	23.4	22.7	21.6
Others	8.0	8.1	5.2	6.7	6.9
Total	100.0	100.0	100.0	100.0	100.0
By type of activity					
Agriculture	1.7	1.5	1.1	1.2	1.1
Building and Construction	3.8	5.3	2.2	2.3	2.3
Manufacturing	18.2	18.5	17.5	20.9	20.0
Mining	40.1	43.7	50.8	49.1	49.2
Trading and business services	31.4	24.6	24.8	23.3	24.2
Transport and communications	1.1	1.5	1.5	1.0	1.0
Miscellaneous	3.7	4.9	3.0	2.2	2.1
Total	100.0	100.0	100.0	100.0	100.0

Note: Figures represent paid-up capital and other liabilities.

Source: Central Bank of Nigeria, Economic and Financial Review 9, no. 1 (June 1971), pp. 10-11, Tables 4, 5.

investment in Australia. The first, as mentioned above, is the one-directional nature of DFPI. This requires no further comment. The second is the recent colonial experience of most LDCs. True or not (and I think it is more true than many care to admit), there is a substantial body of opinion in the underdeveloped countries that the former control of politicoeconomic life of these countries by the governments of the Western countries has not ended but merely been passed on to the multinational investors. Indeed it has been suggested that the recent outburst of economic nationalism in some LDCs is a pent-up reaction to long-term dependence on and control by foreigners. The third feature to remember is the often dissimilar political and economic ideologies in capital-importing and capital-exporting countries. The most familiar multinational corporations originate from and are used to operating in a basically private enterprise system. The host LDCs, on the other hand, are characterized by systems ranging from crude capitalism to extreme Marxism. The abundant opportunities for conflict are apparent. The same theme will recur below.

In analyzing foreign investor-LDC relations, certain assumptions seem inescapable. The first is the pedestrian one that host LDCs are always guided by the desire to promote the economic and social welfare of their nationals. Second, and in the light of the first, it must be assumed that host countries want to maximize the benefits they derive from DFPI at the least cost. Third, the noneconomic objectives of capital-importing LDCs may be as important and as legitimate as the purely economic ones. In this respect, the debate among some economists as to whether nationalism should be considered a "consumer good" or a "public good" becomes irrelevant. It is a time-honored maxim in economics that a preference function should be taken as a datum, as given. The crucial point to stress, therefore, is the fact that nationalism, however interpreted, is an important element in the preference or utility function of most if not all LDCs.

It has become generally recognized that the primary objectives of the multinational corporations are to make profits and to grow. If we accept these objectives as perfectly rational and legitimate—and there is no good reason not to—then it becomes clear why one must assume that the relationship between LDCs and MNCs is one of inherent conflict. Unhappily, the conflict is no more one in which a poor solitary foreign investor is maltreated by an ungrateful host country. Rather, it is one where a nation-state is virtually at the mercy of one or more giant MNCs.

Before we consider the steps being taken and suggested to resolve the real and potential conflicts, it is probably necessary to restate here, rather briefly, the main problems that foreign investment generally and the operations of MNCs in particular pose for the LDCs. It is not my intention to suggest that these problems or "complaints" are peculiar to LDCs. Some have been experienced by, for example, Canada and Australia. But it should be clear that there are other problems peculiar to the LDCs because of their relative underdevelopment or their small size, or both. The main complaints are:

1. Domestic fiscal and monetary policies can be subverted or neutralized by MNCs. In particular, the unharmonized fiscal policies of capital-exporting and importing countries (or just of capital-importing countries) allow profit-shifting among MNC subsidiaries.

2. The long-term effect of foreign investment on the balance of payments in the form of repatriation of interest, dividend, capital, and salaries of foreign staff and consultants is invariably negative.

3. Scientific research often is stifled in the host country, which is thereby denied the "external benefits" derivable from research activities (such as stimulation of scientists and secondary discoveries).

4. The low scientific research activity in foreign-dominated industries of host countries pushes young scientists from LDCs to the industrial countries (the "perverse" brain drain).

5. Given that MNCs are often monopolies and oligopolies where prices do not move flexibly with productivity gains, the benefits of technical progress accrue mostly to foreigners.

6. MNCs, quite understandably, discourage competition among their subsidiaries. Consequently, an MNC is likely to be unethusiastic about export promotion, and will work instead on some market-sharing formula among its subsidiaries.

7. Also in terms of clash of objectives, the maintenance of maximum efficiency by the MNC (an eminently rational objective) may work against such national objectives as full employment and fair income distribution (which are equally eminently rational objectives).

8. The pricing policies of MNCs often operate to minimize the revenue that goes to some host countries.

9. In resource-based industries like petroleum, the production policies of MNCs and host LDCs are sometimes at variance.

10. The "indigenization" of the staff and equity of MNCs is often unnecessarily slow. Unless constant legal and moral pressure is applied (for Chileanization, Nigerianization, and so forth), pretty little will be done by MNCs.

11. After risks have fallen, MNCs are unwilling to renegotiate terms of agreement that allow an unusually high rate of return on capital at the initial stages of operation when risks are high. This is partly the problem of overgenerous inducements that, while depriving host governments of tax revenue, will almost certainly enable the home governments of the investors to realize increased revenue.

12. There has been political interference in the affairs of host countries by MNCs acting either in their own interest or at the instigation of their home governments to foster the latter's foreign policy.

13. No matter how one looks at it, foreign investment involves exploitation (in Marxist terms) of the resources of the host country.

This list is not meant to be exhaustive, and the weight to be attached to the different complaints would vary, depending on one's orientation. However, the important point to get across is that the problems arising from the operations of multinationals are so complex that unilateral solutions by countries, especially LDCs, cannot be effective. There is no easy solution. International action seems inescapable for the sake of host countries, whether LDC or not.

THE SEARCH FOR A MORE HARMONIOUS RELATION

It is easily recognized that the LDCs often face a dilemma. For instance, there is, on the one hand, the nationalistic desire of the LDCs to develop through their own efforts with their own resources. On the other hand, they face the stark reality of shortage or lack of capital, technical skills, and marketing outlets provided by the MNCs. Another dilemma is in the area of joint ventures. Joint ventures are meant to reduce foreign control, but they often have the effect of imposing de facto foreign control on both foreign capital and substantial demestic capital. And yet another dilemma is that LDCs encourage MNCs to plough back their earnings (rather than pay them all out as dividends) in order to reduce the negative balance of payments effects of foreign investment. But this measure also has the effect of increasing foreign equity capital in the economy without the beneficial effect of a new direct investment. One can think of other examples.

The conclusion to be drawn from the discussion in the preceding sections is that some form of transnational institution must be found as a countervailing force to the multinationals and as a complement to individual national efforts. This leads us to the question posed in my terms of reference. In general, I think it is fair to say that over the years LDCs have shown a greater readiness to submit to an international regime than have the industrial countries. The reason is obvious. But there have been frustrations I believe must influence their response to any proposed international institution. For instance, present all-embracing international organizations (such as GATT) tend to be responsive mainly to the problems of industrial countries. On the other hand, institutions established primarily for the LDCs (such as the UN Conference on Trade and Development) have proved just as frustrating. In other words, if any proposed institution is like GATT, it could be effective but will not serve the interests of the LDCs. If it is patterned along UNCTAD lines, it will document problems and prescribe policies reflecting the interests of LDCs, but it will not be effective. So what should be done?

From the point of view of the LDCs, the experience of the Organization of Petroleum Exporting Countries has been the most successful with regard to resolving MNC-host country problems. This would seem to suggest that this is one promising approach for similar industries. The basic idea is that countries with major interests in specific industries need to coordinate their policies vis-à-vis an MNC or group of MNCs. Provided the industries are carefully selected, there is little reason to doubt the effectiveness.

There have been several other suggestions, a few of which deserve some passing remarks here. One is an international office to act as a center for statistics, documentation, and information. Such an office would be of immense value to the LDCs which often have to bargain with MNCs on the basis of virtual ignorance and therefore from a weak position.

Another suggestion relates to the mechanism for settling disputes. Most investment laws and agreements in Africa, and perhaps LDCs generally, provide for arbitration of one kind or another. In internationalizing an arbitration mechanism, two problems will arise. The first is the problem of what legal system to apply—municipal? international? The second is enforcement. Recent official pronouncements from the LDCs suggest that while some will readily submit to an international legal system, others regard their municipal laws as the only final arbiter. This suggests, I think, that a supranational body risks failure in achieving universality if it ignores the interests and sovereignty of nation-states.

It is beyond dispute that foreign investment is a crucial agent in the development process of the underdeveloped countries. The recognition of this fact impels all LDCs to adopt a host of protective measures on foreign investment. But foreign investment in its modern form as multinational enterprise poses a new set of problems, many of which are particularly severe for the LDCs. The MNCs can ensure a more certain future for themselves not so much through a multilateral insurance scheme but by redefining their goals and identifying more with the aspirations and objectives, both economic and noneconomic, of their host countries. As Albert Hirschman has rightly pointed out it is in the long-term interest of MNCs to plan to become less foreign and more national. If such voluntary measures are combined with some carefully planned multinational institutional arrangement, I am convinced that everyone will benefit: the capital-importing countries, the multinationals, and the capital-exporting countries.

12

THE DEVELOPING COUNTRIES' POINT OF VIEW: II

R. Krishnamurti

A brief account of the main developments and features in the flows of private capital to the developing countries during recent years would provide a useful introduction for an analysis of the present situation and an interpretation and appreciation of their attitudes and initiatives with respect to private foreign investment and its international control.

There have been considerable changes and shifts in the character and concentration of foreign private investment in the postwar period. Investment in the developed countries and in the manufacturing and other more technological sectors has shown a significant expansion as compared to investment in the extractive and primary commodity sectors of the developing countries due to the interaction of a number of factors, including the emergence of the United States as the dominant economic power, the remarkable growth of sophisticated modern technology, the development of synthetics, the appearance of the multinational corporation, the formation of trade blocs and common markets in Western Europe, and the impressive rates of growth of trade in manufactured products among the industrialized countries.

Although there has been considerable expansion in absolute terms, the developing countries' share in total private foreign investment, formerly more than 50 percent, has dropped to nearer one-third of the total. Of course private investments are still an important element in capital flows to developing countries. According to the most recent

---

The views expressed in this paper are the personal views of the author and do not necessarily reflect the views of the United Nations Conference on Trade and Development Secretariat, of which he is a member.

data of the Organization for Economic Cooperation and Development (OECD), the flow of net direct investment from DAC (Development Assistance Committee) countries reached $4.1 billion in 1971, a rise of 15 percent over 1970. From an annual average of $1,829 million during 1960-65, total net private capital flows to developing countries rose to an annual average of $2,759 million in the five years 1966-70.

Among the developing regions at the end of 1967, Latin America accounted for over 50 percent of total foreign investments, followed well behind by Africa, Asia, and the Middle East with 19, 14, and 9 percent respectively. Of individual countries in Latin America nearly four-fifths of the total was accounted for by Argentina, Brazil, Mexico, Chile, and the Caribbean. In Africa, 30 percent of foreign investment was in Nigeria and Algeria, with Libya, Zaire, and Zambia accounting for another 20 percent. In Asia, India, Malaysia, Pakistan, and the Philippines accounted for more than 60 percent. When Hong Kong, Indonesia, and Thailand are included, the figure comes to 80 percent. In the Middle East, 75 percent of foreign investment is concentrated in Iran, Kuwait, and Saudi Arabia.

At the end of 1971, aggregate U.S. direct investments abroad amounted to $86 billion, of which developed countries accounted for $58.3 billion and developing countries $23.3 billion. Among the developing regions, Latin America (including other Western Hemisphere countries but excluding the United States and Canada) accounted for $15,763 million (nearly two-thirds), Africa $2,869 million, Asia $3,048 million, and Middle East $1,657 million (see Table 12.1).

Petroleum accounted for $9,163 million, mining and smelting $2,659 million, and manufacturing $5,991 million. Manufacturing investments were heavily concentrated in Latin America with Brazil, Mexico, and Argentina the principal recipients, followed by Colombia, Venezuela, and Panama. Petroleum investments were largest in Latin America, followed by Africa and the Middle East. The African share in manufacturing investments was rather modest ($123 million).

Next to the United States, the United Kingdom is the largest investor in developing countries and in 1968 its direct investments excluding investments in petroleum totaled nearly £1,668 million ($3,977 million). Of this amount 70 percent was in sterling area countries and of these the Commonwealth West Indies and India accounted for approximately 25 percent each, African countries for 20 percent, and Malaysia for 15 percent. The manufacturing sector accounted for nearly 35 percent of total United Kingdom investments in developing countries. In 1965, the latest year for which breakdown of data is available, India accounted for 30 percent, Commonwealth Africa (mainly Nigeria and Kenya) for 12 percent, and Mexico, Brazil, and Argentina for between 6 and 8 percent each.[1]

TABLE 12.1

U.S. Direct Foreign Investments at Year's
End, 1971
(book values in millions of dollars)

	Total	Petro-leum	Manufac-turing	Other	Mining and Smelting
All areas	86,001	24,258	35,475	19,549	6,720
Developed					
countries	58,346	12,954	29,483	11,848	4,060
Canada	24,030	5,134	10,537	5,095	3,265
Europe	27,621	6,202	15,538	5,803	78
Japan	1,818	637	959	222	—
Developing					
countries	23,337	9,163	5,991	5,523	2,659
Latin America[a]	15,763	4,194	4,998	4,454	2,116
Africa[b]	2,869	2,095	123	266	386
Middle East	1,657	1,465	92	98	3
Asia and the					
Pacific[c]	3,048	1,410	779	704	155

[a]Includes all Western Hemisphere countries except the United States and Canada.
[b]Excludes South Africa.
[c]Excludes Japan, Australia, and New Zealand.

Source: U.S. Department of Commerce, Survey of Current Business, November, 1972.

The flow of investments by the Federal Republic of Germany increased rapidly from Dm 1,364 million in 1961 to Dm 5,108 ($1,400 million) in 1970. Of this 70 percent was made in Latin America, with Brazil alone accounting for 30 percent of the total, followed by Argentina and Mexico. Most of these Latin American investments were in the manufacturing sector. Africa accounted for about one-fifth of total West German investments with Libya taking one-half of that amount (in petroleum), and Asia accounted for over 10 percent. (No further details are available on West German investments.)

These statistics indicate that even though investments in petroleum, mining and smelting, and extractive activities account for over 50 percent of total direct investments of the developed countries in developing countries, the manufacturing sector accounts for about 30 percent, a not insignificant proportion. But this is somewhat heavily concentrated in the Latin American and Asian countries, while in Africa that sector accounts for under 20 percent of investments. In the Middle East it is even less significant, since petroleum accounts for 90 percent of the total.

THE ROLE OF LARGE AND NOT-SO-LARGE ENTERPRISES

Despite the concentration of capital investments described above, a point of some importance that tends to get overlooked in current discussions but is particularly relevant in considering private investment in developing countries is that the problems posed by private investment are somewhat broader and more varied than those relating only to multinationals and that while multinational corporations are no doubt a major element, hundreds of foreign enterprises and corporations that would not qualify for the title of multinationals—by virtue of size, resources, centralized management and decision-making, and so forth—are established and operating in developing countries all over the world. It would seem to oversimplify realities to say that private investments and multinational corporations are completely synonymous or coextensive. As Seymour Rubin has pointed out, the problems of the multinational enterprise, as they affect the developing countries, are different from those affecting the developed countries in certain respects, although there are many important overlaps. There are also many more questions of foreign direct investment than of multinational enterprise, assuming the latter term to be broader than the former.[2]

Available statistics are inadequate but suggestive. As shown in in Table 12.2, in 1969 in the developing countries there were 7,769 subsidiaries or associates whose parent companies were located in the United States and major Western European countries. Nearly 50 percent of the 7,769 subsidiaries had parents in the United States, a further 25 percent had parents in the United Kingdom, and 10 percent had parents in France. Among the three regions, Latin America accounted for nearly 60 percent of the U.S. subsidiaries and Asia for about 30 percent. As regards United Kingdom subsidiaries, Africa accounted for 45 percent and Asia for just over 30 percent. Regarding subsidiaries of French parent companies, 70 percent were located in Africa and 23 percent in Latin America. Western German parents firms had

113

TABLE 12.2

Parent Companies in Selected Developed Countries
With Subsidiaries or Associates in Developing
Countries or Territories, 1969

Country of Parent	Africa	Asia	Latin America	Total
Austria	0	7	8	15
Belgium	119	12	25	156
Denmark	11	19	15	45
France	496	50	166	712
West Germany	91	91	199	381
Italy	49	9	82	140
Luxembourg	1	9	6	16
Netherlands	69	47	114	230
Norway	9	3	7	19
Sweden	19	28	123	170
Switzerland	24	32	96	152
United Kingdom	857	605	481	1,943
United States	375	1,099	2,316	3,790
Total	2,120	2,011	3,638	7,769

Source: Derived from Yearbook of International Organizations, 1968/1969, a yearly publication of the Union of International Associations, Brussels.

nearly 50 percent of their subsidiaries in Latin America, and 25 percent each in Africa and Asia. The other European countries—including Sweden, Netherlands, Italy, Belgium, and Switzerland—had fairly large numbers of their subsidiaries or associates located in the developing countries.

Although every caution should be exercised in drawing any bold or dramatic conclusions from the above statistics, one would perhaps be safe in inferring that not all the more than 7,000 subsidiaries are the children of large or giant multinationals. The activities of these over 7,000 subsidiaries in the developing countries can be broadly classified into three categories: those engaged in the extractive industries including oil, metals, and agricultural plantations; those primarily engaged in importing and distributing products manufactured by the parent companies and other affiliates and, in some cases, in assembling or packaging the products imported; and those that manufacture products similar to those previously imported, and perhaps to a certain extent export such products. The three categories are not rigid since varying combinations and degrees of processing, assembling, packaging, manufacturing, and exporting prevail, depending upon the nature of the industry and the state of industrial development of the developing country.

While activities in the petroleum, bauxite, copper, and other mineral sectors and in the agricultural plantation sector are identified with relative ease, it is not possible or easy, for lack of adequate information on other sectors, especially manufacturing, to draw precise, much less quantitative, conclusions as to either the distribution of the capital invested among the large subsidiaries versus the medium and relatively small subsidiaries, or their relative contributions to the growth of processing industries and import substitution as distinguished from simple assembling, trading, and distributing. Probably in the larger or more advanced developing countries of Latin America and Asia, a large number of subsidiaries engage not only in trade but also in manufacturing and, to some extent, export. In many other developing countries not only in Asia and Latin America but also to a lesser extent in Africa, the foreign enterprises probably are engaged in manufacturing a wide range of products involving simple technology and a small scale of production, mainly to cater to their domestic markets. It is generally acknowledged that foreign enterprises set up manufacturing facilities in the developing countries to retain their shares of the developing countries' domestic markets and to get over the tariff and nontariff protections that the developing countries apply to imports in the interest of national industrial development. Probably, many subsidiaries in developing countries, especially in the least developed and those without any industrial base, are only trading and distributing enterprises, and the amount of capital they invest obviously would not be proportionate to their numbers in relation to total foreign private investments in those countries; surely it would be much less. Nevertheless it would seem that the largest multinationals of the United States and Western Europe do not account for the preponderant number of subsidiaries in developing countries, but smaller firms and enterprises do play an important role even in manufacturing activities. This is by no means to deny the dominant lead held by the largest corporations in finance, technology, and other resources.

During the discussions at UNCTAD III at Santiago on the subject of multinationals and restrictive business practices, the representatives of the European Economic Community (EEC) drew attention to the participation of a large number of medium and small enterprises of EEC countries in the industrial and economic life of the developing nation. This is an area where publication of detailed statistics and deeper research would be of profit to both developed and developing countries.

NATIONAL AND REGIONAL POLICIES OF
DEVELOPING COUNTRIES

Developing countries insist, and the international community also has agreed, that foreign private investment should be undertaken in a manner consistent with the development objectives and priorities established in the developing countries' national plans.

It is not possible here to give more than a bare summary statement of the policies and measures adopted by developing countries at different levels of development. Developing countries that have had experience of receiving and utilizing foreign private capital in significant amounts, and that also have fairly definite development goals and priorities, have formulated foreign investment policies, guidelines, and codes. While there is considerable variation in these codes depending upon the political philosophy, economic size, resource endowments, and so forth of the country concerned, there are some broad general elements: (1) foreign firms must offer evidence that they are capable of operating on a sound and efficient basis and that they will contribute to the economic development of the country concerned; (2) foreign investment and technical collaboration are permitted in certain industries and economic sectors but not in others; (3) foreign enterprises must provide for the participation of local capital and management, and for training of staff at different levels; (4) foreign investments must be limited to specified proportions of the value of investments in order to provide for local capital participation, and foreign majority control of equity will not always be permitted; (5) foreign investors' tax obligations are explicit and agreed upon; (6) restrictive business practices such as unreasonably high prices for imported inputs, export restraints and prohibitions of varied types, unjustified use of patent and trademark rights to limit production, export, and import, royalty payments considered excessive—all these are subject to varying degrees of screening and control.

The countries that have introduced the above measures include Bolivia, Brazil, Chile, Colombia, Ecuador, India, Kenya, Liberia, Mexico, Pakistan, and the Philippines.

At the same time the developing countries' genuine desire to attract foreign investment is evident in the numerous and often liberal incentive schemes many of them offer. These include tax concessions, tariff exemptions on imports, and guarantee of profits, remittances, and capital repatriation.

These legislative and administrative measures at the national level in some cases might have had a hampering effect on private capital inflows, but it must be recognized that the foreign enterprises, whether giant multinationals or medium-sized ones, have over the years developed both flexibility and dynamism and instead of shying away from countries and areas where they cannot get effective equity control, have often adapted themselves to the new situations and negotiated mutually acceptable contracts.

New, nontraditional, innovative forms of private capital participation in developing countries in a variety of projects, in partnership with local government, local enterprise, banking or development institutions, and occasionally with development finance institutions of developed countries or regional financial institutions, are being increasingly undertaken successfully, suggesting that equity control may not be such an indispensable condition of private investment. The OECD 1972 review lists in particular joint ventures with local, private or public interests, minority investments with management contract arrangements, production-sharing arrangements, and international ventures in which companies from a single investing country do not have a controlling interest. As Peter Gabriel has said, the fact that the foreign corporation is not welcomed as a direct investor and owner of a venture of theoretically indefinite duration but as a supplier of services—managerial, technological, institutional, and others—involves a major change in the concept of corporate management and there is growing evidence that a variety of alternative arrangements can in fact be worked out on terms satisfactory to both the resource-importing country and the resource-supplying firm.[3] Common to all these arrangements, according to him, are various combinations of the following features: (1) ownership is left in whole or in controlling part in national hands; (2) the duration of the foreign company's presence is limited; and (3) explicit provision is made for renegotiation of terms at specified intervals.

An important regional initiative taken in Latin America (the developing region receiving the largest amounts of private capital) is the Cartagena Agreement on Common Treatment of Foreign Capital, Trademarks, Patents, Licensing Agreements and Royalties in the Andean Common Market, entered into and being implemented by Bolivia, Chile, Peru, Colombia, Ecuador, and Peru. The policies and controls provided in this agreement aim at the steady transfer of control from foreign to Andean nationals and at removing a wide variety of other restrictions practiced by foreign enterprises in the Andean Common Market. Several features of these provisions are in common with measures at the national level described earlier. Foreign investors have not reacted favorably to the Andean initiative, but perhaps it is too early to express any judgment on the working of the agreement.

Mention should be made here of the 25 countries with a total population of 150 million which have been classified by the United Nations as the least developed among the developing countries (LDDCs) on the basis of low per capita incomes (less than 100), low share of manufacturing in GDP (less than 10 percent) and low levels of literacy

(20 percent or less of population aged 15 years and above).* These
countries suffer from special handicaps to economic development;
their capacity to benefit by any commercial policy measure is limited
as is their ability to absorb large amounts of capital despite an urgent
need to survey and explore their resources and build up their social
and economic infrastructure.

Receipts of net official flows of external assistance received by
these countries are only a small percentage of the total received by
all developing countries during 1969-71, and their overall per capita
official receipts were lower than the average for other developing countries and this applied to some of the larger LDDCs. It is generally
considered that these countries are not particularly attractive to the
private foreign investor unless some exceptionally rich natural resources have been discovered and the incentives and returns are really
tempting. Several countries in this group have national policies toward foreign private investment and many would probably welcome
private investments. But their bargaining power is very small, while
they would no doubt, in common with other developing countries, welcome foreign capital on fair and equitable terms and also support
international initiatives to that end.

TECHNICAL ASSISTANCE TO DEVELOPING
COUNTRIES

An important contribution the United Nations family of institutions can make to promote the flow of private investment and technology
to the developing countries lies in technical assistance with respect to
their negotiations with foreign private investors. A large number of
developing countries do not have the requisite skills and expertise for
carrying out such negotiations. It is not realistic to expect the foreign
investor not to negotiate the best possible terms for himself, and in
developing countries where the local entrepreneur is inexperienced,
he is not likely to get the best terms. Even some of the more developed
among the developing countries, which can boast of sophisticated civil
servants and able negotiators, have discovered ex post, after some
years of experience, that they were not as knowledgeable and able
negotiators as they had imagined. Among the least developed of the
developing countries and a considerable number of the other developing

---

*Afghanistan, Bhutan, Botswana, Burundi, Chad, Dahomey,
Ethiopia, Guinea, Haiti, Laos, Lesotho, Malawi, Maldives, Mali, Nepal,
Niger, Rwanda, Sikkun, Somalia, Sudan, Tanzania, Uganda, Upper
Volta, Western Samoa, and Yemen.

countries, both civil servants and local entrepreneurs and industrialists would stand to benefit by information and advice from impartial United Nations experts on the possibilities and opportunities open to them in negotiating reasonable terms, taking into account comparable cases and situations in other countries and industries. In doing this, care will perhaps have to be taken to ensure that the UN experts themselves do not get involved directly in the negotiations between the foreign investor and the local entrepreneur or between the foreign investor and the government of the developing country. The foreign investor might object to the intrusion of an alien element and feel that negotiation is a matter strictly for the parties concerned, nor is it to be imagined that the local entrepreneur or government official would permit his expert or adviser to take over his negotiation. Therefore, these procedural and administrative details can be resolved without too much difficulty.

Already some UN agencies are providing this type of assistance to a limited extent. UNIDO (the United Nations Industrial Development Organization) and the regional commissions have sponsored investment promotion seminars and talks, bringing together interested foreign investors and businessmen from developing countries. UNIDO also is helping by drawing up model conditions of contract for the investment of private capital and transfer of technology. UNCTAD has an impressive technical assistance mandate to carry out in the field of transfer of technology. WIPO (World Intellectual Property Organization) has stepped up its advisory services program to developing countries in relation to patents, trademarks, and allied legal matters. More systematic and considerably expanded assistance to developing countries, not only at the level of general guidelines but also at the individual country level, can bring considerable advantages. It can stimulate the flow of private capital and technology to many developing countries that are ready but at present unable to obtain them; it would help reduce the cruder forms of investment on terms not acceptable to the host countries, which have served to create bad feelings and spoil the investment climate.

INTERNATIONAL INITIATIVES OF DEVELOPING COUNTRIES

Initiatives at the international level by the developing countries have generally been embodied in resolutions within the United Nations by the General Assembly, Economic and Social Council (ECOSOC), and UNCTAD. Particular attention may be drawn in this connection to paragraphs 50 and 74, G.A. resolution 2626(XXV) on the International Development Strategy, and G.A. resolutions 1803 (XVII) and

2158 (XXI). These deal with principles concerning permanent sovereignty over natural resources, as well as the rights of developing countries with respect to foreign investments.

At the third UNCTAD resolution 56(III) was adopted. In this resolution on foreign private investment in its relationship to development, concern was expressed "not only at the total amount of the financial outflow brought about by private foreign investment, but also at its excessive utilization of local financial resources as well as the effects of certain marketing contracts among foreign companies that disrupt competition in the domestic markets, and their possible effects on the economic development of the developing countries." The resolution inter alia urged the developed countries "to take the necessary steps to reverse the tendency for an outflow of capital from developing countries, by fiscal or other appropriate measures, such as tax exemption of reinvestment of profits and other earnings accruing to private capital investments." This resolution also recognized that "private foreign investment, subject to national decisions and priorities, must facilitate the mobilization of internal resources, generate inflows and avoid outflows of foreign reserves, incorporate adequate technology and enhance savings and national investment."

Another important resolution, 73(III), was adopted on the subject of restrictive business practices of foreign enterprises in developing countries, specifically including the activities of multinational corporations. Recognizing inter alia the desirability of action by developing countries at national, subregional, regional, and other multilateral levels to take appropriate remedial measures for restrictive business practices that adversely affect their economies, the conference recommended inter alia cooperation among developed and developing countries through an exchange of information and consultations and other means that could contribute to the alleviation and, where possible, the elimination of restrictive business practices adversely affecting both developed and developing countries. This resolution also establishes an ad hoc group of experts on restrictive business practices whose terms of reference include the identification of restrictive business practices, including those resulting from activities of multinational corporations and enterprises, further study of these restrictive business practices, the drawing up of recommendations and the examination of the possibility of drawing up guidelines for consideration by governments of developed and developing countries regarding restrictive business practices. Significant features relating to private foreign investments and their restrictive impact on the export trade of developing countries would be considered by this expert group.

Mention also should be made of resolution 45(III), the Charter of the Economic Rights and Duties of States adopted by UNCTAD III. This resolution established a working group composed of 31 member-states to draw up the text of the draft charter. Questions relating to the states' rights and duties in the field of private foreign investment are likely to come within the scope of this working group as well.

The fifty-third session of ECOSOC in August 1972 adopted resolution 1721(LIII) on the impact of multinational corporations on the development process and on international relations. Noting the view that the international community has yet to formulate a positive policy and establish effective machinery for dealing with the issues raised by the multinational corporations, this resolution requested the UN secretary-general, in consultation with governments, to appoint a study group of eminent persons intimately acquainted with international economic, trade, and social problems and related international relations, to study the role of multinational corporations and their impact on the process of development, especially that of developing countries, and the implications for international relations; to formulate conclusions that might possibly be used by governments in their decision-making with regard to national policy; and to submit recommendations for appropriate international action. This group is to be convened in 1973.

A most recent initiative by developing countries was taken in the UNCTAD Trade and Development Board (twelth session in October 1972) in resolution 88 (XII). The resolution recalls the relevant previous G.A. resolutions and:

1. Reaffirms the sovereign right of all countries to dispose of their natural resources for the benefit of their national development in the spirit and in accordance with the principles of the Charter of the United Nations, . . . as recognized and stated in the aforementioned declarations of the General Assembly and in those of the United Nations Conference on Trade and Development;

2. Reiterates that in the application of this principle, such measures of nationalization as States may adopt in order to recover their natural resources are the expression of a sovereign power in virtue of which it is for each State of fix the amount of compensation and the procedure for these measures, and any dispute which may arise in that connexion falls within the sole jurisdiction of its courts, without prejudice to what is set forth in General Assembly resolution 1803 (XVII).

It is important to note the reference to the sole recourse to the courts of the individual country in which the nationalization occurred and the reluctance of developing countries to submit their cause of international jurisdiction.

These initiatives in UNCTAD, ECOSOC, and the General Assembly continue to reflect the underlying concern and self-defensive

attitude of developing countries vis-à-vis foreign investment and
multinational enterprises in their territory. The recent resolutions
give added emphasis to the right of the developing countries to expect
that foreign investment will respect and serve the sovereign interests
of the developing country and call for greater international cooperation to this end. They further stem from and reflect the weak negotiating position of the developing countries especially at the bilateral
national level vis-à-vis developed country governments as well as
the private enterprises of developed countries.

The attitudes of developing countries toward private capital also
are heavily influenced by their critical balance of payments situation,
to which their debt service burdens including those on private capital
account (not adequately relieved by official flows) have contributed.
It would be incorrect to look at the problems of private investment
in isolation from the overall developmental needs and priorities and
balance of payments position of the developing countries. These issues
have been so consistently aired in UNCTAD that there is no need to
dwell further on them here.

RELATED PROBLEMS OF DEVELOPED
COUNTRIES

Among the Western countries themselves there remain to be
effectively considered several difficult problems in the field of private
foreign investment, more particularly relating to the rapid growth and
power of multinational corporations, the enforcement of competition
laws, and extraterritoriality. While the problem of extraterritoriality
has been under study for some years now by the Western countries,
discussion on the issues posed by the multinationals has perhaps just
begun. A major first step on which it is to be hoped they would agree
would be to collect systematic and comprehensive data on the operations
of the multinationals and to specify the procedures necessary for this
purpose. This would help to throw light on the subject and further help
to understand the impact of the multinationals on the developing countries.

It would be very difficult in practice to separate the problems
of the developed from those of the developing countries: In many aspects the problems are global and any arrangements and accommodations worked out by the multinational corporations of the developed
countries among themselves within a policy framework set by their
governments would certainly have a significant and far-reaching impact on the developing countries. Decisions on finance and investment, location of plants and manufacturing facilities, labor and employment policies, pricing policies and practices, purchases and sales

of materials and components, market sharing, use of patents and trade-marks—all these will affect the interests of the developing countries.

While the multinational corporations are not the monopoly of the United States, it should nevertheless be recognized that by far the largest number of them are U.S.-based. These are far more richly endowed than their less numerous Western European compeers in financial resources, technology, research and development, marketing and distribution facilities, and the like. Available studies and data on Australia, Canada, the United Kingdom, and the United States have shown that U.S. multinationals account for significant proportions of important sectors of manufacturing output and export in Western European countries. This is causing concern in these countries, even though at the same time they realize the need for and value of U.S. capital and technology, pursue favorable policies toward U.S. investment, and are bound by close ties of friendship in the Atlantic partnership.

Meanwhile, partly under the spur of competition provided by the U.S. firms, partly under the stimulus generated by the establishment of the larger EEC market and the necessity of attaining the scales of production to gain economies, the trends toward mergers and concentration (both vertical and horizontal) have become markedly stronger in Western Europe and may be further reinforced by the enlargement of the EEC. Simultaneously, the countries of Western Europe are applying such competition and antitrust laws and policies as they have mainly to their domestic trade and industry, while retaining freedom in regard to foreign trade. Meanwhile the EEC competition rules also are in force. It can only be a matter of speculation now what the cumulative effects will be of these divergent and powerful political, legal, and economic forces, both internal to Western Europe and those operating from without, on the structure of Western European industry and trade with particular reference to multinational firms and their operations, but these effects surely will be profound for the countries concerned and for the developing countries as well.

The role of Japan in world trade and investment should not be overlooked in this context. Another important element in the dynamic situation involves how much Japanese private investment is made in the developing countries and in which sectors, as well as to what extent and in what manner Japan's policies toward foreign investments in Japan, especially by foreign multinationals, will be modified in the coming years.

These developments regarding multinationals and foreign investment are not unrelated to the fundamental and stubborn issues of trade policy and international monetary reform concerning which negotiations among the major industrial and trading countries and groupings are being seriously prepared for now.

PRIVATE INVESTMENT AND THE SOCIALIST
COUNTRIES

Certain significant developments in economic and trade cooperation between the Western countries and the socialist countries, which
have materialized in the past few years and hold out promise of great
acceleration, are bound sooner or later to have an impact on the policies
and postures of the developing countries. If these prospects material-
ize, the world will witness in the next decade or so industrial and
technical cooperation arrangements, involving very large capital investments by Western countries, for the exploitation of natural resources and sale of sophisticated technology to the socialist countries
including the Soviet Union and China. Already several major projects
have been implemented by the socialist countries with large Western
enterprises on the basis of long-term industrial cooperation contracts.

While these forms of collaboration and capital investment may
not necessarily be susceptible to being transplanted to the developing
countries, the conditions included therein concerning the supply of
capital, technology, and marketing may well prove acceptable to the
developing countries, provided the Western enterprises are prepared
to give serious consideration to these possibilities without rigid or
undue insistence on traditional forms of equity ownership. It could
be supposed that increased East-West (socialist-capitalist) cooperation in investment and technology would help attenuate the hostile and
suspicious political postures and ideological animosities to foreign
investment on the part of developing countries. When the socialist
countries themselves are pragmatic and flexible enough to borrow
private capital and technology, why should the developing countries
shrink from doing so?

AN INTERNATIONAL REGIME FOR PRIVATE
INVESTMENT?

The principal question to which this conference is seeking an
answer is whether the developed and developing countries would be
willing to accept an international regime governing private international
investment and multinational enterprises. In attempting an answer,
especially from the point of view of the developing countries, a number
of points require clarification: What exactly is meant by an "international regime"? Would it consist only of general principles and
broad guidelines that would be internationally accepted in an agreed
forum and later would provide guidance for action by individual nations
or groups of nations without any international juridical obligations?
Or would it imply the drawing up of an international legal instrument

or convention, consisting of rights and obligations enforceable through agreed procedures including possibly conciliation and arbitration? Would such an international regime apply to all investment relationships of all countries, including intradeveloped country relationships as well as developed country-developing country relationships? What would be the scope of such an "instrument" or "regime"—only certain specific issues proving difficult in bilateral negotiations or comprehensively all the major elements involved in investor-host country transactions?

The above questions would seem to provide part of the answer. A comprehensive international legal instrument, it would seem, is not practical politics at the present time for more than one reason, nor would it appear that informed and authoritative opinion believes the idea to be feasible at the present time. It is not evident that the major industrial nations of the West themselves, most of them capital-exporting and investing countries, are prepared to negotiate such an instrument as yet. They have many thorny issues to resolve among themselves. The attitude of a large number of developing countries to such a proposition, especially those active in the international doliborations on the subject, probably would be problematical and possibly could be hostile. Surely this is not to be attributed to their lack of interest in attracting foreign investment or failure to recognize the necessity of an international regime that would in a balanced manner provide fair and reasonable conditions acceptable to the borrower as well as the investor. Their lack of enthusiasm, if their attitude could be so described, would be due largely to their weak bargaining power and their anxiety not to commit themselves to any international contracts or regimes that might adversely affect their already weak bargaining power and possibly their sovereignty. In view of the number and complexity of the issues involved, and the basic differences on some major elements of any such regime which have surfaced again in recent international debates, we should not underestimate the difficulties to be faced in drafting any agreed formulation.

Reference has been made to the possibility of a GATT for Investment, meaning a contractual framework to this end. The present GATT has impressive accomplishments to its credit during the past twenty years in the field of tariff reductions and liberalization of quantitative restrictions; it also has been providing a framework of rights and obligations for dealing with complicated commercial policy issues. However, the same success has not attended its efforts in settling the latter, especially in clear and unequivocal "contractual" terms, and this is no fault of GATT. The main decisions on commercial questions, when arrived at in GATT, represented decisions negotiated on the basis of political and economic realities rather than the on basis of legal rights and obligations. Flexibility and pragmatism, rather

125

than strict judgments on legal claims and their enforcement, have been GATT's recognized technique. It would appear that sensitive and complex issues relating to investment would probably not lend themselves to solutions in terms of international conventions, but would yield better results to pragmatic ad hoc negotiations among the parties concerned. Bilateral negotiations and treaties should not be overlooked in this connection. Experience of the industrialized countries so far in regard to restrictive business practices, antitrust laws, extraterritoriality, and multinationals also would point in the same direction, although this is not to deny the necessity and value of serious dialogue in multilateral institutions. Indeed the United Nations itself has arranged such high-level dialogues through panels on foreign investment.

The above difficulties to an international legal regime should not preclude earnest international consideration to the drawing up—in broad and general terms, without contractual commitments, guidelines, general principles, codes of conduct, and the like—of a framework for both governments and enterprises in developed as well as developing countries. Even here, the differences on such issues as sovereignty over natural wealth and resources, equity control, methods and procedures relating to nationalization and compensation, and international conciliation and arbitration—to name but a few—may make it extremely difficult to reach common ground even on principles and guidelines unless they are formulated at a level of noncontroversial generality. A set of guidelines cannot and is not intended to be a contract setting out specific and precise conditions—the latter are a matter for negotiation by the parties concerned. Even so, guidelines would be of great value. The more concrete and detailed they can be made over a period of time through trial, experience, and international dialogue, the more valuable they could prove to the governments and private parties concerned. As earlier indicated, both UNCTAD and ECOSOC have specific mandates to draw up norms and guidelines with respect to the major elements of private foreign investment and multinational corporations with the help of governments, and this work will be launched in 1973.

NOTES

1. "Book Values of Overseas Investments," Board of Trade Journal, January 26, 1968, and September 23, 1970. United Kingdom direct investments in petroleum, approximately $2.2 billion at the end of 1966, were largely in the Middle East (50 percent) and Latin America (25 percent).

2. Seymour J. Rubin, "Multinational Enterprise and National Sovereignty: A Skeptic's Analysis," Law and Policy in International Business, Vol. 3 (1971).

3. Peter P. Gabriel, "The Multinational Corporation and Economic Development," in Robert E. Hunter and John E. Reilly, eds., Development Today (New York: Praeger Publishers in cooperation with the Overseas Development Council, 1972).

*   *   *   *   *

COMMENT
Constantino Vaitzos

The desirability of establishing an international institution to regulate the activities of transnational corporations must be evaluated on the basis of what such controls could accomplish for the developing countries that national law could not. In addition, international regulations must be compared with the achievements of regional action, such as the Andean Pact. Such international regulatory institutions will not be in the interests of the developing countries. There are minimal benefits to be obtained for the actual functioning and relations between developing countries and foreign firms. Furthermore, there are distinct possibilities of negative effects.

On the other hand, I see a very important role to be played by international institutions in areas such as information, technical assistance, and training, as others have mentioned. All agree that such functions should not be assigned to a particular specialized agency but should be undertaken and promoted within the United Nations. If there is only one body, one institution, there will be a strong temptation for it to establish rules or codes of behavior rather than to limit itself to information, training, and technical assistance.

A question of definition exists: I use the term transnational corporation, not multinational. This is not a semantic difference. The firms we are talking about are not multinational in the sense that they have multinational allocation to research and development, in terms of top management, in terms of ownership. They are transnational firms.

Why are there very limited benefits to be obtained from an international institution to control or regulate activities of transnational firms? Let me first take the case of distribution of benefits among host countries and foreign investors. The host country can obtain direct income benefits either through tax returns to the government, through earnings in local employment, or through lower prices through the activities of foreign firms.

In the case of income earnings for employment, there are studies that tend to indicate the employment-generating effects of foreign firms in the manufacturing sector are rather limited in developing

countries. Certainly the prices are not declining for the consumers
of these countries. Therefore, a very important area of benefits to
be derived by developing countries from the activities of foreign firms
lies in the area of taxes on the profitability of such firms.

Studies undertaken, for example, by the Council for Latin America,
sought to demonstrate that in Latin America the profitability of firms,
particularly U.S. firms, is among the lowest in the world. The figure
given for the 1960s is 7 percent return on investment where taxes
were applied by the host countries. Clearly this is a gross under-
statement of the actual profitability obtained in these countries. My
own studies in Colombia, Peru, and Ecuador indicate an average of
above 40 percent per year of return on investment where actual profits
are being remitted through channels other than dividends and profits.

The term transfer pricing as used here indicates payments not
only for intermediates, which is a very substantial part of the mechanism for remitting profits, at least in Latin America, but also payments
for royalties, interaffiliate debt, other services, and so forth. Apparently these are the major channels of income remission that are beyond the scope of direct income taxation. There are indirect taxes,
such as those on royalties. An example of this is the pharmaceutical
industry in Colombia, where the income obtained from the overpricing
of intermediates amounted to 24 times the declared profits.

Little can be done by an international organization in such situations over and above what can be done by the national governments
or by regional agreements that try to control the transfer pricing
between subsidiaries and foreign corporations. An international organization cannot determine the price of a revolving typewriter ball. This
must be negotiated directly by the host government and the foreign
investor. The host government, in case of standardized products like
natural rubber, sulfuric acid, and vitamin B-12, can set minimum
prices in order to tax the true profitability accruing within its country.

This method also applies to capital investment of foreign firms.
About one-third of the imports of equipment in Latin America in the
1960s were between parents and subsidiaries. The prices here cannot be set internationally; they must be computed at the national level.

As to the benefits to developing countries, I will first discuss
private benefits and second some social benefits. The high profitability rates mentioned are due to a large extent to inappropriate governmental policies of the developing countries. One immediately looks
to the host government for high tariffs or restrictions on imports.
However, the transnational firms have a large role in determining the
scope and extent of such policies.

In studying the situation in Latin America, I saw the manner
in which transnational firms negotiated tariff rates or exclusion of

competitive products by setting figures through transfer pricing. International institutions cannot play a very strong role in these confrontations or negotiations between host countries and foreign investors. Again, the issues must be handled at the national level.

As to the creation of social benefits, no doubt transnational firms have made important contributions to developing countries. However there are many areas where the effects have been quite negative. There are figures on the displacement of entrepreneurial activity within the developing countries. More than one-third of U.S. investments in Peru and Colombia during the ten-year period 1958-67 were acquisitions of national firms and displacement of local activities. The time has come for action to be taken in this area. The Andean Pact has attempted to do so. Furthermore, this is a matter that must be handled at the national level, although exchange of information and mutual support between developing countries would be helpful.

Another area of displacement is technological development. No doubt the foreign firm at the present time is one of the main channels for import of technology into developing countries. But generally the imported technology is in package form: a collective import of different technological components, many of which are outdated. In addition, there is the issue of technological elements that are not industry-specific but task-specific. Here the technology is detailed in design, engineering know-how, feasibility studies, and so forth. These can be developed once a country has the option of testing itself. In this sense the package of technology imported by the transnational firm eliminates the possibility for creation of local technological capacities.

Control is another area in which international action would have little effect and national action would be more effective. However, it would not be in the strict sense of ownership but in the much wider sense of deciding what to export, what to produce, how to produce, and so forth. At the national level this can be done through direct confrontation between the host country and the foreign firm. Reference has been made to export restrictions and the marketing opportunities that the transnational firm offers. I think these marketing opportunities exist although they have been overplayed. Less than 10 percent of the production of U.S. firms in Latin America has been exported, and 80 percent of these exports are from three countries: Mexico, Argentina, and Brazil. Furthermore, investment was concentrated in certain sectors. In Mexico 60 percent of the exports were from the automobile industry; in Argentina most of the exports were meat. Therefore, when talking about exports we should focus on particular sectors in particular countries rather than speak generally. Again, national action or regional action would be more appropriate than international action.

Other areas I would like to mention are national development plans and the need for structural changes in developing countries. What about the negative effects that might be involved in the establishment of an international institution to regulate activities of transnational corporations? The idea of an institution in the form of a GATT is not very attractive for developing countries. There are technical reasons to believe that international organizations like the Organization for Industrial Property (OMPE) have been working against the interests of developing countries. I agree with R. Krishnamurti that actions like that of OPEC in the particular case of petroleum or efforts such as the Andean Pact do correspond to the interests of developing countries. Such actions, however, are not likely to be undertaken at the international level.

Finally, I think that an international organization to regulate foreign investments or transnational corporations would diminish the possibilities for alternatives to the transnational firms. It would legitimize firm, overwhelming presence. It would avoid such diversifications as buying technology in different markets from different size firms, seeking financing from different sources, and looking for marketing outlets as the Mexicans have done with the companies of Japan.

DEALING WITH INVESTMENT PROBLEMS: THE WORLD BANK AND THE INTERNATIONAL CENTRE FOR SETTLEMENT OF INVESTMENT DISPUTES

Piero Sella

I will not attempt here to review or summarize in any systematic manner the efforts, actions, and reactions that have taken place in the international community and among the international organizations in the last twenty years or so in the field of foreign investment. Rather, I would like first to touch on a few aspects of the practice of the World Bank, as a representative of certain types of international organization, in dealing with problems of foreign investment.

The reason I chose the World Bank is not just parochial, since I work there, but because the charter of the World Bank itself provides as one of the purposes of the World Bank the promotion of private investment, which we inside the World Bank and perhaps also people outside it tend to forget. That purpose, however, is somewhat qualified by the words "by means of loans or guarantees of loans."

In fact the World Bank has had a minor role to play, until now at least, in the field of industry. I think the reasons are fairly clear: When the World Bank started dealing with problems of development, the needs of other sectors like roads, utilities, and later agriculture and education, were very large and there was a feeling that industry could better take care of itself than the other sectors. In addition I think that, at least in the beginning, the World Bank management was very much influenced by the idea that governments are not really very good at managing industries and private capital can do a better job; private enterprise is more difficult for us to assist because of the need for a government guarantee.

The World Bank's industrial policy is under review and I do not know what the outcome will be. From time to time there has been an attempt to revive our interest in the industrial sector, for instance around 1956 the the International Finance Corporation (IFC) was created to try to fill a gap in the financing of the industrial sector. The size of IFC's resources has not allowed it to do much in the field

131

of large investments, with which multinational corporations are most involved, although I think it performs a very useful role in regard to medium-sized investments. Another aspect of our interest in industry has been through the financing and promotion of development finance companies.

In fact, as the result of all these circumstances, our participation in large multinational operations has been rather sporadic. And I think this is a first indication of a limitation in the influence that an institution like the World Bank can have, for good—I hope—in the field of multinational investment.

But whenever we have been involved in large multinational investment, for instance in the extractive industry (not many cases), the problem has immediately arisen of what our role should be. Normally when we are approached with a request for financing for, say, a mining project, there is already a basic or preliminary deal between the host country and the foreign investor.

As a provider of funds and a future creditor, we are obviously concerned about the financial viability of the investment, which will probably be the main security of our loan. As a development institution we are also concerned with the benefit that will accrue to the host country, in order to justify the use of our funds.

But beyond that there is a very wide range of choices among which the two parties—the host country and the foreign investor—can choose in order to try to maximize their respective benefits and reduce their respective risks.

In these cases the World Bank found itself in a rather delicate position. While I think we have made our views known to the prospective investor and to the host country where we felt the deal as proposed could not be justified or at least would not justify the use of our funds, we have taken a more neutral position in the hammering out of the details of the deal. Although informally we have been consulted throughout most of this negotiation by both sides, and indirectly we have played a sort of honest broker's role, I was somewhat puzzled by Lincoln Gordon's suggestion that we should take a more active role and always give our blessing or withdraw our blessing from a particular investment on the basis of the fairness of the deal.

The distinction between a justified investment and a fair investment is, I think, a subtle one to draw, and I am afraid it would be difficult for the World Bank, particularly as a creditor in this investment, to go too far in trying to substitute its judgment for that of the host country.

On the other hand whenever we have felt that the host country was not strong enough, in terms of skill and knowledge, to handle effectively the negotiations with the prospective investor, we have insisted that the necessary technical, business, and legal skills be obtained by that country before we consider financing the project.

Now, assuming that an institution of the type of the World Bank were to take a more active role, what would be the standards and objectives it should try to respect or achieve? I do not have an answer for that question.

There has been another aspect of foreign investment in which the World Bank has been involved as a result of its statutory purposes, its constitution as an international organization of rich and poor countries, and its role as financial intermediary between the capital markets or the treasuries of the rich countries and the developing needs of the poorer countries.

Where a particular country that would otherwise have been eligible for the World Bank's assistance—and I stress otherwise eligible—is in conflict with foreign investors as a result of nationalization, expropriation, or similar action, and substantial unsatisfied claims of foreign investors remain outstanding, it has been the World Bank's attitude not to provide its financial assistance if it was not satisfied that the host country was making reasonable efforts to reach a settlement of those claims.

This position, which has been criticized by both developing and industrialized countries, and by their investors—for different reasons, obviously—is a delicate one because the line between judging whether a country is making reasonable efforts for a settlement and deciding what a settlement should be is a thin one, but we have to draw it.

I do not want to argue for this position here or to defend it against its critics. I refer to it because it shows, I think, another limitation on the role of the international financial organizations. Obviously the World Bank action—or rather, inaction in these cases— does influence the attitudes of host countries and investors, but in a rather passive way as it does not offer any positive solution to the problems that exist in the absence of precise and generally accepted substantive rules and impartial procedures for their applications in the field of foreign investments. This may lead to situations where a sense of frustration develops because both investors and host countries find themselves at a total impasse.

There has not been a lack of efforts on the part of the international community to attempt a reconciliation between the need for legal certainty on the part of foreign investors and the freedom of developing countries, and host governments in general, to shape their economic and social policies in accord with their own political goals.

Discussions in the last several years in the various organs of the United Nations, and more particularly in recent years in the UN Conference on Trade and Development (UNCTAD), and the various resolutions that have been adopted in those bodies show, I think, a general recognition of the need for a formulation of principles and rules. But at the same time they show the difficulty of reaching a formal consensus on these matters.

If we compare, for instance, the General Assembly resolution on the permanent sovereignty of national resources and the recent resolution the UNCTAD board proposed and the General Assembly endorsed, I do not see any significant progress toward any general acceptance of principles by which investors and host states can be guided in their dealings.

I would take a similar view of the draft convention of the Organization for Economic Cooperation and Development (OECD) of several years ago, were it not for the fact that most of its provisions have found their way almost literally or even in amplified versions into many economic operation agreements between several members of the OECD and quite a number of developing countries.

This would indicate to me that discussions and debates in international forums have been useful in highlighting problems and different and sometimes irreconcilable positions. It also indicates that further work needs to be done, and perhaps in a more quiet atmosphere such as the International Law Commission (ICC), on the basic international rules that govern state action in these fields.

It also indicates, perhaps, that well-balanced and thoughtful statements like the recent guidelines of the ICC may help clear the air of some political overtones. But practical results at this time are more likely through bilateral action by industrialized countries and developing countries; through unilateral domestic action by the developing countries in, for instance, investment legislation; and, on a more concrete level, through direct agreements between investors and host countries.

There are obviously weaknesses in this approach. There is a danger of a race or competition among developing countries to offer more favorable terms to specific investors. There is a danger of multinational or transnational corporations playing one country against another. But I think these dangers might be reduced substantially by more effective concerted action among the developing countries themselves, among developing countries with similar interests or similar problems. The Organization of Petroleum Exporting Countries (OPEC) is a very successful example in a very special sector; the Andean Pact may be, on a regional basis, a novel example although it is still too new to be assessed.

Another and still unsuccessful effort to tackle some of these problems by international action has been directed at transferring the political risk of the investor investing in other countries, especially developing countries, from the investor himself or his country to the international community or an international organization.

The OECD at first and then the World Bank have been at work for years on a scheme of multilateral insurance of investments. The purpose of such a scheme is to achieve uniform coverage of risk regardless of the nationality of the investment; to diversify the exposure of individual countries by sharing these risks among them; and, by internationalizing the coverage, to improve the investment climate and presumably increase the flow of private investments to the developing countries, or at least improve the terms of private investments in those countries.

Progress on this scheme has been very slow and I do not expect any concrete results in the near future. Among the reasons for this slow progress or lack of progress, may be on the one hand the reluctance of developing countries to share even nominally in the cost or risks of the scheme in exchange for a rather vague advantage that is hard to quantify or even to immediately perceive and may not benefit a particular developing country at any given time.

Moreover, the developing countries have, and I think rightly so, insisted that in any such scheme they should have a substantial voice so as to avoid the danger of a common front of the industrialized countries against a particular developing country, once coverage of the insurance policy is invoked.

Finally, I think for many developing countries there are very serious and traditional political problems in accepting some of what seem essential features of such a scheme, such as subrogation of the insurance agency to the investors' claim upon payment of an indemnity, or settlement of disputes, presumably by arbitration, between the insurance agency and the host country.

On the part of the capital-exporting countries there has not been too much enthusiasm up to this point, even among countries that actively support the scheme—and not all capital-exporting countries do support it actively. My impression, and I think it is shared by others who have worked on this scheme, is that the national systems of insurance or guarantee for investment that practically all important capital exporters have or are about to have meet the needs of their investors, and so nothing additional for the investor would derive from such an international scheme.

Here again I think, even more than in the case of substantive rules on the conduct of investors, unilateral or bilateral action by the states concerned seems much more effective and useful than any concerted worldwide international action.

Perhaps the original approach that the Arab countries have taken to establish a regional insurance scheme for investment may indicate a new and more fruitful way to approach this problem.

Finally, a more modest but fairly successful international effort in the procedural field is represented by the establishment of the International Centre for the Settlement of Investment Disputes (ICSID). This was an initiative of the World Bank and its origin is strictly related to the reluctance of the World Bank to act as mediator or good officer in investment disputes. The convention is basically a very simple instrument. It simply proposes to states—whether capital exporters or capital importers—the acceptance of the principle that a voluntary undertaking by a state and an investor to arbitrate their investment disputes is a binding obligation that cannot be revoked.

Further, the convention provides fairly effective machinery to avoid frustration of arbitration proceedings for lack of cooperation by one of the parties and gives recognition and enforcement status to awards of an arbitration tribunal in the domestic courts of the contracting states. Finally, and I think this is an important aspect, the convention eliminates the right of diplomatic protection of the investor's state whenever a claim can be submitted to arbitration with the consent of both the host state and the investor.

I referred to this as a modest effort because the convention does not per se create any compulsory jurisdiction for the contracting states or the foreign investors, since each contracting state and each investor is free to agree or refuse to go to arbitration or conciliation.

But I also referred to it as a fairly successful effort, not only because 65 countries from all continents have now ratified it but even more because an increasing number of bilateral economic cooperation agreements between industrialized and developing countries, and an ever-increasing number of investment agreements between investors and host states, contain a settlement of disputes clause referring to arbitration under the convention.

While I think the World Bank's sponsorship of this convention and the somewhat unorthodox way it was negotiated may have helped its initial success, the link with the World Bank is now very weak and almost an historical accident.

ICSID provides a useful lynchpin in the increasing network of bilateral intergovernmental agreements or agreements between investors and host states for a mutually satisfactory reconciliation of their interests.

With hindsight one might now wonder whether the drafters of the convention were not too timid and whether something else could have been added, something like a mechanism for renegotiation of agreements. But even now I am very skeptical that anything of that kind could have been achieved in that context.

My conclusions are these:

1. For the time being, multilateral action in the international community would not be able to overcome the ideological and economic conflicts that divide developing countries and industrialized countries and stand in the way of a greater flow of private capital to the developing countries. I think that bilateral agreements, regional arrangements, national investment legislation, and hard bargaining between host states and investors have a better chance of success.

2. International organizations can play a very useful role in collecting and providing information, disseminating skills and techniques for effective negotiations between host states and investors. The proposal of some years ago for an international center on investments of this kind is an attractive one; perhaps the same goal could be achieved through the existing institutions—the UN and its regional economic commissions, for legal information perhaps United Nations Commission on International Trade Law (UNCITRAL) and ICSID. I think there are many bodies already existing that could coordinate their work in this respect.

3. The temptation to use the international financial institutions, which have been established for very specific purposes, as quasi-regulatory or adjudicatory bodies in a field where there is no consensus among the member countries of those organizations on objectives and the means to achieve them should be resisted, because of the danger that the usefulness of these institutions in their principal field of activity will be impaired.

Once a consensus has been reached on some—perhaps limited—questions, then I think the international financial institutions may play a useful role as a common ground to implement what has been agreed. I think the experience of the convention on settlement of investment disputes is a good example.

CHAPTER
14

**INTERNATIONAL RESPONSES TO
INVESTMENT PROBLEMS**
Ibrahim F. I. Shihata

Piero Sella's comprehensive presentation has made it clear that existing and proposed international responses to investment problems were prompted by a universal awareness of the challenge presented by these problems and the need to meet this challenge by international measures. However, such responses were never based on an agreed definition of these problems, even though such a definition may seem the logical prelude to devising effective responses. To be sure, there has been a wide assumption underlying the different approaches elaborated by Mr. Sella to the effect that the problem is in essence a matter of quantity; that international measures are basically needed to stimulate a greater inflow of private capital from rich to poorer countries. Acting on this assumption international efforts seem to have paid less attention to the equally if not more relevant questions of what kind of investment ought to be internationally encouraged, what international rules of behavior the investors should be called upon to follow, and how to effectively combat the possible harmful effects of foreign investments on the economies of the recipient countries.

There has also been a tendency to deal with the issue as if foreign investments constituted one homogeneous whole and therefore deserved the same international legal treatment. No legal differentiation was therefore devised for the old colonial-type investments which enjoyed concessionary terms that would have been unthinkable for Western countries even in the last century. Investments in the extractive

---

Opinions expressed in this commentary are personal opinions and do not necessarily reflect the official views of the Kuwait Fund for Arab Economic Development.

industries, which flourish on the depletion of nonrenewable resources of host countries and have little positive effect on the value added to the national economies of these countries, have not been treated as an independent category either. Nor, for that matter, have multinational firms been singled out for special treatment in view of their strong bargaining power vis-à-vis host countries as well as parent governments. The principle of equality, held dear in the literature on the international legal treatment of foreign investments, has thus been advocated for what are basically unequal subjects.

Mr. Sella's conclusions confirm that the success of international responses to investment problems, like the success of any response to a given challenge, does not depend on their content alone. Of equal importance is the source of the suggested action and the approach and techniques followed in presenting it to the interested parties.

International financial institutions have proved particularly useful catalysts in developing successful remedies within certain limitations. Thus, while the powerful and prestigious World Bank seems to have been the "right" source for initiating such responses as the creation of the ICSID and may eventually succeed in playing a major role in the development of a universal investment code, it does not seem to have met the same measure of success in sponsoring the establishment of a multinational insurance agency. If such an agency is to be financed by the rich industrialized countries that already bave their national insurance programs, these countries themselves or an association of them such as the OECD, may be better suited to act as the exclusive sponsor for creating that agency or adopting more modest proposals like the establishment of an international reinsurance corporation to serve the existing national agencies. The Kuwait Fund for Arab Economic Development has, on the other hand, successfully sponsored the creation of the Arab Corporation for Investment Guarantee on a regional basis, with the participation of the capital-exporting as well as the capital-importing Arab countries. The basic difference is of course that rich Arab countries, not being industrial states looking out for export markets and foreign sources of raw materials, have no national programs for investment insurance and indeed no clear economic interest in encouraging their nationals to invest in other developing countries. They were persuaded to participate in the project by the participation of the poorer countries in the share capital of the corporation and in its other responsibilities.

The source of the response is also particularly relevant in determining the chances of success for the many proposals for the adoption of an international code of investment. Such chances are usually greater when the code is developed by a regional organization to be exclusively applied by its member states. A wider acceptance of such a code is rather unlikely, as is the case for codes devised by sources that are or appear partisan on behalf of the investors or the host countries. Therefore, proposals like the OECD's draft convention on the protection of foreign property or the Asian African Legal Consultative Committee's resolution on the status of aliens may remain merely instruments for the stimulation of further legal thinking on the subject.

The approach followed in drafting the ICSID convention was also a positive factor in its eventual adoption by a great number of states. The close consultation of all the members of the World Bank and the successive regional meetings gave even the smallest state the comforting feeling of participation in the making of the convention. This is a lesson that can be usefully followed in the presentation of other international responses if such collective diplomacy is properly administered by an efficient and trusted secretariat. Continued personal contacts with government officials, especially in the developing countries, is also an important approach for the success of future steps. The particular fickleness and second thoughts of decision-makers in these countries, along with their rapid replacement, pinpoint the importance of this factor.

A response emanating from the "right" source and presented in the "right" procedure may still remain without universal acceptance if its contents are objectionable to any given group of states. The result is that universal regulation will necessarily aim at the bare minimum that can be attained in a particular situation. This may in certain circumstances present a step forward, as in the case of the procedural facilities provided by the ICSID convention. In other situations, however, all sides may be left in a better position without agreement on the attainable minimum. This seems to be the case with the proposed international investment codes. Due to the seemingly incompatible interests of the capital-importing and capital-exporting countries (although they all play host to some foreign investment), a comprehensive and universal agreement on the substantive rules regulating the treatment of foreign investments may not provide a useful remedy to their problems at present. However, this should not mean that the issue ought to be ignored in favor of the procedural approach and the last-defense technique of investment insurance.

There are areas where international regulation is required and seems to be attainable on a group basis, if not on a universal scale. Among these areas the following may readily present themselves for possible consideration, although not all may be equally ripe for immediate action:

1. Some of the existing international responses need to be gradually strengthened if they are to be effective at all. The ICSID, for instance, cannot forever remain without continued jurisdiction, thus repeating the unhappy experience of the Permanent Court of

Arbitration. One of the objectives of its secretariat should be to persuade member states to include in their investment laws and contracts compromissory clauses accepting the jurisdiction of the Center, or to issue declarations to that effect similar to those issued by states under Article 36/2 of the statute of the International Court of Justice. Efforts for the international resolution of conflict of private company laws and for their unification as well as the progressive development of international company law rules should also be activated on the intergovernmental level.

2. If the principle of renegotiation of old investment contracts whose terms have been outdated by economic and political developments is accepted, as I think it should be, there is a clear need for an agreed definition of this principle. Furthermore, conflicts arising in the renegotiation process—being polycentric problems of varied magnitudes, not typical legal disputes—may need for their resolution new types of international forums. Such forums would take up the issue when negotiations fail, not necessarily for the purpose of imposing a settlement but more appropriately for suggesting guiding principles to be followed in further discussions between the parties.

3. More effective efforts may presently be exerted for the resolution of the conflict between capital-exporting and capital-receiving countries in their manipulation of international capital flows for improving their balance of payments. In particular, the measures adopted by certain capital-supplying countries in their attempt to benefit at the expense of the capital-importing countries call for collective measures on the part of the latter or, if at all possible, for international agreements to resolve this conflict.

4. If establishing an international code of behavior for multinational corporations involves formidable difficulties at present, the need for the progressive development of such a code cannot simply be ignored. This is particularly true in the extractive industries of developing countries where there is a fairly high degree of concentration of control of the industries and of their export markets in a limited number of firms in each industry. It is also of special relevance to the exploitation of new resources such as the seabed and the ocean floor. The parent countries may eventually find enough common interest to unite with host states in an agreed regulation of the behavior of these ever-growing giants. Short of such an agreement, the less developed host countries are certainly called upon to devise their own rules and to adopt measures for their implementation. The pioneering initiatives of such organizations as the OPEC in this direction may point to the possibility of further action on a regional or sectoral basis. There is certainly a great deal to be added to ensure systematic and progressive local participation in equity, continuation of the transfer of technology and managerial techniques,

reinvestment of an increasing percentage of profits and prevention of their use in competitive areas in other countries, training and promotion of local personnel, and so forth. However, the effectiveness of such measures depends on improving the professional capacity of the developing countries' bureaucrats and technocrats involved—a fact that calls for the more pressing task of establishing international centers for the training of such staff in the ways of dealing with foreign investments.

On devising international measures such as the ones already mentioned, we should perhaps not lose sight of the fact that some developing countries have spared no effort in the encouragement and protection of foreign investments, by way of issuing favorable laws and statements, entering into bilateral and multilateral investment treaties, and so forth, yet they remain ignored by the investors because of some myth about their unfavorable investment climate or due to ignorance of, or actual lack of, good investment opportunities in their territories. Myth and ignorance can certainly be remedied by international measures such as the establishment of an international center or centers for investment information which may be sponsored by associations of investors or, more appropriately, by the interested developing countries themselves. The actual lack of investment opportunities is a different matter, however. Short of a nonexistant philanthropic investor, the flow of foreign capital to areas lacking attractive investment opportunities can only be expected under generous insurance of commercial risks or outright subsidies. Although such measures might be cited as examples of what aid agencies in the rich countries can do for their nationals investing in less developed countries, the mixture of international charity and transnational private business does not seem to provide a happy solution to this problem.

It is also true—although not commonly observed—that different developing countries have different investment problems and therefore may have good reason to adopt different policies for the treatment of foreign investments. If dealing with foreign investments as if they constituted a single whole was an erroneous generalization, elements of error are equally discernible in the assumption that all developing countries should be expected to react in the same way to the problems of foreign investments or to the international responses devised for tackling these problems.

May I conclude by raising a legal point. Economists and businessmen have spoken of the multinational corporation as one entity with an ease that cannot perhaps be shared by lawyers. For although the term has been used to mean different things, the so-called multinational corporation is in the typical case an integrated system of corporations under the global control of a parent company and is not, legally speaking, one single corporation. However, the formulation of legal standards and rules to direct multinational enterprises toward a more desirable and effective international economic order assumes the possibility of dealing with each one of these integrated systems as one legal entity.

Since that cannot be achieved through any domestic legal system without stretching its scope to such extraterritorial limits as may not readily be acceptable to other host countries, there may be room to initiate thinking of a novel concept of international or transnational corporate personality for the integrated system of the group of domestic corporations that makes a multinational enterprise.

Such a legal person would be a direct subject to the envisaged international law rules, while each of its domestic corporate components remained subject to the domestic legal system concerned, limited in this respect by the higher international law standards. This, of course, is a vision for the future (perhaps the far future) that assumes agreement on the legal criteria for the definition of the multinational enterprise along with some form of international recognition for these enterprises. As such, it may appeal to business circles for the legally recognized international status that it confers on the multinational enterprise as an integrated transnational system. It may also appeal to states insofar as it provides the legal basis for directly subjecting the multinational enterprise to international rules. However, it is not realistic to expect a quick acceptance of this concept by either side at present. I offer it as an elementary thought that may prove under closer scrutiny to raise more problems that it can solve. However, it may deserve that closer scrutiny to examine its potentialities as a useful legal basis for further international responses to investment problems.

*　*　*　*　*

COMMENT
Seymour Rubin

I would like just for a moment to go back over some experience in the field of multilateral attempts to provide some measure of protection for private foreign investment and talk about our present problem in the context of some of that experience.

I start with the 1929 attempt in the League of Nations to provide a code for the protection of private interests abroad, the interests of aliens personally and the interests of property, an attempt that failed dismally despite the fact that there was a very well worked out convention; however, the convention was subjected to so many reservations that it fell by the wayside.

The next attempt, one in which I was personally involved, was that of 1947 and 1948, the attempt to put together a code in the charter of the International Trade Organization (ITO). In the charter as drafted at Geneva there was a quite explicit provision for the protection of private foreign investment providing for the payment of compensation—prompt, adequate, and effective, more or less.

However, in order for the United States, which sponsored that particular provision, to get that provision in that draft, a footnote was dropped down saying that the obligation to make payment was essentially an obligation to make payment in local currency. When that language came back to Washington, the authorities in Washington took a look at the footnote rather than at the language of the draft article itself, and the result was an effort in which I participated very vigorously, with the assistance of a number of people from American industry, to change the language to make it more general, so that on neither the side of the investing country nor the side of the host country would anything be given away. So that the 1948 draft emerged with rather general language, which to my way of thinking—and I must say also to the way of thinking of a number of the industry representatives who worked on the actual negotiation of that clause—represented a rather fair if not very meaningful statement to the effect that proper measures should be taken and property was entitled to protection, and suggested without making any very specific commitments that the property already invested would be given a proper measure of protection, with other rules being specifically set forth for new investments; that is, the draft explicitly indicated that a host country had the right to bar investments in an area in which it did not want investments.

As everyone knows, articles 11 and 12 of the ITO charter were one of the main reasons why the United States rejected that charter. And subsequently there has been the effort of the OECD, the various codes of fair investment practices put forth by the OECD. Some of these provisions seems to me rather obviously unacceptable from the point of view of the host countries, but some have nevertheless been included in some bilateral arrangements.

That history seems to me to indicate the nonfeasibility of working out any kind of generalized overall code of fair investment practices. Even, I may say, if it is in a region—and here I speak to Ibrahim Shihata's observations—if that region includes areas of diverse economic and social systems, as for example the western Hemisphere.

If one includes the Atlantic community and defines the Atlantic community as a region, it may very well be that a code of this sort can be worked out by England, France, and the United States.

My response is that such a code is entirely useless. It is not necessary any more than it is necessary to have an agreement between the United States and Canada; despite the recent wave of criticism of multinational corporations or American corporations operating through subsidiaries in Canada, the United States has never had an arrangement with the Canadians and we have never had any particular problem other than the problem that arises at the present time of the Canadians finding themselves overwhelmed by American investment. In other words, the American investor has never needed the protection of some kind of code in order to induce him to go into Canada.

If these responses are not particularly useful so far as the international investing and investee community is concerned, then perhaps another response would be to particularize. Mr. Shihata has suggested that it would be useful to particularize and perhaps, I would suppose, in two ways. One, to particularize by having individual arrangements or individualized arrangements. Here I refer to such treaties as those of friendship, commerce, and establishment of the United States, the normal treaties we do negotiate; we have quite satisfactory investment provisions in our treaties with Japan, West Germany, and other developed countries.

We have negotiated a few such treaties with the countries of Latin America; none of them have come into effect. These treaties all contain provisions with respect to protection of private foreign investment. They also contain a provision more liberal than that contained in the OECD code with respect to the ability of a country to limit its payments abroad in the interests of its own economic development, or in the interests of the needs of its own people.

But it seems to me that there is some possibility that some arrangements can be arrived at by particularizing that on a regional or a case-by-case basis, by having arrangements between individual investors and individual host countries—the United States on one side and Japan on the other side, perhaps the United States or West Germany on one side and some of the countries of Africa and Asia or maybe even the countries of Latin America, which have other problems as well.

The second way to particularize is to take particular institutions like exit and try to build upon them. I do not feel that this is an entirely promising avenue, but I think it is perhaps the most promising avenue open to us.

I do not feel it is entirely promising because of the limitations in the exit itself, which recognize the reluctance of various countries to sign that particular charter. Exit, as has been indicated, does not compel even a signatory to enter into any arbitration arrangements. A signatory can sign the charter and not put the arbitration provision in its own arrangements with an investing company.

And of course the exit arrangement is lopsided in a way that makes it somewhat undesirable—it applies only in those situations where there is a contract between the host country and the investor. That does not apply to a British investment in the United States, obviously, because the United States government does not get involved in such issues. It does apply to a British or American investment in Uruguay or Botswana. Therefore there is a certain imbalance in the exit arrangement.

Nonetheless it does seem to me that arrangments of this sort—an international institution that would create a procedural basis for parties to come together and talk to each other—is probably the most likely avenue for developments favorable from the point of view of both the host country and the investing company.

15

PROSPECTS FOR PROMOTING
DIALOGUE ON INVESTMENT
BETWEEN THE DEVELOPING
AND THE DEVELOPED COUNTRIES
Walter Sedwitz

Prior to an examination of the prospects for a dialogue between the developed countries and Latin America on foreign private investment, it would be useful to see the problem in broad historical perspective. Since the latter half of the nineteenth century, Latin America has been an attractive area for foreign investment. Prior to World War I, this investment was in railroads and other public utilities, extractive industries, and agricultural commodities such as bananas and sugar. A number of the Latin American governments earlier in this century also obtained substantial funds for development from bond flotations on the private capital markets of Europe and the United States. Unfortunately, these latter obligations were defaulted during the great depression of the 1930s, and until quite recently even the larger countries were unable to resume use of this form of private foreign financing.

After World War II, there were a number of nationalizations of foreign properties, primarily railroads and public utilities, for which the Latin American countries used balances of foreign exchange accumulated during the war. There was also a major shift in the source, sector, and mode of foreign private investment. The United States became the major supplier of capital, the manufacturing sector became a dominant recipient, and direct private investment supplanted bond issues. Petroleum investments, primarily in Venezuela, were an obvious exception to the pattern, and for that matter have distorted all trade and investment statistics for the area.

By and large there were relatively few serious disputes or expropriations during nearly a century of substantial private investment. Even expropriations following intense political pressure were generally compensated, the Mexican petroleum expropriations in 1938 being an outstanding example. Aside from the Cuban case, which was a drastic exception, there have been problems of prompt, effective, and adequate compensation for expropriations only in Peru and Chile, and only with respect to three companies. Both governments expropriated other foreign companies, but apparently with mutually satisfactory compensation.

Nevertheless, the long experience with foreign private investment has created a generally unfavorable attitude toward it in many of the countries. There are many reasons, including rising nationalism with its reaction against foreigners, the dominance of one or a few foreign companies in the economy of a country, company intervention in the politics of some countries, and frustration that the economic destiny of one's country was in the hands of foreigners. Fanning all these feelings since the early 1920s have been ideological considerations based on Marxism, opposing not only the private foreign investment but private enterprise as such, and basically hostile to the United States. There is no doubt today that, however useful and important foreign private investment may be for development, many Latin American countries are wary and psychologically negative toward it. Furthermore the problems are viewed by the Latin Americans much more in political and economic than in juridical terms.

COUNTRY DIFFERENCES

Latin America is not responding in homogeneous fashion to foreign private investment. There are, it is true, certain almost universal tendencies, such as maximizing local participation in foreign companies, diminishing their presence in public utilities and other key sectors, and the like. The large countries, especially Brazil and Mexico, have established ground rules mutually satisfactory to themselves and foreign investors and, given their political stability, are receiving copious quantities of private investment useful for their development. For countries such as Cuba and Chile, which are totally opposed to foreign private investment in the normal sense, no useful dialogue is possible, at least for the time being. For countries of the Andean Group, which has elaborated a common position toward foreign private investment in the so-called Decision No.24, neither the purpose nor the possibilities of dialogue are clear and perhaps a waiting period for results is all that can be expected for the moment. Moreover, Chile and Peru, which have taken additional measures to restrict or eliminate certain types of foreign private investment, remain committed to Decision No.24. There remains for consideration a sizable group of intermediate and smaller countries with varying attitudes toward foreign investment, for whom dialogue with the developed countries would be useful. In the last analysis, of course, each country would agree to the arrangements it believes would best suit its circumstances and interests.

The Latin American attitude toward foreign private investment is the result of many factors. The memory of the Spanish conquest for gold and precious metals and stones is still vivid and undoubtedly contributes to the antagonism toward foreign ownership of the subsoil. In addition, there is Latin America's traditional suspicion, if not deprecation, of business and finance, an attitude that goes back to Catholic Spain. The rather unhappy experience in this century with foreign investments in some Latin American countries has added to the climate of suspicion and fear.

More recently, in the 1940s and 1950s, the U.S. insistence on making private foreign investment in Latin America the key element in assisting the region's development has also given rise to negative reflexes. A contributing factor has been the often strong position assumed by foreign governments in the past in protecting their investors not only through diplomatic and economic pressure but at times also through mild direct military action or threat. The history of the late nineteenth and early twentieth centuries is replete with examples. The more recent U.S. action linking decisions to be taken on loans by international and regional financial institutions of which the United States is a member with private foreign investment disputes in certain countries has tended to aggravate the negative attitude, at least in some countries.

The often heavy concentration of foreign private investment in one sector—banking, public utilities, petroleum—regarded as vital to the economy, together with a relatively opulent presence of a foreign enclave of managers and technicians, has also favored antagonisms. In an environment of growing nationalism, it was to be expected that the climate for private foreign investment in Latin America would not be the best. No matter how enlightened and public-spirited the foreign investor, he faces an uphill fight in many Latin American countries.

Nevertheless, it is interesting to note that, apart from Cuba and Chile, where ideological considerations predominate, the possibilities for dialogue and the setting of ground rules satisfactory both to investor and host country are best in the larger and more rapidly developing countries—notably Brazil, Mexico, and Argentina—and in the relatively less developed and smaller countries. In the former, governments feel strong enough to deal effectively with the foreign investor, and furthermore investments do not loom as large in comparison with domestic private enterprises. But in most countries, governments are likely to be too weak or fearful of various types of pressure to restrict foreign investments. Thus, it is mainly in the middle-sized countries, where economic difficulties have resulted in unsatisfactory rates of development, where inflation and balance of payments problems have been chronic or recurrent, where frustration with the pace of social progress has been widespread, and where foreign investments have been concentrated in one or two large sectors or have constituted a large share of the business sector.

It also seems true that to the extent that development in a country acquires a pace that gives it greater scope for impact, it tends to bring a lessening of chances for expropriation or expropriation without adequate compensation. One need only cite Brazil, Panama, Mexico, and others where economic and social advance are taking the edge off the issue of nationalization. Hence, one cannot consider the vulnerability of private foreign investment as separate from international cooperation in the public sector to speed the pace of development. Recent cases of expropriation or expropriation involving investment disputes have tended to cluster over the 1970-72 period, when "aid fatigue" in the developed countries became most acute, along with frustration with the speed and direction of development in a number of countries.

Today in Latin America most leaders are trying to direct nationalism toward structural change and development. They often find it more effective, especially in the larger and medium-sized countries, to appeal to their people on the basis of national cohesion and self-assertion, as well as the direction of change as a means of channeling energies toward development, than to lose broadly-based support by appearing to make concessions to foreign investment. The will for development and the broad public support required often slackens in the face of openly concessionary policies toward outside investment. This makes the dialogue difficult, although not impossible.

THE OUTLOOK FOR DIALOGUE IN LATIN AMERICA

In the light of the above introductory remarks, the outlook for serious discussion will vary according to the aspects of foreign private investment to be considered. Here we can distinguish the establishment of ground rules, the settlement of disputes, and agreement on the role of foreign private investment in development.

In some ways, the dialogue might be greatly facilitated if agreement could be reached on the role of foreign private investment. This question, however, is greatly complicated by previous positions of the developed countries, especially the United States. The U.S. emphasis during the 1950s on the use of private rather than public foreign funds for development aggravated Latin American sensitivities against private investment. Moreover, each country has evolved its own relationships, which vary widely concerning the sectors and conditions

of foreign private investment. More recently, as the need to diversify
and expand exports in manufactures has become an urgent priority,
the countries have evidenced a growing realization of the potential
importance of foreign private investment in this sector. They are
realizing that the removal of trade barriers to developed countries'
markets is not enough. Their export industries must be able to compete with those of other countries, including the developed countries.
This in turn involves technological and managerial resources.

With reference to the contribution of foreign private investment
to development, the Council of the Americas has sponsored several
studies. A study of the impact on the region as a whole and country
studies for Mexico and Argentina have been published, and one on
Brazil is close to completion. All have shown a definitely favorable
impact. But the dialogue in these efforts has been mainly among research economists.

Another facet of the same problem is the ways and amounts in
which external private investment supplements external public finance.
The outlook for substantial increases in public sources for development is not bright. Yet the needs of the developing countries for external finance are increasing. In this connection, a proposal made by
U.S. Senator Jacob K. Javits in April 1971 is worth exploring. As
part of a broader project, he suggested that a small representative
group of knowledgeable persons of the Organization of American States
system be designated to define the role of foreign private investment
and the foreign capital, technological, and managerial inputs required
by Latin America over the next decade. With appropriate research
staff support, this could be a very useful exercise. The consideration
of the report of such a group by governments and private representatives of the Latin American and developed countries would greatly
benefit the understanding of the problems.

With reference to the establishment of ground rules mutually
satisfactory to host countries and investors, except for Chile, Peru,
Bolivia, Equador, and Columbia (the five countries already excluded),
it appears that for the time being at least the Andean Group countries
would not think it necessary to discuss further the subject of ground
rules as such, although various aspects of the implementation of Decision No.24 (which concerns the sale of foreign assets to local investors after given periods) might be the subject of discussion and
consultation, provided of course that the basic concept of the rule is
not violated. The remainder of the countries would probably be dis-
posed to discuss both the broad and specific aspects of ground rules.
The question of the forum and whether the approach should be bilateral
or with the countries as a group would have to be carefully considered.

More general approaches to the ground rules aspect of the problem have included the Panel on Foreign Investment in Developing

Countries, which met under United Nations auspices in Amsterdam in February 1969. This panel dealt with the importance of foreign private investment in development and the encouragement of it in developed and developing countries. The United Nations itself, in "International Strategy for the Second U.N. Development Decade," attached considerable importance to private foreign investment and action to facilitate it by developing countries, investors, and developed countries. The United Nations joined the OAS and Inter-American Development Bank in sponsoring a follow-up dialogue in Medellin, Colombia, in June 1970. Still another seminar was held in Rome in January 1971 and another in Caracas in February 1973. At this latter meeting consideration was given to a draft code on the ground rules for foreign private investment proposed by a special commission of the International Chamber of Commerce.

SETTLEMENT OF INVESTMENT DISPUTES

It is with reference to the settlement of investment disputes that the prospects of dialogue are less favorable in Latin America. Here we are faced with the century-old Calvo doctrine which limits treatment of expropriation of foreign nationals to that accorded to nationals. More important, it has been used to reject the jurisdiction of third parties and international tribunals for consideration of disputes. Thus, no Latin American country (except the ex-British territories) has ratified the convention for the International Centre for Settlement of Investment Disputes (ICSID). Latin American countries have been reluctant to accept arbitration. In the current pending disputes, all forms of arbitration or mediation suggested have been rejected. The decisions of the governments of Peru in the International Petroleum Company case and Chile with reference to Kennecott and Anaconda copper companies were unilateral and thus far not subject to extra-national review.

The several attempts by the capital-exporting countries to negotiate a multilateral investment protection code have failed. For example, the effort of the European countries and the United States in the Conferences on the International Trade Organization Charter in 1947 and 1948; the efforts of the United States in the Bogotá Conference of 1948 and the Buenos Aires Conference in 1957. At the direction of the IA-ECOSOC (Inter-American Economic and Social Council) some years ago, the Latin American countries were canvassed on their interest in a multilateral investment guarantee treaty. The reactions revealed little or no interest.

152

DEVELOPED COUNTRY RECEPTIVITY

For many years the developed countries as capital exporters have been interested not only in promoting the foreign private investment of their nationals but in devising understandings on conditions and arranging methods of protection. Promotion has included bilateral insurance and guarantee systems and attempts, as noted before, at multilateral agreement including both developing and developed countries.

During the postwar period and especially the past 15 years, the unprecedented expansion of the Western developed countries has absorbed a proportionately much greater share of private investment, thus reducing the proportion available for the developing world and especially Latin America. Private investment, always sensitive to conditions, has flowed to countries offering political stability and the best economic prospects of success. Spearheading the investment of this latter period have been the multinational corporations, which together with their subsidiaries have helped to push total production of foreign enterprises to about double the total value of world trade.

The United States detente with the USSR and China has opened up new prospects in those countries for foreign private investment. Already a mammoth undertaking running into billions of dollars has been worked out between the Occidental Petroleum Company and the Soviet Union. Another vast investment to bring gas across Siberia is in prospect involving a Japanese consortium. One might anticipate investment of comparable magnitudes by Western companies in China. The flow of huge amounts of foreign private capital to the Soviet Union obviously makes less capital available to the developing countries. It may also diminish the sense of urgency by the developed countries to concern themselves with trying to convince negatively inclined countries of the usefulness of foreign private investment in their development. Total funds for private investment remain limited and will flow where they are wanted and conditions for success are optimal.

The vast operations of the multinational corporations and the consequences of their actions on many countries, developed and developing, have caused increasing attention to be focused on them by governments. The U.S. government and the European Economic Community (EEC), in recent negotiations for the next round of GATT, have agreed to study jointly the problems created by these corporations. Likewise, the international business community is concerned, as shown by the dedication of the twenty-second congress of the International Chamber of Commerce in 1969 to the problems of the international corporations. A constructive study of the alternatives for harmonizing the operations of these complex enterprises with national sovereignty and economic policy may in effect go a long way in resolving the issues in regulation of foreign private investment itself in both the developed and the developing countries.

WAYS OF ENCOURAGING THE DIALOGUE

For purposes of constructive dialogue, two levels should be distinguished: (1) the broader questions of policies and conditions for investment and (2) the resolution of conflicts arising in specific cases. Fundamental to both is the need for a much better understanding of the operations of international companies and for better statistics. The U.S. government is virtually alone in furnishing such data and even these could be improved and made more timely.

For the Latin American countries, a good forum for policy considerations could be the annual country reviews of the International Committee for the Alliance for Progress (CIAP). These studies attempt to analyze all major factors affecting the growth and development of each country. In accord with the wishes of the countries, with reference to investment primary attention thus far has been devoted to public investment programs. Hindering analysis of all private sector activity has been a general lack of data but, as with other important questions, this problem can be attacked and overcome. The CIAP reviews could examine and make recommendations concerning public policies relating to foreign private investment, but they are not appropriate for dealing with problems created by the operations of individual business enterprises.

With respect to the capital-exporting countries, whose cooperation is important in working out these problems of acceptable control, perhaps the DAC forum would be helpful. The Development Assistance Committee (DAC) secretariat has already prepared very useful statistics on the flows of private as well as public financial resources from the developed to the developing countries. As in the case of CIAP, however, major analytical attention appears to have been devoted to public sector financing and the flow of external public funds. While DAC might concern itself with policy questions, quite likely it could not deal with problems arising in specific cases of investment disputes.

Still another important approach in encouraging the dialogue involves the organizations of the private sector. In these, businessmen from the developing and developed countries can discuss the kinds of policies most suitable not only for governments but for the businesses themselves. In the international organizations such as the International Chamber of Commerce, and regional organizations such as the Interamerican Federation for Trade and Production (CICYP), the international corporations could do much, not only to propose plans to adjust their practices to the needs of the developing countries but also to create a better understanding of their operations among the businessmen and governments of those countries.

With reference to the settlement of investment disputes, a different forum and procedure are required. For many countries, evidently, the International Centre for Settlement of Investment Disputes may provide an acceptable mechanism. By June 30, 1972, 63 states had ratified the Convention on the Settlement of Investment Disputes between States and Nationals of other States, which provided for establishment of the ICSID. Yet although the convention was opened for signature in March 1965, ICSID registered its first request for arbitration proceedings only during 1973. For the Latin American countries and perhaps others that have not been able to accept the convention, other procedures must be sought, something less formal and nonjuridical.

One possibly helpful procedure might be a fact-finding service, which could perhaps be established in the World Bank. This could be made up of technical staff versed in operations of international companies and the development problems of the developing countries. In case of a dispute either party could request a fact-finding report. Hopefully, both parties would furnish all information and points of view available. Such a report could be made available to all interested parties, private and governmental, to the international lending agencies, and possibly to international private banks. Unlike arbitration, where both parties must accept the procedure and terms and are bound by the decision once they accept, there would be no award and no one would be legally obligated to take action. This procedure would also differ from mediation where a third party actively seeks to bring the disputing parties to a mutually acceptable settlement.

While this very informal fact-finding service may appear ineffectual, it may nevertheless be a major improvement over a purely unilateral handling of the dispute, which may produce no settlement and lead to reprisals and other damaging actions against the developing country, as well as lack of satisfaction for the individual or firm whose property has been taken or damaged. It is also possible that this informal approach may encourage the parties to accept mediation or even ultimately the arbitration of ICSID.

It would also appear that there is a lot the private sectors in the developed countries can do to regulate themselves in their relations with less developed countries (LDCs). It is highly possible that business groups in the developed countries can make great progress among themselves without the participation of the LDCs. There is some incentive to do so. To the extent that a single foreign enterprise in an LDC conducts itself in an unusual way, it tends to heighten tensions over private investment generally and prejudice the possibilities of

TABLE 15.1

Current Situations in Latin America Involving Nationalization, Expropriation, or
Negotiated Sale of Property in Which U.S. Corporations Have a Direct or
Indirect Interest, January 1, 1960-June 30, 1971

Country	Company	Year of Takeover
	Total nationalization or expropriation of companies with majority U.S. ownership interest	
Bolivia	Bolivian Gulf Oil Co.	1969
	International Metals Processing Corp.	1971
	Mina Matilde Corp.	1971
Chile	Alimentos Purina	a
	Cía. Minera Andina	1971
	Cía. Minera Exótica	1971
	Ford Motor Co.	a
	Industrias Nibco	a
Ecuador	All-American Cables & Radio	1970
Peru	International Petroleum Co.	1968
	W. R. Grace & Co.	1969
	Total nationalization or expropriation of companies with minority U.S. ownership interest (nationality of majority share and percentage of U.S. ownership in parentheses)	
Chile	Cía. de Cobre Chuquicamata (Chile; 49% U.S.)	1971
	Cía. de Cobre El Salvador (Chile ; 49% U.S.)	1971
	Soc. Minera El Teniente (Chile; 49% U.S.)	1971
Guyana	Demerara Bauxite Co. (Canada; 46% U.S.)	1971
	Companies with majority or minority U.S. ownership interest that are negotiating or have negotiated sale of Equity interest to host government (nationality of majority shares in parentheses; date given is year action initiated)	
Chile	Armco (U.S.)	1971
	Bank of America (U.S.)	b
	Bethlehem-Chile Iron Mines Co. (U.S.)	1971
	Cia. de Telefonos de Chile (U.S.)	b
	First National City Bank (U.S.)	b
	RCA Chile (U.S.)	1971
	Soquimich (Anglo-Lautaro) (Chile)	1971
	South American Power (U.S.)	1970

Note: Other claims involving various disputes, including tax claims, labor disputes, performance disputes, concession rights, and insolvencies, are not included in this listing. Also not included are certain cases where majority interests have been acquired by governments under mutually satisfactory agreements.

aIntervention by government, but no formal expropriation.
bPreliminary discussions leading to probable sale under way.

Source: Nationalization, Expropriation and Other Takings of United States and Certain Foreign Properties Since 1960 (Washington, D.C.: U.S. Department of State, Bureau of Intelligence and Research, November 30, 1971).

TABLE 15.2

Settled Situations in Latin America Involving Nationalization, Expropriation, or Negotiated Sale of U.S. Corporate Property (January 1, 1960-June 30, 1971)

Country	Company	Year of Takeover Sale, or Other Action	Year Settled
Argentina	Argentine Cities Service Development Co.	1963	1967
	Continental Oil Co. of Argentina — joint	1963	1967
	Marathon Petroleum Argentina Ltd. — venture		
	Esso Argentina, Inc.	1963	1967
	Pan American International Oil Co.	1963	1967
	Tennessee Argentina, S. A.	1963	1967
	Transworld Drilling Co.	1963	1967
	Union Oil Co. of California	1963	1967
Brazil	American and Foreign Power	1959	1964
	Companhia Telefonica Nacional	1962	1967
Chile	Andes Copper Mining Co. Chile acquired 51% with	1969	1969
	Chile Exploration Co. provisions to purchase		
	remainder	1969	1969
	Branden Copper Co.—Chile acquired 51%	1966	1969
	Valentine Petroleum and Chemical Corp.	1964	n.a.
Mexico	American and Foreign Power	1960	1960
	Asarco Mexicana both	1965	1965
	Industrias Penoles Mexicanized	1965	1965
	Compania Azufrera Mexicana both	1967	1967
	Compania Explotadora del Istmo Mexicanized	1967	1967
Peru	Banco Continental—negotiated sale	1969	1969
	Peruvian Telephone Co.—negotiated sale	1969	1969

Source: Nationalization, Expropriation and Other Takings of United States and Certain Foreign Properties Since 1960 (Washington, D.C.: U.S. Department of State, Bureau of Intelligence and Research, November 30, 1971).

all foreign enterprise, not just of the specific company in question. If the possibilities for dialogue and decision on the regulation of foreign private investment appear to be limited between developed and under-developed countries, some progress surely can be made in discussions within the business communities of the industrial countries.

Given the diverse factors that determine the vulnerability of investment and the extent to which these escape both economic and legal parameters, a flexible and modest approach to the problem of investment regulation seems to be the most feasible and desirable at this time.

Regarding the establishment of a GATT-type international organization to bring some degree of order to the problem of international investment, this certainly should be the objective. But several intermediate steps are still needed to bring about the economic, political, and psychological conditions for such a mechanism to work effectively. First and foremost, more concerted and genuine international efforts are needed to bring about more sustained economic and social advance. Public bilateral and multilateral assistance is essential in this regard to begin to improve the climate for private foreign investment. Existing arbitration arrangements must be allowed to demonstrate their effectiveness, where they are being issued. In the absence of such facilities, fact-finding services could become the nearest approach to opening the dialogue further. The private foreign investor must begin to judge his entry into a country on the basis of how his investment may contribute to excessive concentration in one sector, overall size and profile in comparison with the rest of the economy, conditions of entry, and the general economic, social, and political climate. In this regard, there is need now to concentrate attention on the draft International Chamber of Commerce (ICC) convention, which sets up certain basic and rather flexible principles and criteria affecting the investor, the investor's own country, and the host country. While advances in this direction are made, every possible regional or international forum should be used, especially DAC and CIAP, but also the UN annual review of performance under the Second Development Decade, to widen and deepen the dialogue.

* * * * *

COMMENT
Edward Korry

"What whispers burial to some," Baudelaire wrote, "cries out to others life and light." I confess to an uncommon optimism after listening to the observations made here and reading the well-reasoned points made by Walter Sedwitz. The turn of recent events persuades me neither to seek to bury nor to praise the multinational enterprise (MNE) but to view it as a fortuitous accelerator in man's progress toward an integrated world society.

How does one who served as U.S. Ambassador to Chile for three years before the election of Dr. Salvador Allende as president and for more than one year after that event arrive at such a Micawberish conclusion? Personal experience and perception of a number of trends of the past fifteen years conspire to fashion that outlook.

Until recently, the United States was the overwhelmingly pre-eminent power in the world, militarily, politically, industrially. Largely by design of U.S. policies, the European Economic Community and Japan are now rapidly closing the resource gap to emerge as equals in a universe with many centers of political initiative and decision-making. The higher growth rates and greater reinvestment efforts of Japan and Germany are propelling these countries, to mention only the two most notable, into the American and other markets. They no longer come as mere investors in portfolios but increasingly as owners of factories and service industries.

This interpenetration is creating a symmetry among the non-socialist industrialized countries of the Northern Hemisphere. It is shaping conditions in which similar rules of the game can be applied, in which regulations can be expanded, sharpened, or added to deal, at first on a regional basis and then more generally, with the problems involving the MNE—market domination, double taxation, speculative movements of capital, and so on. Such harmonization should reduce the psychic distances between North America, on the one hand, and Europe and Japan on the other; the consensual process, unless interrupted by political changes of a significant nature, should lead to still greater integration of an important segment of mankind.

The common origins of civilization that the United States and the USSR do, after all, share and that is more widely recognized by the peoples of all Europe, is in part behind a second great shift in which the MNE is playing a role as integrator.

Only fifteen or so years ago, the United States participated for the first time in a trade fair in one of the "satellite" countries. One or two Americans returned from that novelty in Poznan to seek to persuade their compatriots that cooperative ventures between American companies and socialist trusts were not irrational illusions, that the objective conditions in central Europe were becoming propitious for some transactions in which investment of equipment could be repaid in products or materials. In briefing and board rooms, they were regarded as eyeless visionaries. Now these same organizations have pushed their horizons to anticipation of a Marxist Eldorado where joint ventures, coproductions, and old-fashioned barter will demonstrate

159

the MNE's superiority and profitability. Wherever the pendulum of
reality should be today, the symmetry that increasingly governs the
actions of nonsocialist developed countries is also a natural precursor
of the stability that seems to characterize relations in this particular
period between them and the socialist world; this phenomenon is a
second important trend that is converting the MNE into an integrative
force.

U.S. economic and political objectives in Europe (and Japan) in
the 1950s coincided, had a clearcut national interest justification, and
were sharply defined: To recreate European (and Japanese) strength
and to construct barriers to the extension of communist power. When
the United States achieved these goals and when the USSR ended the
Pentagon's nuclear monopoly and demonstrated that it would employ
its forces to maintain the political status quo in Europe, the locus of
cold war contest shifted from the developed to the developing world.
Within a short period, the major protagonists discovered that for all
their power, the politicomilitary costs of worldwide confrontation
politics were mounting to an unsupportable level. Not only were the
demands on national resources too onerous but the strains imposed
by the international contest jeopardized the very institutions and values
at home that were the promoters of all the jousting. The imperatives
of domestic stability drove managers in government and corporations
on both sides of the ideological divide to contemplate alternative policies that could be more efficiently handled and more responsive to
popular needs. Marxist-Leninist planners, emboldened by their success in stabilizing their relations with NATO nations and enfeebled
by the dissatisfactions of would-be consumers, looked longingly at
the capital, the machines, the techniques, and the markets of the West;
they began to shop for solutions to the nagging problems of production,
distribution, and discontent. The MNEs and governments of Europe
and Japan, no less concerned about the explosion of mass expectations,
heeded this call of a new marketplace. And once Western European
MNEs arrived, the United States could not be far behind.

Because the MNE expects to operate in the Northern Hemisphere
in an environment of evolution and negotiable equilibrium, and seeming
erraticism and instability in the southern half of the globe is all the
more disconcerting and frustrating. What has happened, the older
generation of MNE directors ask, to those decades when comparative
quiescence and acquiesence provided profit and opportunity to the
trading companies, the developers of raw materials, and the providers
of local services, when resignation was twin to poverty, and apathy
the father of political stability? The answer is that anticolonialism,
nationalism, populism, and statism have swept away those "good old
days."

Today the thesis that economic and social ills are correctable has been thoroughly disseminated as part of the worldwide information explosion. There are many ears at the ready among the silent majority of mankind in that underworld of poverty, pain, and anger that is thrusting at our affluence and indifference.

In the LDCs, the means used by the Soviet Union, or China, or Cuba, to accumulate capital seem to represent a workable alternative to poverty, to development gains devoured by high rates of population growth, and to income distribution based on the trickle-down experience of the industrial revolution in the West. Regimentation of an economy can force a surplus. The worst excesses of such forced savings are, rightly or wrongly, thought by developing countries to be avoidable.

Hence, the much publicized deals between MNEs such as Occidental Petroleum and the Soviets are just as likely to be viewed as notable for the lack of any role for direct foreign investment as for the recourse by the Kremlin to the seemingly indispensable MNE.

The United States has sought at times to anticipate or respond to the changes in the Southern Hemisphere by moving fitfully toward the concept of an integrated world society in which there would be no client states, in which all regions would benefit from truly international institutions, and in which multilateral instruments of change would function equitably and effectively.

In 1966, for example, the United States adopted for Africa a policy that eschewed for the first time since the inception of the cold war the notion of competition with communist powers in every corner of a vast continent. Instead, it proposed for Africa a multilateral triad of the International Bank for Reconstruction and Development (IBRD), the United Nations Economic Commission for Africa, and the African Development Bank, to serve as the major continental and subregional planner, coordinator, and developer. Calling for greater cooperation among all Western aid-giving nations while specifically keeping the door open to eventual participation by socialist countries, Washington phased out most of its country missions and pushed for concerted international support of development by subregion and by sector.

Implicit throughout the new U.S. approach and explicit in the most pertinent instances was the expectation that international (and indigenous) private enterprise would be crucial to African advances. The multilateral triumvirate was to provide leadership to the aid-givers, to furnish expertise to the Africans for their negotiations with MNEs, to initiate or encourage the most promising preinvestment surveys, to act as a shield against large-scale waste of resources, and to serve as a clearinghouse of data. But flows of private capital were indispensable to all these efforts. The World Bank and the African Development Bank would be counted upon to take minority equity positions alongside the MNEs in certain investments.

161

Progress toward these goals has been rather slow and undramatic. But African governments have, on occasion, foresworn their own power projects to plug into the grids of neighbors; roads are built now to join subregional networks; airlines represent several countries; a continental telecommunications system is taking shape. It is axiomatic, however, that a customs union or a subregion cannot be artificially forged. There should be a minimal threshhold of development shared by participants and a modicum of political compatibility. Hence progress toward regional units has not been as significant as, say, the acceptance of a meaningful developmental function by the World Bank since Washington embarked on this new policy in 1967.

In Latin America, where U.S. influence was preponderant, where some of the preconditions for regionalism were more advanced, and where institutional competence was well ahead of the African models, another set of American proposals was put forward with high-level support in late 1969:

> It is in our interest to encourage regionalism, greater cooperation, and more viable economic institutions in Latin America. There are already some incipient, viable regional organizations in Latin America—the Central American Common Market, the Andean Group, and, for some purposes, the River Plate group. We should seek to deal with them as groups whenever possible, rather than with countries individually. This would foster more coherence on their part; and it would reduce the involvement of the U.S. in their domestic affairs.
>
> Brazil, because of its size, diversity, and importance, does not like to be included in any multilateral arrangements. There is no theoretical bar to classifying countries of Brazil's dimensions as regions for the forseeable future, a classification that would be responsive to their self-appreciation and consistent with our conviction that the U.S. should neither dogmatize multilateralism nor abandon its own bent of pragmatism.
>
> CECLA [Committee for Economic Coordination in Latin America] is a grouping of all Latin American countries, created by them to develop common views with which to confront the U.S. The Latin Americans preferred CECLA to the Inter-American OAS [Organization of American States] in order to bar the U.S. from participating in the first round of reaching a Latin American consensus, and to permit U.S. participation only in the second round—the dialogue. The arrival at a common

position and the subsequent meeting of the InterAmerican ECOSOC in November, 1969, was an example of the process of consensus leading to multilateralization. While CECLA has slipped into an adversary posture with the U.S., while it addressed its demands only to the U.S. and not to other industrialized nations, and while it ignored what Latin America might do to improve its capacity for economic growth, it is to the U.S. interest to encourage CECLA. For by a continuing discussion as well as by the logic of events, CECLA may be encouraged, for example, to press the European community for a generalized system of trade preferences and for the reduction of quota and nontariff barriers. . . .

Negotiations for debt-rescheduling provide predictable opportunities that should be exploited to engage the more permanent interest of European countries and of Japan. Similarly the Inter-American Development Bank should be prompted to look for more durable links with European countries, beyond its present limited success in gaining access to the European financial markets. Because of the domination by U.S. private enterprise of many investment sectors, the U.S. should try to educate its businessmen to welcome, if not to attract, participation by firms from Asia or Europe so that the total flow of resources increases and the Latin outlook becomes more global.*

Gradually, these arguments have been assimilated by officials in Washington responsible for policy toward Latin America. They came to adopt this view because the "special relationship" with Latin America could not be isolated from the worldwide consequences of World War II, because we could not continue to delude ourselves that decolonialization in Africa and Asia did not affect the paternalistic preeminence of the United States in Latin America.

Although Washington could and did argue with reason and with right that its presence in the area was not analogous to that of the European empires in Africa and Asia, that it did not have any "colonies," it could not persuade nationalists, populists, and Marxists

---

*The author was requested in the autumn of 1969 to draft the executive branch's position on the future of all U.S. foreign aid and the justification for any programs. The above excerpt comes from the draft prepared in response to the specific National Security Study memorandum request.

in the area that there was a significant distinction between the need for psychological and economic liberation and the more conventional desire for political decolonization.

The North American gaze is usually fixed on Europe and, to a lesser degree in normal times, on Asia. Once in a great while when the U.S. vice president is mobbed in Caracas or when U.S. armed forces are engaged in the Dominican Republic or are eyeballing with the Soviets, we interrupt our East-West line of sight. These diversions are so fleeting that we are often deceived by appearances.

The much-heralded triumph of U.S. diplomacy and determination in the staredown of Khruschev did, in fact, mark the end of an era in Latin America. For the citizens of that region, the long-term import of that incident over Cuba was and is that Fidel Castro has succeeded in surviving; indeed, they argue that he improved his durability, and that he did so on his terms. For Latin Americans, the capacity of one of their number to defy the Colossus of the North, the ability to impose his will, overrides all else, even the stagnation of the Cuban economy and the country's dependence on the Soviet camp.

The pervasiveness of Castro's success did not propel North Americans to abrupt change. Most MNEs, for example, continued to count upon the power of the U.S. government, the pull of the U.S. market, and the pertinacity of habit to protect their fundamental interests. The Alliance for Progress, with its social awareness and its promise of a tremendous transfer of resources, was regarded by some executives as a safety valve; others looked to the new Agency for International Development (AID), and later Overseas Private Investment Corporation (OPIC), insurance of fresh investment as a guarantee; many depended upon the Hickenlooper amendment and similar retaliatory baggage to be effective dissuaders.

It was rare that a U.S. firm felt that any radical shift in customary concepts of property, equity, management, or marketing might be considered. When Kennecott Copper responded to the 1964 Frei platform of Chileanization by selling 51 percent of its holdings in Chile and entered as a minority stockholder into a joint enterprise with a state corporation, most North American businessmen in Latin America were outraged. But the episode came to be viewed as a curious if unsettling exception, and when Chile later agreed to permit the larger Anaconda Company to retain 100 percent ownership of its existing operations, the sit-tighters were sure of their security. Similarly in 1968 when the Peruvian junta nationalized oil properties of the International Petroleum Company and not only refused compensation but demanded retroactive reparations many times the worth of the seized company, the event was generally seen as an oddity laden with very special emotional and historical pegs.

Again, it was disquieting to some that the Hickenlooper amendment was not applied by the Nixon administration. But it was regarded as far more threatening and peculiar that one or two U.S.
officials in the area were insisting that the time had arrived for a
demonstration of imaginative flexibility by U.S. corporations. The
response to the suggestion that it would be beneficial to both the U.S.
business enterprises and to the larger interests of the home and host
countries to devise new modes of relationships was not merely cool;
it was, as I can attest, downright hostile.

The circumstances that governed Chile in this period were
particularly instructive. Washington had made its single greatest
Alliance for Progress commitment, in per capita and psychic terms,
to Chile; that country was a solid yet vital political democracy; it had
progressive social and economic policies; and in a place where copper
dominated all else, the U.S. copper firms (as in the case of other
industries) were fulfilling if not overtaking the schedules for their
enormous investments guaranteed by the U.S. government. Yet the
odds were that this first experiment in Christian Democracy in the
hemisphere would not be extended by the electorate in the next presi-
dential balloting in 1970.

These were the broad brushes of the background against which
U.S. firms and Latin American officials were first asked in 1967 to
consider alternatives to the either/or options of the day. It was suggested that rather than await inevitable showdowns over nationalization,
various fadeouts should be considered, that such fadeouts of extant
investments be structured according to the particularities of the
industrial sector, the history of the activity, and the level of development of the nation.

Ambiguity could be an integral feature of such consideration,
it was emphasized. For example, if a foreign enterprise already
operating in a country agreed to gradually sell its equity, there could
be a previously agreed period of cooling-off when the 50 percent level
was about to be reached, a period in which the foreign partner could
assess its experience and decide whether it wished to be bought out
entirely or would be satisfied with a minority role. Alternatively,
the purchasing entity, be it state-controlled or private enterprise
could, by the original contract, reflect as to whether it wished to continue with a straight buyout or whether national pride had been sufficiently satisfied to put aside political aspirations in favor of access
to technology, to higher levels of training, to greater markets, to
integrated management skills on a worldwide scale.

Corporations operating in Latin America that were ready to
study such alternatives were little more than phantoms. Moreover,
the U.S. firms were not pushed in that direction by any influential
segments of the Congress, the Executive, or the Washington

bureaucracy. Thus, when Anaconda in the spring of 1969 was suddenly confronted by the Frei government with a demand for a renegotiation of the copper accords signed only two years earlier, we had what is usually described as a touchstone case, one that did, quite rapidly, affect other regions and other industries once the company and the Chilean government had set their courses.

The decision that the two parties reached by mid-1969 incorporated an unusual degree of inventiveness and statesmanship. Anaconda agreed to sell all 100 percent of its immense holdings in the country to the state; it consented to hand over 51 percent of its shares immediately against a maximum schedule of 12 years of payments for them; it entered a binding accord that made it mandatory for Chile to buy the remaining 49 percent once a certain payments level had been attained for the first 51 percent; and it pledged to provide technical and other assistance on a compensated basis.

This voluntary disinvestment as part of an investment process, as part of a rational evolution of relations between an industrialized and a nonindustrialized area, was a genuine MNE landmark. In the context of this conference, it proved that the MNE could be an agent of progressive change.

I maintain this position even though the rules of the game were again upset within 18 months when Salvador Allende became President of Chile. The United States and a good many U.S. companies discovered that the bargaining power that is always supposed to be with the rich did not exist in the form that most took for granted.

First, there was no united front among the North American firms: Some wished to stay; some wished to clear out; some were ready to negotiate. Second, there was no unanimity of purpose among the MNEs from the industrialized world. Some from Europe wished to capitalize on the plight of their beleaguered U.S. competitors and there were some based in Japan no less ready and willing to exploit the opportunities. Third, the U.S. government found little sympathy for its view that international law demanded adequate compensation arranged for promptly and in effective means of payment; a nation of less than 10 million citizens with a leader pledged to what he defined as a progressive and democratic sharing of the national wealth aroused considerable sympathy in every corner of the world.

Most of the headlines have been devoted to the two copper companies and to International Telephone and Telegraph (ITT), all three of which received no compensation. Overlooked were more than a dozen other agreements involving U.S. companies that were negotiated with the Socialists and Communists—Marxist-Leninists, if you will—who control the government of Chile. These accords involved some fairly substantial investments and some major corporations, among them Bethlehem Steel, Ralston Purina, ARMCO, Cerro Copper, the Bank of America, the First National City Bank of New York.

Even more important, in seeking to work out acceptable exits for the two largest copper companies, the Allende government was urged to consider disinvestment formulas that went far beyond anything anyone had put on the table in any other country. Some elements of this thinking have surfaced recently in the agreement that OPIC has just announced in settlement of its outstanding insurance held by the Kennecott Company. For the first time, I believe, the U.S. Treasury, via OPIC, is guaranteeing notes from a foreign state corporation and authorizing their sale to private commercial bankers. This means has been utilized to eliminate a major problem between the governments of the United States and Chile, and between North American taxpayers and their government. Had the Chilean government defaulted on the note due Kennecott last December 31, it might have triggered full payment of the approximately $80 million insurance issued to Kennecott by the Chilean state corporation at the time of the formation of the joint copper company in 1967. Instead, OPIC guaranteed the notes so they could be sold at commercial discount in the commercial market. The net effect is that the U.S. government reduced the total liability by a not insignificant percentage, and it reduced the immediate liability of the taxpayer to a fraction since insurance would be paid only on a note per note basis each six months for many years if Chile defaulted, rather than an immediate lump sum.

Let me say parenthetically that some multinational corporations have been terribly maligned. Kennecott, for example, for which I have no need to make any special brief, had only six foreigners in Chile at the time the Allende government nationalized its holdings. Only two of the six were North Americans, and they were part of a labor force of more than 8,000 of whom 500 were trained Chilean supervisors. Every job that could be considered managerial or skilled was three deep in trained Chileans—in computer programming, in the most advanced copper technology, in administration, and at every level of the enterprise in the mine, the smelter, and the office. This example was not unique.

But to return to my central point, the multinational enterprises began to negotiate in Chile matters they had consistently refused to consider only two years before. Company after company expressed willingness to accept arrangements that would have been denounced as lunacy under normal conditions.

I spoke earlier of the evolving symmetry in the nonsocialist world, of the legitimization of the MNE by the socialist camp, and of the profound change in the U.S. role in the world, a factor that is going to become ever more apparent and meaningful.

To these major trends should be added the influences that many hope will eliminate the compartmentalization of north-south relationships as in the case of the European Economic Community and Africa, of the United States and Latin America, and of Japan and Asia. Unfortunately the United States has failed so far to play its promised role in the African Development Bank, and the Inter-American Development Bank is attracting European and Japanese support in an unspectacular manner. But in time, once the industrialized nations fully comprehend their responsibilities and obligations, another kind of symmetry should emerge: Each of the three major nonindustrialized regions will have equal access to the major industrialized sectors and each will be given more or less equal responses from those areas.

Pushing all countries toward this more universal structure is a new-found awareness that most of the problems of the postindustrial age are universal in nature; they involve the atmosphere, the oceans, the environment, the natural resources, and the flow of ideas.

The MNE will both lead and be led by this inevitable process. The speed and manner in which MNEs arrive at new equilibriums with the nonindustrialized countries will, to a large degree, be determined by how they and their governments can define their own rules of the game. They cannot expect rational "rules" from the poorer when they have not yet succeeded in setting their own or applying them in a just and equitable manner for the less advantaged nations.

I anticipated that MNEs from the United States and Japan or Europe will enter jointly into more ventures with partners in the less developed world; it will be part of a growing process of multilateralization of investment and endeavor. Perhaps there will also be a multilateralization of guarantees. For the LDCs, there will be a greater availability of expertise for international negotiation, as well as a greater awareness of pertinent information and a greater disposition within each of the industrialized countries to provide political support for the just aspirations of the LDCs. And finally, there will be an equalizing of some of the market forces, in favor of the LDCs that have natural resources or large numbers of potential consumers.

I expect these trends, far more than any attempt to codify the process of negotiation, to fashion a political environment that will enable the MNE to contribute to the process of making mankind out of man.

*   *   *   *   *

COMMENT
Raul Prebisch

I am encouraged by Ambassador Korry's optimism. He has observed that there is a very interesting evolution in the relationships between the multinational corporations and governments, especially with the socialist governments. It is my impression that there is more flexibility and imagination in these corporations than in many governments, and in my view the fact that these corporations have started work in socialist countries may have a profound impact on Latin American countries. This will take time. Changes in the form of this relationship are needed. The multinational corporations, as they have been working in the past, could not succeed in establishing a constructive relationship with Latin American governments, especially with socialist governments. A change is necessary and for this reason I attach great importance to discussions and dialogues of the kind that are taking place at this conference.

This change in attitudes has started and I believe the idea of "fading out," within certain limits and proportions, is a good one. Ambassador Korry has given only part of the information on this matter and I will complete it. The truth is that he was one of the first—perhaps the first—to develop this idea, but only within a narrow circle of friends. Indeed, I had the privilege in 1967 to listen to his ideas about this matter, presented with his customary lucidity. I have ample proof Ambassador Korry, while ambassador to Chile, was instrumental in shaping new ideas in this matter of investment.

As I mentioned before, it is indispensable to look for new forms of relationships. This becomes apparent not only in discussions with economists but also with eminent financial authorities in our region. A few months ago I was impressed by what President Antonio Ortiz Mena of the Inter-American Development Bank (IDB) said on this matter. Even though the texts of the two speeches he gave have not yet been made public, I have been given authority to make use of their contents.

The need not only to give information to the developing countries about the nature of the multinational companies trying to develop their activities in these countries but also to establish a system of technical assistance for developing countries is duly recognized and advocated by the presence of the IDB at this meeting. Mr. Ortiz Mena has said, for instance, that the IDB should be prepared to give "assistance in working out terms for new arrangements between the host countries and the foreign companies, and of providing a secure framework for the implementation of such arrangements."

I consider this a declaration of importance. He is not only presenting a proposal but developing an idea I consider very interesting. He added that in order for international finance institutions to enter this type of technical assistance, "it is necessary to preserve and strengthen their character as truly multilateral institutions. For the effectiveness of their participation will depend not only upon their technical skill, but, above all, upon the confidence of all the parties concerned that the action of these institutions will be independent, free from any external pressure and interference wherever they may originate."

I believe Mr. Ortiz Mena knows very well what he is talking about and the following sentence is a worthy proof: "It is therefore obvious that the capital-exporting countries, in pursuing their policies of channeling increasing amounts of financial resources through the multilateral system, should refrain from bringing in political considerations which sometimes accompany bilateral cooperation." In other words, he would like to see the multilateral character strengthened and freed from individual pressures in matters of paramount importance to developing countries.

In the same speech, Mr. Ortiz Mena spoke very frankly about the role of multinational corporations in the exploitation of natural resources in Latin America. He is in favor of the corporations but on a new basis. For instance, he advocates the participation of multinational companies in only part of the capital, together with a form of service contract to allow the developing countries to exercise greater control. He said that in many cases the multinational companies exploiting natural resources had used sizable financial resources provided by foreign sources other than their own. And that, according to the formula he is advocating, these other resources should be channeled to local entities in developing countries, in order for them to participate, with a majority interest, from the beginning of the joint venture. In order to underline the importance of this participation he goes so far as to recommend, for that purpose, the need for the international finance institutions to lend to governments.

As is well-known, the attitude of these institutions up to now has been to abstain from lending where private capital was available for the exploitation of natural resources. Mr. Ortiz Mena advocates a drastic change by which the international lending institutions would make capital available and thus pave the way for access from other sources, in order to strengthen the position of developing countries. He visualizes a combination of two factors: (1) technical assistance to help countries analyze proposals from the multinational companies, clarify the terms of their proposals so that they are correctly interpreted by the officials of developing countries, and (2) any kind of assistance, on the technical side or the economic and financial side, to establish a proper balance in the bargaining position of the developing countries.

As I mentioned before, the president of the IDB has not presented these points as proposals but as ideas that should be discussed properly. To a certain degree, this idea of Mr. Ortiz Mena corresponds to the explanations presented earlier by Lincoln Gordon, who maintains that the era of concessions in the exploitation of natural resources is over and that new forms of action should be found in order to deal properly with this problem. I am deeply impressed by the vigor and clarity of Mr Gordon's observations and concur with his conclusions.

Another aspect of a clear evolution in thinking pertains to the takeover of local enterprises by multinational companies. I have witnessed in Latin America, and in my own country in particular, the takeovers of local firms in which both technology of production and organizational know-how were well known. This resulted in a series of grave consequences. First, a takeover carries with it political implications, when there is ability in the country to manage the enterprises concerned and even to develop them further. Second, the impact of the takeover on the balance of payments is sometimes rather serious.

In some Latin American countries we have seen a curious way to create a favorable climate for foreign private capital, and in particular takeovers. I refer to a devaluation of local currency far beyond the needs imposed by internal inflation, and thus to cheapen for the foreign investor the value of the local assets, so as to facilitate the takeover. In this particular case, we should not put the blame solely on the multinational corporations but point to the lack of vision, the lack of understanding, or perhaps other shortcomings of Latin American governments.

I believe the idea that governments are entitled to define where they need foreign capital, or where they do not wish it, has been widely accepted; consequently, in case takeovers do happen, they are due to the wrong attitude of these governments rather than to the policy of the multinational corporations. If these corporations find the door wide open they will enter, and it is not their business to see what the advantages or disadvantages are for the developing countries.

Lincoln Gordon has rightly put emphasis on the role of foreign private capital and multinational corporations in export ventures. I fully concur with him, and would like to see, in this particular aspect, a form of association between foreign and local private capital. In actual cases local capital sometimes is in a minority position, but if the principle of partial fadeout is accepted, the situation could be corrected in the course of time. I for my part do not consider that total fading out is a good idea, especially in those cases (such as export activities) where developing countries need to continuously absorb new technologies, because the channel for the absorption of technology should not be risked. I am referring not only to the technology of production but also to the highly complex and delicate technology concerning the exploitation of foreign markets. This brings to my mind another related idea.

The technological as well as the financial inferiority of the local entrepreneurs compared to the foreigner is well known. If we leave

171

the local entrepreneur alone, with his limited resources, he will be in a most unfavorable bargaining position in relation to the other side of the joint venture. This is why we in Latin America have been stressing the need for an organization—a financial organization with a multilateral character—that would have both the authority and resources to take part of the equity and transfer it to nationals of the country in the course of time. In this way a joint venture may start, let us say, with only 10 percent of the capital in the hands of the local entrepreneur. However, a sizable part of the capital would be handled by this new institution until such time as the transfer of capital to the nationals of the host country can take place.

The IDB has elaborated on an idea concerning a subsidiary of its own for this purpose. The IDB is lending to local entrepreneurs, but it is not able to hold shares or part of the equities. The idea is to create a subsidiary, connected and financed by the IDB, in order to facilitate this operation. Unfortunately, this idea has not yet been duly considered. When searching for new forms of action on this matter, I attach considerable importance (as a complement to other ideas) to pushing this one, even though some of its aspects as elaborated to date may have to be altered.

Finally, I would like to say that for the past few years I have been attending conferences of this nature. The first ones were of a rather confrontation character, where developing countries presented all the shortcomings of the multinational companies—all the ills that we have seen in the past and that are always present in our minds— and developed countries mentioned all the extralimitations and arbitrary acts of the developing countries.

Perhaps this confrontation has been useful, since I now see with great satisfaction that in more and more meetings this type of confrontation has been losing strength. Indeed, at this particular conference it has somewhat disappeared. On the other hand, everybody is trying to see which are the real problems and how to solve them. This is why I consider this type of meeting, as well as others with the presence of businessmen in addition to intellectuals and public officials from both sides, to be extremely useful. In this sense, I share Ambassador Korry's optimism because I have seen great advances in this matter.

Let me mention a specific case. In 1955 I had to advise my government about economic policy and I recommended introducing service contracts in the exploitation of oil. However, no important company would even attempt to participate. In a relatively short span of time this has changed. If we look at the matter in a historical perspective, the mere fact that socialist economies are willing to enter into this new type of relationship is very meaningful. Perhaps this will take a little more time in Latin America, but I am hopeful that a proper revolution in this matter will be possible.

The possibility of having new forms of relationships independent of economic and social systems is very important because in Latin America we see a plurality of systems. I hope that any new foreign investment forms will be flexible enough to adapt to different economic and social systems.

16

SUMMARY OF
PANEL II
Samuel Stern

Panel II considered the problems of the less developed countries and concluded that their problems regarding foreign direct investment by multinational corporations are different in kind from those of developed countries for a variety of reasons: the recent colonial experience, the preceding history of exploitation, differences in cultural standards, burgeoning neocolonialism, discontinuity of governments, disparity in negotiation talents, lack of reciprocal inner penetration and investment, and the relative size of investments to the total economy.

The issues for most LDCs are fundamental questions of whether to permit the investment at all and, if so, what the percentage of foreign ownership ought to be. Also, whether to have a built-in disinvestment formula, how to prevent restraints on exports, how to control the supposed siphoning off through transfer payments, how to renegotiate existing arrangements that are felt to be no longer responsive to controlling circumstances, whether to expropriate an existing investment and, if so, with what compensation. And these are not the more subtle and sophisticated issues of how to deal with transnational restraints on competition, problems of dual taxing authorities, and overlapping regulatory jurisdictions. It was universally accepted that foreign investment is still vital to the process of development and structural transformation in the developing world in order to provide capital, particularly high-risk capital as in natural resource exploration, to provide technology, and to give access to and knowledge of international markets.

Foreign investment in the developing world is increasing, even though not at the same rate as in the developed countries. The available statistics are surprising, and encouraging. For example, measuring the decade from 1961 to 1971, in terms of U.S. direct investment in less developed areas, there was a 92 percent overall increase and an increase of 134 percent in the nonextractive areas.

The fundamental question in the panel discussion was: Can international controls, either in the form of a code creating enforceable rights and remedies or in the form of an international regulatory body, help the less developed countries? The universal response from the representatives of such countries was negative, for two principal reasons: (1) their experience has shown them that such international approaches are either ineffective or biased in favor of the developed world and (2) arrangements on the fundamental issues (which I have mentioned as of particular interest to them) must come from ad hoc or bilateral negotiations in which the developing countries participate directly. The bargaining power and negotiating technology of developing countries may be enhanced by providing a role for relatively small groupings of LDCs with shared interests on a regional basis, as in the Andean Code, or a product-oriented basis, as in the Organization of Petroleum Exporting Countries.

Nevertheless, it was felt that there are modest international steps to be taken to facilitate the process and advance the development of more generally accepted standards in this field. First, and without qualification, access to more information was widely regarded as vital. The establishment of an international clearinghouse for information was suggested. It should be easily accessible to host countries, companies, and interested third parties for supplying statistics on investment and for terms of particular arrangements, including the most important contracts with industry.

Second, and considered equally important, is the provision of technical assistance and training to less developed countries involved in negotiating with potential investors. Beyond this limit there was disagreement as to whether anything else could be done on an international organization basis. The suggestion that the World Bank act as a referee for proposed transactions was strongly resisted. The World Bank representative objected fundamentally because there are no generally accepted standards to apply. If there were, he thought the role of the World Bank might be expanded beyond its present role wherein the World Bank's participation in a particular transaction might imply basic approval of the transaction but not of its detailed terms. But he felt that to attempt to use a financial institution like the World Bank as a quasiregulatory body, where there is no consensus on standards, would undermine its basic role as a financial institution. The representatives of developing countries again objected on the basis that bias would tend to favor developed countries in any such examination.

There was a somewhat optimistic note that the problem might be beginning to improve and in the future may not be as serious as presently perceived, despite the continuing gulf in abstract principles. Many straws seem to be in the wind, including a socialist bloc interest in greater participation in world trade and in joint ventures, the decline in the previously unique position of the United States as a global power, the willingness of multinational corporations to come to terms as in Chile from 1969 through 1971, and the increased expertise of the LDCs. It was felt that these and other changes would ultimately minimize the need for any special international control of multinational corporations in their relations with the developing world. However, it must be emphasized that this kind of pragmatic approach is hammered out in the meeting place, rather than in an effort to formulate abstract principles.

INTRODUCTION
Seymour Rubin

There has been considerable discussion about the necessity or possibility of some kind of international organization, and considerable disagreement as to the need for such an organization and the direction it might take. From the point of view of one who has been dealing with problems of multinational enterprise, having in mind the complaints of the host countries, and with the possibility of setting up an organization (or a set of rules) to curb the power of the transnational enterprise, it has come as a surprise that the organizational proposals are regarded by some representatives of the developing world more as a threat than as a benefit.

This conference has very usefully elucidated this subject and brought it to the forefront for some of us in a new way. The consensus that seems to exist with respect to information-gathering and its importance and the establishment of some kind of mechanism for making this information more readily available to those who need it is, I think, a hopeful sign.

Perhaps the representatives of the international organizations here might emerge from this conference with some kind of encouragement to get together and perhaps establish a working party in order to see what information is at present being gathered—which I suspect is a great deal—and more important, how it is made available to those who can make best use of it.

However, there are clearly much more important, substantive problems; some of these have been alluded to, some have not. One is the feeling that renegotiation is in the wind, or that something should be done to encourage the concept of renegotiation, perhaps to channel concepts dealing with the idea of renegotiation.

Another thought that occurs to me is the possible relevance of what we are talking about in connection with multinational enterprise to the problems taken up by the Stockholm Conference on Ecology and the Environment sponsored by the United Nations. Perhaps there is something to be said in those directions as well.

In any case, various suggestions have been made: The suggestion of Ambassador Korry that market forces will eventually mitigate the problems we sometimes see in the headlines these days; the suggestions of others that some kind of organization might be put together to take care of some of the problems; the suggestion of Mr. Solomon that there might be some kind of organization to take a look at takeovers; or that of Mr. Prebisch that there might be some kind of organization to assist in the process of disinvestment. All of these are before us.

The immediate problem of today is the question of whether there should be some kind of new organizational structure and, if so, what kind of organization.

18

SUPRANATIONAL CONTROL OF
THE MULTINATIONAL ENTERPRISE

Jack N. Behrman

Various proposals for controlling the multinational enterprise have been put forward by those who oppose its existence, by those who consider it the most desirable mechanism for ordering the world economy, and by those who wish its rough edges to be smoothed by consideration for national interests.[1] None of these start from the assumption that the interests of the nation-state are paramount and that the multinational enterprise is but one stage in the development of industrial enterprise which is likely to be changed even before it reaches maturity. Each of them is based on assumptions about the shape of the international economic order that do not include the fact that three critical changes have occurred in the international economy during the past decade.

The first of these changes is that the power of the United States is no longer sufficient to force on the rest of the world the principle of multilateral, nondiscriminatory trade and payments. The second is that many nations are placing regional economic integration above international economic goals. The third is that a new nationalism has arisen because governments have assumed increasing responsibilities for economic and social welfare in their countries.

The decline of the relative economic significance of the United States means that mercantilist sentiments and approaches will come to the fore again, mitigated only partly by regional integration. Few countries outside the United States have been dedicated strongly to the principles underlying the postwar international economic institutions, and even the United States has violated them when it was to its advantage to do so.

Regional integration will both widen and restrict investment and trade opportunities. The rise of international production has shown governments that trade is increasingly the result of investment patterns and that the bases of comparative advantage can be altered through the movement of factors of production. Governments have discovered that it is possible to induce investment by the multinational enterprise, thereby altering significantly the patterns of trade and flow of international payments. Regional integration objectives can therefore be supported by policies directed at international investment.

Concern over the multinational enterprise (MNE) would not be so great if national governments had not been asked to assume expanding responsibilities for the welfare of national economies. From the classical responsibilities of national security, personal protection, judicial system education, and maintenance of competition, the responsibilities of governments have ballooned greatly and are continuing to expand. This new nationalism is not a return to simple mercantilism but an increasing imposition on governments of the responsibility for economic growth and social welfare of citizens. These new duties require the governments to increase their means of control, both extensively and intensively. The MNE, being outside the effective reach of any one government, poses a challenge to governments in meeting their old and new responsibilities.

CRITERIA FOR NEW CONTROLS

Given these responsibilities, governments must also be concerned over their participation in the benefits of world economic growth. So far, governments have not been willing to accept the distribution that would occur under laissez-faire or oligopolistic control by the MNE. The absence of laws of distribution similar in clarity and acceptability to the laws of production has plagued capitalist and socialist countries alike for nearly 200 years. Neither group has grasped the nettle firmly, but it is unlikely that we will be able to restructure the world economy appropriately wihtout attempting to meet this problem head on.

Neither free market, nor nationally oriented, nor MNE-oriented decision criteria will provide an acceptable approach for the distribution of benefits among nations or groups in the world economy. No one of these approaches adequately includes the noneconomic goals sought by peoples and nations. These other goals include an equitable distribution of benefits, effective participation in decisions affecting them and in the process of producing wealth, and a sufficient degree of autonomy to permit diversity in solving local social, political, and economic problems. Although the world is pulled toward unity for the sake of efficiency, they will accept unity (for example, at the supranational level) only if it is also guarantees the desired diversity (at the local or national level).

The quadruple criteria of efficiency, equity, participation, and autonomy are intertwined. Any attempt to place one above the other three and to establish a world economic order on it alone will be unacceptable. Even if the MNE or a free market economy could or would use the world's resources in the most efficient (or effective) way, it would not be acceptable unless the result also made all people better off than before. The recent break-up of the Central American Common Market results from an attempt to follow the prescriptions of integration theory, freeing trade and capital movements; the experiment proved to each of the three countries that they were no better off than before in absolute terms and were worse off in comparison to the other two. Welfare theory demonstrates only that all can be made better off, not how it is to be done.

Even if all were made better off by gifts from the richer to the poorer, the distribution would not be acceptable. International charity is not a sound basis for building an economic order. Sharing at the hands of the most efficient is demeaning. Equity must be achieved through participation by all concerned. This participation cannot be merely at the level of how to redistribute the larger pie; it must include active roles in the production of the larger pie. And these roles must be roles providing self-respect, creativity, and the opportunity for fulfillment. The opportunity for fulfillment and creativity imply that the local solutions to social, political, and economic problems may be quite different from place to place. To permit this, there must be a sufficient degree of autonomy—which implies that there is not only a key role for the nation-state but also for provincial, municipal, and community governments.

Presently, the world is pulled two ways along a continuum from local government to international government—or from particularism to internationalism and back again. In between, other forces pull toward nationalism and toward regionalism. No control system for the MNE can satisfy all these criteria at each market level: local, national, regional, international. But the MNE can be guided in such a way that it does little violence to these criteria at the local and national levels and contributes directly to their achievements at the regional and international levels. At least the tradeoff between benefits and costs will be seen as desirable.

Under this approach (developed further in the last section of these observations), the MNE would be seen not as the problem but as part of the solution—a means of achieving mutual goals at the regional and international levels. What is needed are not merely controls to curb the excesses of the MNE but means of directing it to the pressing problem of creating a new international economic order. Such an approach would be a step in the direction of creating the needed community of interest within which multinational enterprises can find a productive place.

Presently, the MNE is seen as merely an institution built on a legal fiction, having no legitimacy in and of itself and endowed only with the powers bestowed upon it by national laws. It can gain legitimacy only by acting in an acceptable manner—which means helping peoples and governments to reach the goals they seek. Within a nation, the corporation is legitimized by being approved under the laws and within a community of interest. Neither of these exists at the international level. Until they are created, the MNE will likely be factured or repelled. Any international agreement prior to steps toward a community of interest will likely constrain the MNE greatly, forcing substantial changes in its character and operations.

It should be noted that if an agreement were limited to countries within the Organization for Economic Cooperation and Development (OECD), which have or will soon have MNEs of their own, the possibilities are different. But one still needs prior agreement on the nature of the economic order envisaged. For example, are these countries willing to permit major decisions as to the location of industrial activity, research and development, prices, employment shifts, and so forth to be made by the MNEs? If so, agreement to facilitate their operations could be achieved. To the extent that they wish to constrain activities, to achieve greater governmental influence, the agreement would introduce provisions covering such items as movement of funds, intercompany pricing, location of research and development, right of entry, merger and acquisition, royalties and allocation of expenses. Any effort to discriminate against foreign-owned facilities would probably be prevented by the fact of mutual investment in each other's countries, although this possibility cannot be ruled out.

Whatever agreement might be reached within the OECD would still be reached more easily if regional or national industrial policies had been determined beforehand or if nations announced acceptance of the decisions of the MNE on location of industrial activity among the member countries. However, my observations here are addressed to supranational agreement including also the LDCs, and possibly the Eastern European countries, Russia, and China. To attempt an OECD agreement would signal an even greater cleavage between the rich and the poor—not only as to prospective wealth but also as to control by the rich over progress in the world economy, and at the hands of a private sector not fully accepted by the rest of the world.

CONSTRAINING CONTROLS

Without an international community of interest, national interests will predominate in applying the criteria against which the MNE is measured. An international agreement to protect national interests will be highly restrictive and probably push the MNE back toward the international holding company form of ownership and control.[2]

The agreement would probably start from the proposition that MNE affiliates are legitimized by local law but the control exercised by the parent company is not. A first principle, therefore, would be permission to discriminate against MNE affiliates based on the fact of foreign control. This discrimination would include restrictions on the right of establishment and, once in the country, would take the form of exclusion from bidding on governmental purchases, from industrial or research and development subsidies, from tax incentives, and from other preferences extended under national industrial policies.

A second provision would curtail acquisition of locally owned companies, takeovers through purchase of publicly held shares, mergers of foreign-owned affiliates with locally owned companies, and concentrations involving several locally owned companies and foreign-owned ones. Antitrust policies would be applied more harshly against foreign-owned affiliates, although the agreement might not provide for such treatment.

These two provisions would codify the removal of the principle of national treatment offered to foreign investors. This principle was acceptable to colonial countries only under duress and to independent countries only when the form of investment was either the classical type of raw material exploitation or the international holding company type, under which the affiliate was left largely independent of parental control.[3] The principle of national treatment has been violated under the OECD Code of Liberalization whenever it has been in the interest of a member to do so. Many sectors are reserved for investment by nationals, and current efforts in Europe to promote computer production have brought numerous discriminations.

An extension of the principle of discrimination would occur in provisions requiring national participation in ownership and management of foreign-owned affiliates, with different percentages applied to different industrial sectors. The most sensitive sectors among advanced countries at present appear to be electronics, chemicals, autos, food processing, aircraft, pharmaceuticals, and petroleum processing and distribution. To this list, the LDCs have added public utilities, mineral exploration and development, iron and steel, retailing, insurance, banking, and other services.

Further discrimination has arisen in the access of foreign-owned affiliates to local financial institutions; this differential treatment would likely be codified. To further prevent monopolization of a segment of an industry, LDCs are particularly concerned to limit the grant under a patent, and substantial disagreement remains among advanced countries as to the appropriate definition and duration of a patent. Codification would not be likely to result in acceptance of U.S. criteria.

To prevent the shifting of profits to reduce taxation among host countries, provisions would be introduced to control intercompany prices, allocation of expenses, returns under licenses, intercompany loans, changes in valuations of assets or inventories, movement of investment funds among affiliates, and so forth. Rather than the provisions settling on the least constraining laws among the signatory countries, compromise would bring more restrictive regulations than companies now face. And tax rates would likely be harmonized upward.

To prevent cartelization of markets at the hands of MNEs operating in oligopolistic conditions, licensing agreements would be brought under governmental surveillance as to the rights transferred, royalties, and limitations as to exporting, pricing, quality control, materials used or imported, and so forth. And use of such agreements to retain managerial control for the foreign licensor, despite a minority equity position, would be prevented.

Such an extensive agreement on how to handle the MNE would invite pressure from the international labor unions to include within the agreement provisions as to collective bargaining, codetermination, and international fair labor standards.[4] The international unions are now pressing for company-wide bargaining over the world; an international agreement would be a useful vehicle for requiring this mode of negotiation. At least it would be an opportunity to require disclosure of international operations as the basis for negotiation; to prohibit imports from one affiliate to break a strike or bargaining deadlock at another; to restrict plant closings, shifting of sourcing of components, and "runaway plants"; and to harmonize wages and working conditions on the principle of "equal pay for equal work." Related to the problem of runaway plants is the question of whether industry should be brought to labor or labor to industry; some agreement might be included as to the acceptable inducements member countries could use to alter investment location decisions.

Given the potential for increasing disagreement between MNEs and the international trade secretariats or local unions, negotiation of an international agreement would open discussion of arbitration or mediation facilities at an international level.

To achieve a greater participation in the development and innovation of scientific and technological discoveries, the signatory nations would undoubtedly want provisions to reduce the control by the parent company over research and development programs of affiliated companies in host countries. Not only would they want more local R&D activities, independent of the parent's efforts, but they would also want control over the use of those developments within the hands of nationals.

To reduce the threat of interference by the U. S. government (or other parent company government), the international agreement would undoubtedly seek to limit the extraterritorial reach of any one government through its laws on antitrust, export control, capital controls, or depollution.

A sure way of reducing the power of the parent company and of foreign governments is to force majority local ownership or to inject the government itself into ownership of the foreign-owned affiliate. Both are occurring over the world, with governments taking more and more active and direct participation in key sectors—petroleum, banking, mineral exploitation, basic industries, and transport services.

Codification of such constraints on the MNE would transform it into a different kind of business entity.[5] It would have neither the interest nor the capability of operating as it has over the past decade in trying to develop a worldwide production and marketing strategy.

GUIDING CONTROLS

If the MNE is not to be virtually destroyed, means must be found of guiding its activities so they are acceptable to host countries, in ways that permit their essential (and desirable) characteristics to be used effectively in pursuit of mutual goals.

The essence of the MNE is that it is a mechanism for integrating industrial activity across national boundaries, directed from the parent company. Therefore, the MNE is an entity readily adapted to the goals of regional or international industrial integration. It is not particularly adapted to national or local industrial development, at least not any more so than any other form of national or international business. A simple direct investment, licensing agreement, management contract, or locally controlled joint venture can be just as effective in meeting the goals of local market and national market development as an MNE.[6] Most MNEs do include within their total activities a number of straight licensing arrangements and simple direct investments, producing only for the local or national markets; these operations are separated from the integrated activities among the advanced countries of the world. Governmental control over these non-MNE types of activities can be appropriately left to local or national authorities, as has been the case in India, Brazil, Mexico, and Japan. It may be desirable to include them within the scope of an international agreement, but the purpose would be to facilitate exchanges sought by the host governments—not necessarily to pave the way for private business decisions divergent from local or national interests. But to use the MNE to achieve local or national objectives means subjecting the host country to a world market orientation, reflected in MNE management techniques, product lines, and decision criteria, which may be less appropriate than those found in smaller, more flexible companies.

Although MNEs can be helpful at the local or national levels in offering management and technical skills, their special capabilities and contributions lie in industrial integration across national boundaries. The objective of any supranational control system should be to use these special characteristics in pursuit of the declared goals of regional and international integration, keeping in mind the criteria spelled out above; by this process, the MNE would be legitimized.

The MNE can be used effectively in at least two major areas. One is in problems of industrial growth that cannot be solved at the national level and require cooperation at the regional or international level; the other is in a concerted effort to bring the developing countries into full participation in the process of industrial growth, in ways that minimize the costs of that growth. Both of these objectives will involve gestation of joint projects and the selection of industrial policies that will guide the international division of labor, will help to develop new activities in the LDCs, and will mitigate the impacts of this process on the advanced countries. A corollary problem in reaching both objectives relates to the impact on the environment, including the ecological, social, and political aspects. Both joint projects and new industrial policies can be pursued at the regional or international levels. One purpose of either approach would be to develop means of moving industrial activity to population centers among and within nations rather than the movement of people to where industry is located. We have now reached the stage where we find it unacceptable to let the decisions as to the use of human and natural resources be made in a "free market" or by business entities relying on "efficiency" criteria based on only a partial costing of the economic inputs and the social and environmental impacts.

Formation of an Organization of International Industrial Integration (OIII) is proposed to deal with the creation of joint projects and industrial policies. Given the variety of existing institutions that are concerned with one facet or another of these problems, the OIII would not have to assume full responsibility but would be a central coordinating body where rules could be formulated by members applicable to the various situations that would arise. It is within these objectives and under these rules that guidelines from the MNE would be developed. It makes little sense to propose controls over the MNE without some idea of what we want such an organization to do or the decision criteria we want it to use.

The OIII's first responsibility would be to collect and disseminate information on the activities of MNEs, the types of problems that require joint projects, and the means of including LDCs in the

process of international industrial integration. It should initially limit
its observations to key sectors and problem areas. It would be concerned with obtaining information on market divisions, shifts in technology (both in location and in sophistication), governmental or corporate interest in joint projects, and problems arising in the internationally mobile industries—that is, those with a tendency to shift
location over the world, which must be done if the LDCs are to participate equitably in industrial progress.

These shifts are even more critical if there is, in fact, any
necessity to slow down the rate of world industrial growth. The slow
down must, of course, come in the advanced countries rather than
among the LDCs; extensive adjustments would therefore be required
in the former, and much cooperative action would be required to make
the adjustments acceptable. Even if there is no necessity to slow the
rate of growth, many of the problems that will be piling up can be met
only with concerted action; the LDCs will be bypassed unless they are
brought consciously into industrial sectors that utilize the more advanced technologies, helping them to build a base for their own technology.

The data gathered would be employed to help meet the two basic
objectives above: (1) joint projects and (2) the international division
of labor. No adequate guidelines exist for either today. The OIII
would seek to establish such guidelines, evolving new forms of industrial cooperation for the new international economic order, based
on the four criteria detailed above.

Specifically, among the joint or "integration" projects are those
related to depollution of land, air, and water; resource development;
regional development; aerospace exploration; defense industries;
industrial infrastructure; and coproduction projects between the East
and West. Depollution relates to the removal of existing pollutants
rather than merely prevention of more pollution; prevention can be
handled by national and international agreements concerning effluents,
product use, and control devices. But removal of existing pollutants
will require extensive new industrial activities across or along national boundaries. For example, depollution of the Rhine will require
cooperation among several European countries and efforts by different
types of companies in each. Reduction of administrative problems
can be achieved by use of multinational enterprises with affiliates
in several of the cooperating countries. Similarly, depollution of
the oceans and the air over Scandinavia, which carries acid rain and
black snow, will require extensive detection schemes merely to trace
the causes.

Location of resources, about which we still know very little,
and their development can be more effectively accomplished cooperatively, under the direction of large international companies. Similarly,

development of the seabed will require intergovernmental cooperation and can effectively use the capabilities of the MNE. International production consortiums have been used in both defense-related and commercial fields, in infrastructure, sophisticated products, and services: transport, electrification, missiles, aircraft, and satellite communications.[7]

Development of large geographic regions, encompassing two or more nations, will be more effective if use is made of the MNE; examples include the Choco Valley in South America, the Andean ranges, the Amazon Valley, the Mekong Delta in Indochina, the Sahara, and the Nile Valley. Aerospace exploration will require such large inputs of money, men, and materials that cooperative efforts will be found desirable; again, the MNEs' technical and managerial capabilities will be found useful.

Development of national security industries serving several countries within a regional association will be most efficiently carried out cooperatively, as will the erection of adequate infrastructure of communications, electrification, and transport across national boundaries. In addition, MNE capabilities can be used effectively in the systems analysis required to examine the costs of industrialization in a given locale or region, assessing the transport, housing, education, health, social, and other support services needed in the urban-industrial process. Forewarned with such information, policy-makers will err less often than in the past, and the MNE will be seen as a major contributor to finding the best use of resources.

Finally, the massive inputs required in the industrialization of Eastern European, Russia, and China, which seek coproduction arrangements with outlets into Western markets, can be effectively generated by the MNEs.

In each of these examples, the fact that the MNE operates in several countries, among which would be those involved in a joint projects, opens the possibility for sharing of production, control, and decisions as to technologies used and trade patterns to be developed among the members of the project. This ready capacity to share out the participation among the member countries makes the MNE an effective mechanism in achieving managerial efficiency and producing equity in benefits. Since it can be guided to produce efficiently, with equity and with participation in policy decisions by all countries involved, the MNE is a potentially useful mechanism at the regional and international levels. No other existing institution is currently able to meet so many criteria simultaneously.

However, it will not do so on its own; it must be guided by governments to perform in this manner. Governments will not only be the clients but also the rule-settlers and overseers. Guided in this manner, the MNE will respond quite effectively. Any alternative effort to generate the same joint projects will require ad hoc creation of administrative groups, which is costly not only in time but in scarce managerial manpower. Some of these projects will require governmental participation in managerial decisions, or at least a management style governmental team collaborating with the industry team. These experiences should develop a sounder appreciation on the part of the MNE and governments of the capabilities, interests, motives, and needs of the other, building a stronger base for international industrial cooperation.

The second area of international (or regional) industrial integration is that of selecting the industries to be developed under new criteria of the international division of labor. The problems of location of industrial activity plague not only regional associations such as the Andean Group and the European Economic Community but also those concerned with developing key industries (high technology or mass consumption and those concerned to see that that LDCs are permitted to share in the process of industrial growth. Given that decisions stemming from these concerns will require adjustments among advanced countries and between them and the LDCs, a major responsibility of the OIII would be to ease the shifts—minimizing the costs in both the advanced and less developed countries of the shift in activity on the primary industry, on secondary and tertiary activities, and on communities affected. There is currently under study a proposal for creation of an International Industrialization Institute that would have responsibility for research on a new pattern of international division of labor and the impact of industrialization on developing countries. It would not, however, be a policy-making body; while it might make some recommendations, it would not be in any position to translate them into national or international policies for it would be composed of professional researchers. If such an organization were established, it would directly complement the terms of reference of the OIII, which would be a policy-oriented body composed of government officials seeking to determine the bases for the international division of labor, to increase the participation of the LDCs in the process of industrialization, and to ease the problems of transition in the advanced countries. To facilitate its discussions as to the role of the MNE in this process, the OIII should have information on tax policies affecting the MNEs, the types of technology employed, the existing and projected location of different types of activities, emerging markets, cost differentials, and projected patterns of trade in materials, components, and final products in the key sectors selected for examination.

The initial focus of the OIII should be on the development of industrial facilities that support a greater role for the LDCs in regional and international markets. (There are ample resources for

191

assistance to LDCs in the development of industries oriented to local-
or national-markets, and these do not involve significant use of MNE
capabilities.) Industries that are mobile internationally and are oriented to the international market are by and large the same ones in
which the MNEs are most active: chemicals, autos, textiles, food
processing, electronics, rubber products, heavy machinery, pharmaceuticals. (Shoes, iron and steel, and metalworking are exceptions.)
The problem of how to deal with shifts in the international location
of industrial activity cannot be readily resolved without taking the
MNEs into account. Fortunately, their existence facilitates a solution,
for the fact that they operate in several countries simultaneously
permits ready tradeoff of activities in one country with another, facilitating an equitable sharing of benefits and spreading the participation
of countries in the industry.

At present, the national reaction to pressures arising from the
shifts of industrial activities—both among the advanced countries and
between them and the LDCs—is a protectionist one in the form of
"voluntary, orderly marketing arrangements." Rather than the international textile agreement being an exception, as it was touted initially, it embodied a principle recently applied to iron and steel, shoes,
mushrooms, electronics, chemicals, and other items—not just by the
United States but also by Europe against Japan and several LDCs.
What is needed instead is an orderly process of relocating industrial
activity, as Japan is itself beginning to realize with reference to its
relations with Southeast Asia. This approach would include a concern for where polluting industries should be located within a region,
if at all.

At present, the European countries are concerned over the
future development of several key industries (such as computers)
and the role played within them by the multinational enterprises. The
LDCs are trying to decide which industries to develop and how to
divide their efforts between the national, regional, and international
markets. Offers by some of the multinational enterprises, such as
Ford and General Motors, to allocate production among several
countries in Southeast Asia and in Latin America so as to produce
an Asian and a Latin American car have not been readily received
by the governments of the countries involved. The major reason is
that the governments do not feel they would be able to control the
activities of the single giant international company that would be in
charge.

If there were an OIII that could counsel the governments on ways
of guiding such an effort, the MNE could be more readily relied upon
to meet specific product needs in a region, using regional resources
and capabilities. It would be able to show the precise tradeoffs between greater efficiency and equitable sharing of benefits, if such a

tradeoff were necessary. It will be found that sharing of production will not always produce inefficiencies and that greater participation will generate greater markets and higher productivity.

With such regional repartition of an industry, it would be conceivable to integrate parts of it with worldwide production and sourcing, after the companies involved were able to show the government concerned precisely what the tradeoffs would be. To achieve such an understanding by governments, it is likely that governments will want to participate in boards of directors or managerial deliberations so as to keep themselves fully informed of costs and benefits.

Once it is determined among a group of countries (regionally or internationally) that a particular industry requires rationalization among them, the MNE can be used quite effectively to carry out the program. For example, in the Latin American area, the Andean countries have determined that some 20 industries must be placed under specific programs to assure their development within the region under criteria of efficiency, equity, participation, and autonomy. Each industry is to be divided by sector among the five participating countries, each country receiving the right to establish production of specific components or subassemblies or product lines. All five agree as to the acceptability of that division of labor among themselves, and each is given a headstart on the others in its allocated sector. Since one objective is to export final products outside the region at competitive costs, all countries are permitted to enter any sector after a period of seven to ten years. Unless a country has met competitive levels of efficiency in its allocated segment of the industry, it is likely to lose its position.

The MNE is readily adapted to such schemes as these, for it can allocate production facilities among several countries and also open marketing outlets both within the region and outside. Having facilities in several countries, it can make certain that costs remain competitive among them and that none is squeezed out by fortuitous events. The Andean countries are investigating the desirability of forming regional MNEs of their own, but they will lose the advantages of ready access to international markets in some sectors (such as autos) if they do not tie into the present MNEs, which can be done either through regional regulations or by international agreements.

If the MNE is used in these ways, a high degree of specialization occurs—not along lines of comparative advantage in the classical sense but under criteria that are both economic and noneconomic. This specialization is not without danger to the MNE's total operation, for any interference by one government or a local labor union can disrupt the entire worldwide operation of the firm. Therefore, some protection against such disruption must be built into the agreements.

It will be argued that specialization among sectors of a given industry is not the most efficient way of organizing industry among countries and that some specialization should be based on locating an entire industry in one country and another sector in another country. While this is certainly correct in theory and might be practicable in some industries, governments will insist on participation in each of the key industries on which industrial development is based. The failure of the Central American Common Market is critically tied to the attempt to select "integration industries" that would be allocated one to a country; it became impossible to find suitable industries that each would accept as its fair share of industrial development in the region. It is much easier to repartition sectors of an industry than an entire industry—easier not only politically but also from the standpoints of equity and efficiency. In addition, this approach demonstrates and perpetuates the type of interdependence that should characterize regional integration—just like the situation within the common market of the United States, where segments of almost all industries are spread throughout the country.

Although the OIII would not itself make decisions for the MNEs involved, it would be the intergovernmental arm for setting the guidelines and incentives necessary to induce appropriate action by the MNEs. Later, it might become a type of international arbiter between the international trade secretariats and the MNEs over comparative wages and working conditions over the world; it might also be a forum for discussion of the extent to which codetermination would be desirable in given industrial sectors.

To some extent, the success of the OIII would be measured by the relaxation of pressures on the MNE from special interest groups that previously felt themselves harmed or challenged by MNE operations. In these key industries, it may well be that the most successful way of removing the tensions surrounding MNE operations will be to place governmental representatives in management of local affiliates so that adequate information as to the participation of the company is funneled back to the government. Such a move should halt the efforts to break up the MNE or to separate its contributions into portfolio capital, licensing agreements, and management contracts—either of which would be counterproductive and lose the essential capabilities of the MNE in achieving integration.

Set within such a control system, and guided to a resolution of these major problems, the MNE would be seen as an entity that does not create tensions but relieves them. The initiative to achieve this result, however, is with governments through regional and international agreements.

NOTES

1. Stephen H. Hymer and Robert R. Rowthorn oppose this in "Multinational Corporations and International Oligopoly," in Charles Kindleberger, ed., The International Corporation (Boston: MIT Press, 1970), pp. 84ff. George Ball praises it in "Cosmocorp: The Importance of Being Stateless," Columbia Journal of World Business, November-December 1967, pp. 25-30. Paul M. Goldberg and Charles Kindleberger would smooth it; see "Toward a GATT for Investment," Law & Policy in International Business, Summer 1970, pp. 323ff. And Seymour Rubin doubts the need for any new controls; see "Multinational Enterprise and National Sovereignty," Law & Policy in International Business 3, no. 1 (1971), pp. 1-41.

2. I have examined in more detail "Alternative Approaches to Controlling the MNE" in a forthcoming paper presented to a seminar at the Wharton School, University of Pennsylvania, December 1972.

3. The distinctions between these different types of investment and the MNE are detailed in my article on "The Multinational Enterprises: Its Initiatives and Governmental Reactions," Journal of International Law and Economics, January 1972, pp. 215-33.

4. David H. Blake has presented the unions' views in "Trade Unions and the Challenge of the Multinational Corporation," The ANNALS of the American Academy of Political Sciences, September 1972, pp. 34-45.

5. Several views of the pressures that will likely transform the MNE are analyzed in The Annals, September 1972, pp. 93-138, by Lawrence Krause, Chadwick Alger, Joe Nye, and Robert Walters. Howard Perlmutter projects a transmutation into "global industrial systems constellations" (pp. 138-52).

6. Richard Robinson makes a similar argument supporting the "fade-out" approach (The ANNALS, September 1972, pp. 67-79) and argues that the LDCs should see separate contracts for capital, know-how, and management.

7. A study for the U.S. Department of State on "Multinational Production Consortia" summarizes the lessons of NATO experience in coproduction. (Bureau of Intelligence and Research, Office of External Research, November 1971.)

* * * * *

COMMENT

Jerome Levinson

What is most striking to me is the extent to which there seems to be a consensus developing that is quite different from the premise upon which this conference started. The premise was that controls are desirable, and that they should be formulated on a universalistic basis. The issue seemed to be what kind of controls, what kind of entity.

To the surprise of some people, particularly those dealing with developing countries, it turned out that there was great skepticism about the desirability of a universalistic approach to controls. What seems to come out very strongly is that we are fed up with organizations. The organizations exist, consultations exist; the question really is whether any of these can be made to work. It seems to me that the problem must be broken down into a number of elements. It is a question of bargaining power, of the capacities of different countries and groups of countries for bargaining with respect to the multinational corporations.

In the Latin American region, for instance, one element of skepticism rises from the fact that after the last two decades there is not really a regional approach. How do you define national interests when countries have such diverse development strategies as do Brazil, Mexico, and the Andean Group? I think it would be virtually impossible to get a consensus even within the region on an approach toward the multinational corporations (MNCs). Brazil certainly would not agree with the Andean approach, or even with the developing Mexican approach.

The same thing happened in the European discussion. If in the two most developed regional approaches, the EEC and the OECD (where the countries have been struggling to evolve regional approaches and where institutionalization is generally considered most advanced) —if in these regions one cannot even approach a regional attitude and policy toward multinational corporations, how then can we talk about a universalistic approach and new organizations?

It seems to me that this is really the most striking consensus that has been reached. And it therefore gets down to a question of where the bargaining disparities lie. I do not think that Brazil, for example, feels any weakness in negotiating with the MNCs; it feels perfectly competent to negotiate with the MNCs to set the policies. It does not feel threatened. We see Mexico moving increasingly toward defining a position. We find that the MNCs are perfectly adaptable to these national development strategies. Mexico and Brazil offer them sufficient advantages, therefore it is in their interest to make the adaptations.

The real problem comes with countries that do not have that individual bargaining capacity: countries like Peru, Bolivia, Colombia, and Chile. And so they have combined their forces in Latin America in a regional approach. I think what we see in the Andean Group is really the initiation of that kind of bargaining by a group of countries that previously was pretty open to foreign investment.

One of the most striking things, I think, is the question of defining the rules of the game. It is not whether any individual rule is desirable or not desirable, but whether we can establish some stability so the rules will be the same ten years from now. I think this explains the paradox that the MNCs find it easier to negotiate with the socialist countries than with the Latin American countries. The socialist countries have achieved a degree of stability, although ideologically one might find it curious that there can be a basis of accommodation between the two systems, in terms of the expectation of stability. The MNCs know what they can expect here ten years from now. In a context like Latin America, with startling internal changes in which there are sudden shifts in the distribution of internal power, external entities like the MNCs are associated with one group and do not know what might happen. The power position within society might soon be reversed, and the MNCs associated with a group that is displaced find themselves displaced in terms of the internal power relationship. There is a great deal of uncertainty, and this is much more difficult to deal with, in terms of policy and psychology, than is the relative stability of an ideologically antithetical group of countries like the socialist countries.

The discussion has really focused around the policies of the recipient countries. When we talk about MNCs, in the back of our minds we think of the American-based, American owned, American-managed MNCs. And the question has been: How does the environment react to them—what controls, what restrictions, what inhibitions are put up?

What I see developing convergently at the other end is the question of how a parent country reacts in terms of a rethinking of the extent to which it wants to promote investment. I think this is not confined solely to the United States. I suppose Sweden has gone further than any other country, saying that a group that wants a government guarantee for its investment must meet certain conditions in the foreign country that are similar to those in Sweden, in terms of such matters as labor conditions. Neither the United States nor any of the other industrialized countries have gone that far.

But one is beginning to see a more discriminating approach. The Overseas Private Investment Corporation (OPIC) has different rules concerning the basis on which it will extend guarantees for investments in what it considers highly sensitive areas, such as the extractive industries. And OPIC is beginning to build in divestiture conditions, through those investments.

I think we are seeing a series of ad hoc accommodations, to the points at which the countries feel the crises arrive. And instead of reacting only after the crisis, there is now the beginning of an attempt to anticipate and work out rules to avoid crises.

That leads to what seems to me to be the conclusion of this conference: We are in an intermediate stage in which universalistic rules are really utopian. A consensus will not be reached between developing and developed countries, or among the developing countries, or even within regions of developing countries. National interests, national strategy, and national conditions are too diverse. What we are going to see over the next decade is an attempt to work out ad hoc arrangements to deal with immediate crises. Perhaps a decade from now there might be a series of agreed principles, particularly resulting through the communications revolution, and it will be possible to disseminate the experience of each country. For example, the Canadian dialogue about the virtues and nonvirtues of foreign investment parallels the dialogue within Latin America in the previous decade. And in a sense Australia is just catching up in terms of beginning that debate.

Ten years from now this conference may be more timely. I think that in terms of timing, and in terms of regional and individual variations, we may be ten years ahead of ourselves. That seems to me to be the dominant impression of this conference.

*   *   *   *   *

COMMENT
Seymour Rubin

I trust that ten years from now someone will say we were ten years ahead of ourselves. This is a rather unusual conclusion for a conference; mostly they are about ten years too late. I should say, partially in defense of the organizers of the conference and in response to Jerome Levinson's remarks, that such a conclusion was not outside the ideas of the organizers of the conference.

I think Don Wallace, Jr., and those who collaborated with him in putting the conference together did not expect that there would necessarily emerge the conclusion that there should be an international agreement, a new international organization, or any other form of international collaboration or lack of collaboration other than that which exists at the present time. The idea was to explore the situation to see whether some new forum, some new set rules should be suggested and, if so, what shape that organization or those rules should take.

I do think that Mr. Levinson made a very interesting point that I find strangely analogous to that made by Ambassador Korry. His point was that market forces were likely to bring a convergence of views between the host countries and the transnational enterprises— they would find their views coming closer into harmony. I take it, at

least in part, that Mr. Levinson is saying that the reexamination in
the home base country—in the United States, Great Britain, or Sweden—
of the role of its own private foreign investment is tending to arrive
at some conclusions strangely similar to those reached in what we
might call the recipient countries.

Clearly, I think the view expressed by the authors of the Burke-
Hartke legislation proposed in the United States, and some of the views
expressed in the Andean private investment code, bear a certain similarity although from opposite viewpoints.

* * * * *

COMMENT
Peter Ady

The discussions at this conference seem to me—although they
have a great deal of due praise recognizing the merits of private investment, the dynamism of private initiatives, and so on—to reveal
certain hesitations about the operation of the system as it is developing. I think we are really concerned with the flexibility of private
investment, which is developing along new, multinational lines as an
adjustment to the quite evident desire of governments to moderate,
channel, and alter the forces of private enterprise.

One way of adjusting to the pressures of individual governments
is to become transnational; another way is to diversify into a number
of different industries. The private concern is then an animal that
is very difficult to identify. These changes make it very difficult to
know who you are dealing with in any legal situation; for example,
the different associated or component companies in the multinational
enterprise are subject to different national laws.

Another difficulty is how to allocate costs, for example, over-
head costs between enterprises that are operating in several different
countries and perhaps are also highly diversified by product. Such
considerations are very relevant in the context of the developing
countries, which find it difficult to deal with these giants anyway. It
is particularly from their point of view that I speak. This leads me
to support the points made by Lincoln Gordon, who stressed the need
for more information, better evaluation, and generally more publicity
about the activities of multinational enterprises. One form this special
information should take and is taking is the development of international
accounting.

We have had national accounting developed to a very high degree.
Most countries now produce accounts on a standardized framework
for the United Nations. Even the less developed countries are producing better and better national accounts. The stage is being reached

199

where the integration of these national accounts is becoming possible. Work on this is being done in the International Association for Research in Income and Wealth. It is also being done at the OECD Development Centre, for example, and at the United Nations.

In due course this is going to enable us to answer some of the questions that have been raised and to settle some of the disputes, some of the discrepancies. The secretary for the Andean Group, Constantino Vaitsos, said that whereas the proclaimed profit on private capital in Latin America was 7 percent, his calculations brought profits out at an average of 40 percent. This is the kind of discrepancy that we can really sort out only by going and looking at the figures. Clearly there are some differences in definition or some flows that are being missed. Further, the correct percentage depends on whether you are using net worth as the measure of capital for the denominator, or whether you are using inflow of actual cash and so forth. This is not the place to go further with the technicalities. But earlier attempts at doing these accounts have led to surprising discrepancies. For example, at OECD Angus Madison's efforts to arrive at the balance of payments for the developing countries as a group came up with an errors and omissions figure in 1962 that is something like to 3 to 4 thousand million as against an export trade total of 25 to 30 thousand (Banca Nazionale del Lavoro, 1966). This is a very large unaccounted discrepancy and one on which more work must be done.

Another point I think really should be stressed is the fact that even regional groupings of developing countries may not be strong enough or large enough to deal with the multinationals. While the Andean group and OPEC have been notably successful, other countries might benefit from developing joint enterprises. This is not popular with firms on the ground that governments are too large to make comfortable partners. Yet the opposite is the case in the developing world: For a developing country the presence of a multinational in its midst is like having a Gulliver in Lilliput.

* * * * *

COMMENT
R. Krishnamurti

It is very important to draw a distinction between private foreign investment and multinational corporations. The two are not synonymous or coextensive. From whatever little data we have on the operations of private enterprises in the various developing countries of the world, a very large number, probably 30 or 40 or 50 percent of the enterprises, are not affiliates or subsidiaries of the so-called multinational enterprises, according to Jack Behrman's definition.

I think this point was also made by Fernand Braun, the representative of the European Economic Community, who said that private
enterprises, small and medium-sized firms, are functioning and
making a contribution to production, to trade, to transfer of technology, in various developing countries including Africa and Asia.

As far as the operations of the multinational corporations are
concerned, it is necessary to draw a distinction between the problems
faced by the developing countries and those faced by the developed
countries. Any arrangements that might be worked out among the
developed or industrialized countries themselves, whether at the
level of private enterprise or within the broad policy accepted by
the industrialized countries, do not quite meet the needs of the developing countries. The policies adopted by the multinational enterprises with regard to investment, the location of plants, the use of
patents and trademarks, market delegation, and transfer of technology are bound to have very serious impact on the development interests of the developing countries. It is therefore not possible to deal
with these problems as if they were not totally distinct. Any arrangements that might be worked out on a mutually acceptable basis among
the firms, affecting only the developed countries, may not fully take
into account the interests of the developing countries.

It seems to me that the discussions at this conference have
tended to be dominated by Latin American interests and preoccupa-
tions, and I cannot help feeling that sufficient attention has not been
given to other continents.

* * * * *

COMMENT
J. Ade Oyelabi

I want to correct an impression that apparently was given in
my previous observations. That relates to the desirability or non-
desirability of an international effort. I have heard people say that
the representatives of the less developed countries at this conference
appear not to support an international effort for controlling the multinational corporations.

I want to stress my view that there is a clear need for some
form of international effort. That does not imply that there must be
an international organization or institution; all I am saying is that
there is a need for supplementing national and regional efforts. My
suggestion does not rule out the efforts of nation-states or regional
organizations.

I think that the capability of the larger Latin American countries to bargain with the multinational corporations has tended to lead some observers to the conclusion that most developing countries have the ability to bargain. I want to emphasize the importance of information to the developing countries. Most of them are small, most just do not have the ability to negotiate, to bargain with the multinational corporations. This is why I suggested a kind of documentation or information center. I do not care who supplies the information, a regional group or an international organization. An individual under-developed country, particularly in Africa and Asia, cannot have access to this kind of information unless it is supplied by an international organization.

I have also commented that the relationship between multinational corporations and LDCs is one of inherent conflict. I believe there are disputes, no matter what kind of arrangement is made. Therefore, the problem is: What kind of mechanism should be provided for settling these disputes? I think for most of these countries, national laws will be supreme and the final arbiter. Having said that, I must also say that in practice, African countries particularly are very pragmatic. In contracts they usually provide that in case of disputes, a third party will be appointed, acceptable to both the host country and the foreign investor.

I agree that multinational corporations like stability—they want to be sure of the environment in which they operate for ten or fifteen years. I also agree that it is better to have renegotiation provisions included in the original contract, but I would like to point out that in many existing contracts such provisions do not exist. If they do not exist, and a host country decides that renegotiation is necessary, what do you do? Here I would plead with the multinational corporations to be a lot more understanding and not bluntly refuse to negotiate.

*   *   *   *   *

COMMENT
Willis Armstrong

Every day in Washington we have problems in connection with, say, Peru or Panama regarding investment and its treatment. One of my functions is to serve as chairman of the committee on expropriation, which is an interdepartmental committee in the U.S. government.

I do think it very important that conferences of this kind try to avoid if possible, the folklore approach to these questions, the cliché approach, the advertising man's emphasis on the virtues of "private enterprise" or the evils of "multinational corporations" or whatever. Everybody starts with his own prejudices, and ordinarily a discussion of this question is susceptible to a ventilation of prejudices rather than a discussion of the issues.

I think it will be very helpful over time if everybody concerned can be as dispassionate as possible in looking at the facts of a given situation. We cannot resolve all problems on purely economic grounds, and Jack Behrman has given good evidence of the importance of the other values in which everybody really is interested, and must be interested, if we are to have a workable world society.

But I do think it is highly important for governments and academic and business people to keep talking and communicating, and to keep moving toward an understanding of how to reach equitable and practical solutions to practical problems, which ultimately will probably defy and definition as to whether they correspond to any particular set of principles.

Therefore I agree that the conference may be much too stimulating for that reason. And it may be helpful in guiding future discussions.

I think one element that must be mentioned is the great change that is occurring and will be occurring in the field of energy. In the past, capital formation arising out of energy exploitation occurred largely in the developed countries; in the near future capital formation will be occurring largely in the countries of the Middle East. And what will happen to that particular capital formation and its international implications are very interesting.

Of course we in the United States hope that we can develop atomic energy over time sufficiently so that we will not need to import any oil at all. That unfortunately is too far away. So we must try to resolve energy problems on a cooperative basis.

19

**MULTINATIONAL CORPORATIONS IN
DEVELOPING COUNTRIES:
AN INTERNATIONAL APPROACH**
Edwin Martin

I have been asked to present suggestions for international arrangements to deal with the new problems raised for the world community by the growth of multinational corporations in power and scope. I undertake this task under two substantial handicaps:

First, I am partial to the view that the nature of institutions, at least new ones, should reflect to a considerable extent the nature of the work they are expected to do, in this case the nature of the multinational corporation problems they are expected to work on. But this conference has not yet determined those problems.

Second, my experience with multinational corporations is almost entirely limited to their activities in developing countries. While investments there may not equal in volume those in developed countries, I believe that the issues their presence has raised, while similar in some respects to those in developed countries, have many unique features that generally make them even more complex. Therefore, I think it will be worthwhile to discuss only the developing country situation, leaving others to judge how useful my conclusions may be to the problems arising in developed countries.

I start with my assumptions as to the principal sources of conflict between multinational corporations and the countries in which they wish to or do operate. I think we may usefully treat separately the problems arising at each of three stages of the overseas investment process, although of course there are overlaps. They are entry, operation, and in relatively few but well-publicized cases, eviction.

Entry. Entry negotiations create several issues:

1. Is the investment desirable in terms of a country's development objectives? There seems to be general agreement that to require this is an unchallengeable sovereign right of each developing country. One hopes, however, that governments have a sensible set of priorities and a bureaucracy that can and will apply these priorities fairly in each case.

2. What specific points should the entry agreement cover? Investors may request financial inducements to invest, such as help with land and utilities, tax holidays, tariff waivers for imported capital equipment, tariff or other protection against imports of competing products, protection against future investors in the production of competing products, permission to control exports.

Host governments may wish to incorporate requirements for training, employment and promotion of indigenous personnel, requirements for or limitations on import of materials and components and on export of output, controls over repatriation of dividends and capital, various special financial measures in the case of subsoil resources, and local equity participation arrangements, applicable now or in the future, to list a few key points. All of these provisions require complex, technical, and potentially controversial negotiations.

3. How long does it take to reach an entry agreement, time often being crucial to an investor?

4. What assurances can be secured for the permanent validity of what is agreed?

5. What are provisions for settling disputes?

Operations. With respect to operations, it hardly seems possible to identify more than a few main issues. These may concern one or more of such subjects as import licenses for materials and spare parts, prices of inputs and outputs, availability of local credit, permits for additional investment, labor standards, and employee relations. The essential problem is that in most developing countries governments play a very large role in the economy. Businesses of all sorts must get new pieces of government paper at every turn. Usually foreign firms have even more requirements to meet as the result of their entry agreement. The problems are sometimes stimulated by local competitors, suppliers, or consumers, but basically they involve bat - tles to get the needed paper, and in time, from the bureaucracy. The issues seldom come within the jurisdiction of judicial structures, administrative or other. Often legal codes and the court system, even when possibly applicable, are not well adapted to prompt decision on the types of issue raised by the operations of a modern business enterprise.

Eviction. Eviction, which must of course have a compulsory element, may be achieved in several ways:

1. Making operation unprofitable or otherwise creating unacceptable operating conditions so that sale of operation is chosen by the foreign investor as best solution, often referred to as creeping expropriation. Not so creeping, but often with similar results, is intervention to assume full management control without change in legal ownership.

2. Nationalization at host initiative without prior harassment and after agreed arrangements for payment by public or private purchaser have been reached.

3. Nationalization with compensation to be worked out later, often called expropriation.

In all of these cases, apart from regret at being evicted, the central issue for the multinational corporation is the size and nature of the compensation to be received. By definition this is not an issue when a nationalization of type 2 takes place, but although sometimes there can be a fair bargain struck, in most cases the multinational corporation finds itself at a disadvantage in negotiating on the value of its property, especially as regards future earnings foregone.

For the host country, the principal issue is weighing the pros and cons of the takeover for the future development of the country, economic and political. These should include not only the immediate direct costs but the effect on future foreign investment and the future profitability of the property under national management, cut off from the overseas connections it previously had.

What are the principal causes of the conflicts that so often seem to arise between multinational corporations and their host governments at all three of these stages? From the standpoint of the positions taken by the foreign investor, they include:

1. Natural desire to make profits out of the fact and risks of being a multinational corporation by making major decisions about technology, products, new investments, production volumes, marketing programs, research, and so forth at central headquarters in the way it is believed will maximize profits for the corporation as a whole, without any special weight for the effects of such decisions on any one of the countries in which operations take place, including not uncommonly the home country.

2. Desire to make as large profits on investment as possible and to be free to repatriate them at discretion. This normal corporate objective is often reinforced in the case of investments in developing countries by the desire to reduce as quickly as possible the amount of capital exposed to the unknowns of operation in a foreign country and especially the dangers feared from changes in governments or in governmental policies that are not well understood, may not be too stable, and on which the company usually feels it has few means of exercising effective influence.

3. Desire to operate as much as possible as the company would at home, both to reduce the risks of the unfamiliar and because it makes for a more comfortable life for the responsible expatriate executives and their home base backstoppers.

Developing country positions often reflect, among other things:

1. Fear that as corporate giants the truly multinational corporations are so big, economically powerful, well staffed with brilliant

engineers, economists, lawyers, and so forth that negotiation with them at no point can be in fact on an equal basis. This inferiority complex is often justified by actual serious deficiencies in negotiating skills, with the result that agreed arrangements too often do not do justice to legitimate developing country interests, causing resentment when this is later realized.

2. Apart from lacking the professional skills of experts, in many developing countries ruling elites, including politicians and bureaucrats, have had no training or experience of modern business, have no close friends or relatives with such experience. The "best" people have strong prejudices against "business" as a way of making a living, and hence frequently take positions at all three stages seriously damaging to the legitimate interests of foreign investors without any real comprehension of these interests or their significance. Often there is also no locally owned and managed modern business community to whom the government can turn for advice on economic policy generally and treatment of foreign business specifically—advice that it is politically possible to accept as being in the national interest.

3. In many countries, especially those whose foreign exchange earnings and government budgets are largely dependent on exports from their subsoil resources or whose modern business sector is largely foreign-owned, local leaders fear, with some justice, that decisions by distant managements of multinational corporations, not influenced at all or only very secondarily by the national interests or development objectives of the host country, can seriously damage the country's whole economy and hence its political and social stability. This fear is accentuated in many countries by the absence of a strong, modern, locally owned and managed production sector, which could provide a feeling of security against foreign economic domination.

4. In many countries there is a considerable tendency for natural suspicion of foreigners by public opinion, politicians, and bureaucrats, often reinforced by ideologies that are suspicious of, if not wholly opposed to, private capitalism, and especially its embodiment in the multinational corporation, which is both capitalist and foreign.

From the existing rules of international relations, there is little help to be expected. There are numerous commitments to the peaceful settlement of disputes, which set limits to the means utilizable in cases of disagreements over foreign investments, although peace does elude us on other issues rather too often.

There is also general agreement in many solemn documents to nonintervention, to the ultimate sovereignty of each nation over its territory and people in it. But there are also a number of international documents attempting to set forth traditional international "law," designed to protect individuals and their property, especially in the case of foreigners, against an unlimited exercise of sovereignty, although without the sanction, necessary to true law, of an international judicial system and police force to back it up. Hence head-on conflict between the two principles has so far involved mostly words and various scattered economic pressures.

Thus, there is not only no general system of agreed and enforceable rights and obligations to govern relations between states or citizens, corporate or otherwise, of different states, but in the specific matter of the operation of multinational corporations there are sharp differences as to what these rights and obligations should be. These differences are not just a matter of legal niceties or failure to keep up with the changing needs of the world business community; they are fundamental, highly political differences in concepts. Moreover, they are not just between developing and developed countries but divide each group, in theory and practice, and not just as between capitalist and socialist countries.

This situation applies especially to the various rights and obligations arising in connection with eviction actions. Unfortunately, most of them arise over investments in natural resource development and it is here that differences are most pronounced. Anyone who doubts this need only compare the resolutions on the subject passed by UNCTAD I and III and that proposed at the Twelfth Session of the UNCTAD Trade and Development Board by the eleven leading Latin American countries with the U.S. policy statement of January 1973.

As long as the international community is as divided on these issues as it now is, I see no role for international institutions either in drawing up rules or codes or in trying to settle specific conflicts. One can only urge that bodies in whom the developing countries have trust, like the UNCTAD and regional UN commission secretariats, do the research necessary to demonstrate the net magnitude of the economic advantages or damages that may accompany evictions. Each country will, of course, make up its own mind and take the action that seems to it most in the national interest, political as well as economic, as we all do every day in big and little things, but it should be able to have before it the full economic facts about the choices.

Usually, however, when one has reached the eviction stage it is too late for foreign investors to avoid difficult adjustments. One can more easily prevent matters from reaching this extreme position by courses of action at earlier stages to build a relationship of mutual confidence based on day-to-day cooperative working relations. But this may not always be possible with the best of intentions and efforts, and it seldom does the multinational corporation any good to undergo a sudden conversion as the precipice looms closer and closer.

But are there ways in which such permanently easier relations may be promoted by international action? I caution that the word is "promoted" and not "assured." Much the heaviest burden will always be on the individuals directly involved.

One must look at the basic nature of the problems at these earlier stages in order to have an idea of what international institutions might do about them.

First, there is basic opposition to all foreign investment by those who oppose the capitalist system and attack all private investment and by ultranationalists who reject foreigners in any role. Specific actions will not change such ideological convictions, but over time good performance by multinational corporations may weaken the influence of both these groups on government policy. More accurate facts may also help to do this. The Development Centre of the Organization for Economic Cooperation and Development (OECD) hopes to publish shortly two reports on the economic and social costs and benefits of foreign private investment. UNCTAD researchers have also shed useful light on this question. More work on this line is greatly needed, although of course it is necessary to be prepared to face the fact that such research may show that some such investment has had negative effects.

Second, there are numerous ways in which the objective of maximizing the return to the multinational enterprise is in direct conflict with maximizing the economic and social benefits to each country in which it has an operation. Both may gain from an investment but both wish to gain more and can do so only at the expense of less gain by the other. This is the critical issue. Each party must understand the technical details of and the reasons for the positions taken by the other in order that satisfactory compromises may be worked out. This requires changes in attitudes on both sides and improvements in the knowledge and understanding of those responsible, especially in developing countries. This is required not just so that they can appreciate why certain demands of the multinational enterprise are reasonable but also so that they can be sure to recognize demands that are not reasonable and explain why they refuse to grant them. No permanently satisfactory relationship is possible without such a fair sharing of costs and benefits. Fortunately, more and more multinationals are recognizing this fact and seeing that their best interests lie in a long-term operation. The acquisition of knowledge and experience by developing country authorities is also progressing. But on both sides much remains to be done.

The specifics involved here, whether a question of entry negotiations or operating conditions, are numerous and complex. They may well differ in nature and importance not only from country to country but from project to project within the same country. No international authority can be expected to intervene usefully in such matters. No general rules are applicable.

A few cases may be dealt with by the local legal system, such as enforcing provisions of entering arrangements or eliminating unjustified discrimination under local law. But this is often a long and expensive process with uncertainty about the outcome.

A few others may be resolved by arbitration and conciliation arrangements at the local level, but these are seldom well-developed nor is their objectivity widely accepted.

A few may also be susceptible to treatment under the arbitration scheme of the International Bank for Reconstruction and Development (IBRD), but thus far this appeal to international action rather than local decision has not seen much use. Perhaps its existence may have served in other cases as a deterrent to unjustified action.

But even taken all together, these procedural devices can do little. It is often suggested that the whole climate could be greatly improved by adoption in the UN framework of a code of good behavior for corporations and their host governments. But a code has legal connotations. To be effective, it must deal concretely with potential differences. As has been seen, few of the problems lie in the legal area or are capable of legal treatment. And even on these there is no chance of getting agreement of either developed or developing countries, or even less of both, on provisions sufficiently concrete to have any impact on attitudes, let alone to be the basis for decisions in concrete cases.

The central immediate task is to improve the capacity of developing country authorities to deal professionally with the issues at stake and to be able to offer objective policy advice when it is requested. A start has been made along the latter lines by the establishment of an advisory service on foreign investment in the United Nations and by the support of the United Nations Development Program (UNDP) and many bilateral donors for schools of business and public administration and special training for public officials in subjects related to this problem.

But the effort remains dispersed and not sharply focused. I suggest that there be established an international organization under fully impartial sponsorship and leadership. Its role would be:

1. To engage in providing training and advice to officials of developed and developing countries and multinational corporations on this range of questions.

2. To improve the capacity of, or to create where necessary, institutions in developing countries to do training and research in this field.

3. To engage in serious research of a specific nature on matters that are the subject of the most common and difficult conflicts of interest, real or apparent.

4. To sponsor continuing dialogues between operating officials in developing countries and in multinational corporations in continuation of that organized by the UN in Amsterdam in February 1969, and on a regional basis since then.

5. To give encouragement and technical assistance to revisions of local business law and to national conciliation and arbitration schemes, even though progress will not exclusively benefit multinational operations.

Such an institution should see its role as getting others with special capacities or funds to do what it believes needs to be done, and in a coordinated way. Insofar as it must get into advisory activities in developing countries, as distinct from research, collection, and exchange of information and appraisal of how things are going and what gaps need filling, it should look to the UNDP for resources from within its country-programming system.

Three subjects for further analysis stand out in particular, in current public discussion among those interested in development, as requiring intensive work:

1. Much work has been done by the IBRD, experts at the OECD Development Centre, and elsewhere in developing detailed procedures for appraising public development projects for which aid is being requested. It would be of great help to developing countries to have available detailed manuals for project appraisal that they could follow in deciding on proposals for foreign investment, covering all the major economic and social factors at issue including analysis of special inducements and requirements sought in each case.

2. Closely related to this is the interest in many quarters in adapting technologies to the real costs of labor and capital in developing countries and in considering also the social costs of present high rates of employment and underemployment. There is need for general guidance on the extent to which and just how these considerations should play a role in entry negotiations. Such criteria can affect not only choices between proposals, based on technology to be used, but also modification in proposals and changes in the incentives now so often offered, nearly all of which cheapen capital investment far below its real cost to the developing country rather than encouraging the use of more labor.

3. One of the most difficult conflicts of interest, again arising primarily as part of the entry discussions, has to do with export policy. It is natural to the multinational corporation to wish to serve its global markets from what are, for it, the cheapest sources of supply regardless of the effects of such market allocations on the economies in which its plants are located. It is equally natural for the host country to want to maximize its exports; thus an increase in export earnings is often a main advantage to it of a proposed foreign investment. This particular "restrictive business practice" has been studied somewhat by the UNCTAD secretariat but no easy compromise is visible, needed as it is.

Multinational corporations commonly complain about the slowness with which most issues are handled by developing country officials, whether in the entry or operation phase. The importance to business planning of speed in making decisions is often not well understood. The use of more common sense in disposing of most operational issues, involving to a large extent either implementation of entry understandings or normal controls over the economy, is also frequently demanded.

I fear improvement of relations in these senses must depend on gradual increase in general bureaucratic efficiency and specific professional skills, on the expansion of the local business community and its influence on government, and in general on a modernization of society at all levels. Underdevelopment will continue for some time to have its costs, not customary in more developed countries. Foreign investors can help by understanding the novelty of many of the problems with which the bureaucrats are faced, by associating well-trained local personnel with their operations and, where possible, sharing ownership, and by encouraging the local private sector through subcontracting, business schools, and so forth.

Another important consideration for the multinational corporation, not always recognized as such by developing countries, is stability in the rules under which it must operate. No one can do much about changes caused by the rather frequent replacements of governments, which are often rather basic and not just "outs" taking over from "ins." Smaller alterations in the rules are apt to become less troublesome only as those in authority acquire more experience and a better knowledge of the conditions for the successful conduct of a business, domestic or foreign.

Apart from the indirect contribution of the advisory, training, and research institution already proposed, I see no special new role for the international community in these two areas of speed and continuity, and very little for the governments of foreign investors.

Thus, I conclude that a new international organization is desirable to provide help to multinational corporations and to developing countries on their common problems, but not to give directions, set standards, or make decisions. In view of the objectivity necessary to its acceptance by all parties, I would think it could best function as a part of the UN Secretariat.

*   *   *   *   *

AN ADDED STATEMENT
Edwin Martin

It seems to me that the very important distinction that has been made between the activities of the multinational corporations and the activities of the smaller foreign private investors in developing countries can be explained by the fact that in the case of one, the government is the elephant while in the other it is the corporation that is the elephant, and this does make a difference.

There was an amazing degree of consensus in Panel II. I would like to stress a few points and quarrel with a few others, without challenging the basic conclusions. In the first place, I do not think one can sufficiently emphasize the lack of consensus as to what should be rules, principles, and guides of conduct for multinational corporations in developing countries. It is far from being a difference between developed and developing countries. Nor does it just involve differences between developing countries with different socioeconomic systems.

As Seymour Rubin has indicated, the differences are very wide between, for example, Sweden and the United States, and there are even quite considerable differences between the representatives of countries as alike as the United Kingdom and the United States on, for example, the issue of accepting 51 percent local ownership. I would also emphasize the differences between companies of a single country, as Ambassador Korry did in reporting on a Chilean experience. I can recall a case in a Central American country a decade ago in which two American corporations were active, in the same identical line of business. One of them felt that a projected government move would destroy it and that the government must be put out of office by some means. The other, which had a somewhat larger investment, saw no problems. How do you draw rules out of this kind of a difference of opinion toward specific situations? I think it is quite impossible to contemplate doing so.

I do think, as others have indicated, that there is increased flexibility on the part of both some developing country governments and many multinational corporations in finding solutions to the inherent conflicts between their interests, but I would not expect too rapid progress in this direction for several reasons, all basically political. I do want to emphasize that I do not think the issues here are essentially efficiency or issues that can and will be dealt with by market forces. The political factors are the dominant factors in relationships between developing countries and multinational corporations, and I think this situation will persist for some little time in the future. Nearly all developing countries face difficult issues in reacting to and absorbing or rejecting the modern technological society, which is represented in their midst as much as anything by the multinational corporations.

They are trying—with varying degrees of success and varying priorities—to obtain the material benefits of modern industrial society without too much damage or harm to traditional values on which they put high priority. Some of these traditional values are values now being reemphasized in our society at the expense of growth. Jack Behrman has mentioned some of them—the question of equality, the question of participation, the question of community values and community welfare—and so long as this is the case, there will be, I think, great difficulties in developing a consistent, general, single reaction to multinational corporations among developing countries. The developing countries are each seeking a society to meet their own needs and ambitions. They will be experimenting. They will fail and look in other directions, and so long as this uncertainty persists—and I think it will persist for quite a long time—I do not think one can look for a stable political climate in the developing countries as a whole for a great many will be in a state of rather considerable flux. Reflecting in part this, but also other factors, I think one must anticipate quite a lot of change in political structures. Apart from finding a national personality, the question of organizing an effective political structure, democratic or otherwise, is one on which we have been working in the Western world for several centuries; the developing countries are trying to organize now under great pressures, great frustrations, and very rapid changes in their ways of life and their external surroundings. This is going to induce political instability for a very considerable time ahead in a good many of them. It must be faced as a fact of life that continuity in the attitudes, politicians, and governments with which multinational corporations will be dealing is not to be expected as the standard experience.

I think too that this is all taking place and will for some time take place in an atmosphere of intense nationalism. Nationalism is, on the whole, a commodity the developing countries have borrowed from the developed ones. Mr. Behrman refers to the new and more intense nationalism in developed countries, and it is certainly much deeper in most of the developing countries. This is to a considerable extent a reaction to previous dependence, whether formal or informal, and a desire to establish themselves as really independent, with the ability to make independent choices and participate in the world as distinct entities. Intense nationalism such as one finds in most developing countries naturally expresses itself and is often symbolized by attitudes toward foreigners; multinational corporations are foreigners and cannot really dress themselves up any other way.

Consequently, this nationalistic spirit will consistently present serious problems for the operation of multinational corporations. These problems are, I am sure, accentuated by a feeling, often true, of weakness in dealing with multinational corporations—the lack of professional skills to which reference has been made. This accentuates the inferiority complex type of attitude toward the outsider.

It has been suggested that the recent opening up of the Soviet bloc to the multinational corporation might do a great deal to improve attitudes toward them from left-of-center groups in developing countries, making it possible to deal on a nonideological basis.

I find the analogy false and not a reflection of the true situation. The only real analogy to the Soviet bloc in Latin America, for example, is Cuba. It is a much weaker, less stable communist system than that in the Soviet bloc countries, and therefore unable to accept the risks of having multinational corporations operating in its midst. It is because of the Soviet bloc's strength and confidence that its members are willing to do this, and this has, I think, nothing to do with the principle of acceptability of multinational corporations. Rather I would think that if any conclusions are to be drawn by the developing countries, the conclusions would be that if the Soviet bloc can obtain the benefits of the capital and technology of the multinational corporation, then we can certainly have a communist system without losing this asset. It makes it easier to contemplate a communist system and still retain the benefits of the multinational corporation. So I do not find this particular development a justification for any degree of optimism.

In addition to the points about diversity and the obvious great uncertainties of the attitudes of developing countries toward multinational corporations in the future, I think there is one other reason why codes, rules, and machinery to formally adjudicate are not apt to be particularly helpful at the present time. This is the impression that I have from my experience that the kinds of issues with which one can deal in pieces of paper of this kind, to be enforced by various kinds of judicial machinery, are not necessarily the most difficult issues multinational corporations face. The more important ones— sometimes lumped under the label of "creeping expropriation" but sometimes not going that far—are the day-to-day dealings with the bureaucracy, the delays, the difficulties, the lack of understanding. These matters cannot be dealt with by formal mechanisms of any kind. They will only be dealt with by increased sophistication, confidence, and efficiency in the government bureaucracy. Again, it is a political problem, but a political problem that will only be resolved over a long period of time. One does not build a capable well-coordinated bureaucracy rapidly. There are even some people who would suggest that not all the developed countries have achieved this goal as yet.

However, I do agree with those who feel it would be desirable to have some kind of body of an international sort to collect information, insofar as this can be done effectively on the critical issues, to do research or see that research gets done. I do not necessarily envisage an operating group in the sense of direct operation but a group that is doing research on some of the critical problems and coordinating research by others. It should also be in a position to see that adequate technical assistance is available and that training facilities are made available—either by itself or by a variety of other forums, and we will need many. The object should be to try to create a more effective bargaining relationship, a better informed bargaining relationship on both sides. I am convinced that a lot of the current difficulties are due to this lack of capacity for effective bargaining, mostly on the part of the developing countries, but not always. I have seen multinational corporations that also are singularly ineffective bargainers in situations in which other companies in the same industry were doing quite well.

I may say that this does not necessarily mean public assistance for the developing countries. One of the most effectively bargaining countries I know of is a socialist, Marxist country that in its negotiations on critical extractive industry problems uses the best Wall Street law firms it can find and has done an extremely effective job of protecting its own interests. I suspect that companies negotiating with it will find that their situation will be more permanently satisfactory than if the Wall Street law firms had not been hired. This is the kind of situation in which it will be advantageous to put more developing countries.

It has been suggested that some part of the World Bank family could perform the role of the international institution I have projected. I do not agree. I think it is absolutely essential that this body, to be effective both with developing countries and multinational corporations and with the others who are working in this field in academic and other circles, must not only be objective but also believed by all to be objective, which is not always the same thing. Whether one likes it or not, or believes this would affect its judgment, the facts are that the World Bank is located in Washington, D.C., the capital of the major capitalistic power. Just about all top officers are Americans except one who is British and another who comes from a Commonwealth country. More important, by far, the executive board votes are dominated by the industrialized powers: They have the majority. Therefore, it will not be accepted as wholly impartial on delicate political issues of this kind. Furthermore, these are delicate political issues and it seems to me that getting involved in them in any controversial way would undoubtedly impair, as its policies already have in a few cases, the World Bank's ability to operate effectively in improving the development performance and financing the development programs of the developing countries.

For the opposite reason in terms of trust, the secretariat of the UN Conference on Trade and Development (UNCTAD) is in my judgment equally unacceptable as an objective source. Not because the secretariat is not objective but because it is looked upon, by both the developing and the developed countries, as the instrument of the developing countries in the United Nations system. This is unfortunate

but it is a fact. I must say I personally see a great merit in the proposal made by Luis Escobar of having the secretary-general of the
United Nations set up a semiautonomous body to perform this function.

Only in this global framework and at the very top do I think one
can get the kind of attention that is needed for this set of problems.
If one gets that, there are three or four subjects I would particularly
like this group to give attention to in addition to the more routine
operations that have been described and discussed here. Whether it
performs these functions itself or contracts out, or sees that other
people are doing them, is in my judgment irrelevant. The first question
is sometimes referred to as the restrictive practices issue, but I
would rather refer to it more broadly as the question of the competitive
situation. It is to the interest of the multinational corporation to use
its multinational character to divide up markets in the way that is
most profitable. It is to the interest of the developing countries, and
we press it on them, to export as much as possible. These interests
are often in conflict. I am convinced that a great many royalty, licensing, and subsidiary arrangements do contain market limitation arrangements. Even when they do not so far as subsidiaries are concerned,
a word from the home office is all that is necessary and this is, I
may say, not just a developing country problem.

For example, on the Development Assistance Committee (DAC),
Canadians say they find great difficulty in going all the way on untying
aid loans, as many other countries are prepared to do, because so
many of their companies are subsidiaries of U.S. or United Kingdom
companies and they feel that the home offices would find production
in the United States or United Kingdom, with the larger markets there,
more economic than in Canada and thus would not permit the Canadian
firms to bid in competition with the main factories in the United States
or United Kingdom.

In addition, there is a serious competitive problem in developing
countries due to the smallness of the markets. Some have tried to
solve this problem by bringing in several companies. In Argentina I
think there are some twelve companies producing automobiles. There
was competition, but because of the smallness of the production runs
this meant that a Rambler sedan cost $7,000. This is not a unique
case, either in the automobile industry or in many other industries.
We have not begun to solve the problem of reasonable pressures for
efficiency in developing countries with their small markets, either
through multinational corporations or combinations of multinationals
and national corporations.

Of course this is largely made possible by high tariff or other
protective arrangements in the developing countries, which are often
demanded by the multinational corporation. A corporation may sell
out to the government because it did not get a sufficiently high tariff

on the product it was producing. This has happened often; it is not a good justification for a takeover, but there is a serious competition problem here.

I would suspect that finding solutions to the competition question would go a long way toward solving another potentially serious problem. Nobody knows the dimensions, but the questions of intracompany transfer price and the reasonableness of royalty and license payments are critical issues. But if there were sufficient competitive pressures, the local affiliate could not pay excessive prices to the home office for any of these purposes. This is a very difficult problem and may be almost impossible to solve under present circumstances; it is not a solution in my judgment to say that national governments must deal bilaterally on this matter. Most developing country governments are not possessed of a bureaucracy with sufficient effectiveness to enforce strong antitrust provisions on pricing or market-sharing agreements, and so the multinational corporations tend to escape them. It is not even easy in the developed countries.

Another problem is the question of takeovers of domestic companies. This probably is a problem of varying importance in varying countries, but it seems to me that it is of the greatest importance for the multinational corporation that it operate in a climate in which there is a strong domestic business sector. This gives a government and its citizens confidence that they are not under foreign domination. It also gives a government a source of politically acceptable advice on good economic policy, a source it does not have in the multinational corporations, which will always be suspect no matter what the nationality of their management is. Without strong domestic business there are great troubles in establishing a sound business climate. We must not only find ways to limit multinational corporation takeovers of domestic entrepreneurs but rather induce them to build up the domestic business sector in every way possible. This again could be an objective to be sought by the proposed international organization.

Related to this family of problems is that of renegotiation. How can one get a fair basis for renegotiation? Here again are internal conflicts of interest. It will not be simple to make progress on this, but perhaps we can provide information, analyses, and studies that will help produce the necessary flexibility for amiable renegotiation of arrangements. Both sides may need help in this respect.

Lastly a much more complex issue is the question of technology and technology transfer. There are some very difficult problems created by multinational corporations, often in cooperation with host governments, in establishing incentives for inappropriate technology—inappropriate in terms of the factor prices of capital and labor in the particular developing country. This creates social as well as economic problems. It derives in large part from tax incentives, tariff incentives, and others offered to foreign investors, often in competition with other developing countries. For this reason, joint international action is probably required if anything is to be achieved. At the moment nobody is taking serious initiatives in this area and it seems to me of the greatest importance that a number of steps be taken in the tax and economic policy field to try to help promote selection of the technology that is appropriate in view of the high real cost of capital, the high real cost of foreign exchange to pay for capital equipment, and the abundance of labor in most but not all developing countries.

I find two defects in Jack Behrman's proposal. One is that, given the diversity of attitudes I think still persists in developing countries, I find great difficulty in anticipating that any considerable number of developing countries could agree on a program of location of multinational enterprise activities, or on the arrangements for these activities. The regional approach to multinational planning is not apt to be successful for any period of time or any wide area.

Second, I think that, even more fundamentally, most of the developing country regional arrangements would prefer to use domestic and not multinational corporations to carry out these projects and would keep the multinational corporations on the fringe of the operations. I think it is significant in this situation that one of the main arguments being used against the Latin America Free Trade Area (LAFTA) and in favor of the restrictive provisions of the Andean Pact is that the only corporations within their territories capable of taking advantage of a wider market are the multinational corporations. Virtually the only commodities on which LAFTA has reached agreements are those on which multinational corporations are active and willing to have agreements made because it permits them to allocate production more freely among various subsidiaries. The beneficiaries of the free trade areas will be the multinational corporations and not the domestic ones, and this is not and will not be politically acceptable.

I would like to conclude by pointing out one other political and anthropological factor that I think must be taken into account in trying to judge how rapidly we are going to make progress and along what lines it will have to come. I increasingly have the feeling that in many developing countries, although not all, the society is at a stage where the developed countries were a long time ago, in which the man who is engaged in business, either production or trade, is doing something that is socially second rate and not prestigious: It is not a good thing to become a businessman or have a son go to a business school or get into trade since these areas are looked down upon. This means two things: first, that the best brains do not go into business; second and much more important, that the people who go into the prestigious occupations, government and the liberal professions, have no knowledge of business, do not know anybody who is in business, and therefore have no comprehension whatever of the effect of government action on business planning and incentives. This is a complete failure of comprehension and I suggest that this attitude is not as far away from some developed societies as one might think. I can recall fifteen years ago I was living in the United Kingdom and a friend who was president of one of the largest department stores in London was turned down for membership in a country club. The club had just agreed to take in people in wholesale trade but retail trade was still not quite respectable. Now this is much deeper in most developing countries than that. It was this way in the Middle Ages in the now developed countries. This attitude is changing in the developed countries; it will probably change in the developing countries, but slowly and almost surely not in the same way.

And until this change takes place, there will always be difficulties in getting satisfactory conditions for business operations—foreign or domestic but particularly for the foreign because they appear even stranger. This, I think, is one of the big problems we face. We can only work ahead at it and continue to try to make progress. It will be possible, even though slow, because for many developing countries the foreign enterprise will be an asset. But others will decide that it is not an asset and try to copy other patterns from the industrialized world, because there are other patterns to copy, and we must accept that this will be the course of history.

*　*　*　*　*

COMMENT
Philippe de Seynes

I am very substantially in agreement with the position taken by Edwin Martin.

In a way, some of the steps being discussed here in order to improve the relationship between multinational companies and host countries are already taking place, or will shortly be taking place, within the United Nations system. I am not here claiming any monopoly for the organization to which I belong, but I believe that plans discussed and worked out in other places must, from now on, take into account the fact that the topic of multinational corporations, and their impact on international relations and on the development of less developed countries, is now squarely planted within the UN system and that the system will deal with it in the various ways available to it. This is no longer a situation of tabula rasa.

The history of the United Nations is one of reconquest of the authority granted to it by the charter but soon after denied to it by the struggle of the great powers that in the early days dominated the principal organs of the institution.

After the recent decisions of UNCTAD and the Economic and Social Council (ECOSOC), the present situation in regard to multinational corporations appears very similar to what happened to international trade in the beginning of the 1960s. Previously, international trade was considered officially the preserve of GATT or of the OEEC (the first incarnation of the Organization for Economic Cooperation and Development, or OECD). With the change in the membership of the United Nations, this position became untenable and the United Nations Conference on Trade and Development was born in 1964. Thereafter the subject of trade and payments, shipping and insurance, was continuously and thoroughly investigated within the United Nations in all the ways available to it—political debates, professional studies, negotiations on specific points, technical cooperation programs. It is a safe bet that the same process will be followed in regard to multinational corporations although it is not certain whether any changes in the institutional set-up—such as the creation of a new instrumentality—will take place.

The recognition of the multinational corporations as an important phenomenon of international economic relations—at least equal in scope to classic commercial exchanges and much more far-reaching in some political and social implications—and its emergence as a major topic of international discussion and action is, as so often is the case, the result of a combination of chance and necessity. The chance was the "aberration" of one of the largest and technologically most advanced among the multinational corporations, and the fact that an important conference, UNCTAD III, was being held at the very moment when the aberration was discovered in the capital of the aggrieved country. But the necessity was there all the time, at least for the last ten or twelve years, and in fact the subject matter of foreign investment in less developed countries, of permanent sovereignty over natural resources, has been evoked episodically and sporadically within the UN system.

Permanent sovereignty is of course an important, sacred concept in the light of the United Nations charter. However, governments interpreted it in such widely differing ways that it has not been possible up to now to give it a real operational meaning embodied in a consensus. Moreover, there is another possible approach that is also important in the United Nations and should be pursued simultaneously: That is that private capital should be properly inserted in a general scheme of international cooperation for the benefit of less developed countries. It should be viewed as a device through which developing countries can join the world community, or at least increase the benefits of their membership within this world community. Incidentally, this is also true of some of the more advanced countries that are gradually overcoming their neurosis in respect to American takeovers. In their case, the concept of national sovereignty is hardly relevant since these countries are capable of refusing the mergers as well as of fully reciprocating, thereby creating a situation that would not be as asymmetrical as it is today.

In the case of less developed countries the asymmetry is obvious and for most of them durable; therefore, the problem presents much greater political and psychological difficulties. In spite of this, and particularly in the present predicament characterized by increasing external debt burden and stagnation in the official transfer of capital from rich countries, a great number of less developed countries tend to view multinational corporations not just as a threat to their sovereignty but also as a means of joining the world community and acquiring the package of financial resources, technology, managerial skills, and access to markets that the multinational company sometimes delivers so expeditiously and efficiently.

Therefore, there is a real ambivalence in attitudes, nurtured and perpetuated by the sometimes extravagant claims made by the multinational companies, more particularly by their assumption that there is automatically and in every case a coincidence of interests between what they want to do in a country and the way the country sees its own destiny. Possible conflicts of interest in my view are at present much more significant than possible conflicts of law. Potential conflicts of interest may even increase, as approaches to development change and the search for new styles of development is carried forward. Many less developed countries are at present seriously questioning the path they have been following. They are no more confident that the pursuit of growth in GNP or the spread of modern technology produces a beneficial spinoff on their social conditions. They are more often than before concerned with the creation of jobs, sometimes at the expense of average productivity, and with the type of social policies that will ensure to the masses of people the provision of ordinary consumption of goods: food, footwear, clothing, shelter, education, and hygiene. These new policies are not necessarily creating the most congenial climate for international corporations to operate. It is not a natural trend for the multinational companies to use large masses of local workers because this is not always the most productive way of doing things and because it may involve the companies in some difficult political or psychological syndromes. I am not saying that multinational corporations are not or will not become able to adjust themselves to these styles of development, but I cannot share the tranquilizing philosophy that suggests more faith than I have in an early normalization of relationships.

Beyond these considerations pertaining to practical relationship, there is a larger and not easily assessable factor, that of power, the concentration of power, which cannot leave the United Nations indifferent. This is independent of social and economic benefits or losses, independent of the good or less good behavior of international companies, independent even of the impact of those companies on national sovereignty. In the face of a phenomenon of power there must be checks and balances, countervailing power and a measure of international surveillance. I was somewhat disappointed by the very negative comments made in respect to the possibility of establishing any form of international regulation. I believe that there are such possibilities already, and that these possibilities should be investigated and negotiated as rapidly as possible. If we really want an international market for capital investments and the flow of technology, we cannot just rely on laissez-faire. No open social framework can probably function without some institutions.

As John Evans and I have noted, as far back as 1948 the Havana charter expressed the need for some regulation in international business, and the fact that the matter was left dormant for all these years in the face of the expansion of the multinational companies is not, in my view, a reflection of the impossibility of doing anything, but rather of the expression of an interplay of forces that are not immutable. In fact there are growing signs in the business world as well as the political world that the need for some form of international surveillance is gradually being recognized. This is the context in which the United Nations is going to operate in this new phase of its history.

It is not difficult to discern some of the directions this intervention will take. The most easily accessible one lies in the function of technical cooperation, which has been significantly developed in the United Nations. In this case cooperation will mean strengthening the hand of governments of developing countries for their negotiations with multinational companies, developing within these governments some measure of countervailing power. Obviously, governments of oil producing countries no longer need such cooperation as they have come to analyze for themselves with great accuracy their true bargaining position as a result of changing circumstances in technology as well as demand, and to recognize the advantages of joint bargaining. But in other fields our experience is that governments of less developed countries are not always fully aware of the contractual arrangements or other forms of association with multinational companies that are open to them. Missions undertaken in some of these countries at their request indicate that they can significantly benefit from a thorough reexamination of their national laws, regulations, and practices. They have welcomed the possibility of discussing such matters with knowledgeable experts and of comparing their own experience with that of others. Training courses with the same objectives in mind, open to governmental as well as business executives, will presumably be systematically organized on a regional basis and discussions to this effect are already underway in both Southeast Asia and the Caribbean region.

We also have indications that some governments would like to go further than that. They want advice and assistance of a completely objective nature in their negotiations of specific contracts with the companies, and we are seriously studying the possibility of working out modalities to ensure that such services might be available to governments that want to make use of them, without directly involving the United Nations itself.

Then comes the question of the forum, and I have already indicated that the United Nations constitutes a forum and that this forum is going to be available in more than one way for study and possible negotiations pertaining to the question of multinational corporations. This is not of course the composite forum suggested by Senator Jacob K. Javits, where governments and business would discuss general policies as well as specific cases, nor the new GATT that Charles Kindleberger and others have outlined. Still, it is a forum where the various aspects of policies and problems—including the possibility and desirability of such other forums—can be evoked and debated at the political level on the basis of professional studies. Such a United Nations forum will no doubt, as before in other fields, hasten the changes in basic assumptions and attitudes leading to new policies, rules of behavior, and institutional arrangements. This UN forum is a continuing and ubiquitous one with its global, sectoral, and regional instances, and although its behavior often appears disconcerting to outsiders, its cumulative effect in conceptualizing problems at the international level has been impressive.

The secretary-general of the United Nations has been directed by ECOSOC to appoint a group of "eminent persons"—and I quote this language because it is the first time that it appears in United Nations legislation—to sort out the various problems pertaining to international relationships and the development of less developed countries, and on which multinational corporations may have an impact. The outcome of this study is certainly going to be a systematic development of the work to be undertaken under the umbrella of the United Nations forum. I know that serious apprehensions have been generated by this intrusion of the United Nations system because the image a certain public has formed of the United Nations is often one of a body where ideology, if not demagoguery, prevails. I think this image on the whole is wrong. There is of course a certain ideology that comes from the aspirations of the Third World majority, but this ideology is not necessarily irrational nor a priori inimical to international business.

I have worked myself to dissipate whatever mutual suspicion might exist through symposiums organized in Amsterdam, Medellin, and Tokyo, through the joint committee of the International Chamber of Commerce and the United Nations, which meets once a year. But of course this is not enough. Being an incurable optimist, I firmly believe that the developments we are going to witness in the United Nations in relation to multinational companies will contribute toward more understanding and more rationality in reciprocal attitudes.

One reason for my belief that the United Nations is a proper forum in relation to the problem of multinational companies is that within the United Nations this problem can be viewed in the broadest possible context. It can and will be seen within a framework where all aspects of international cooperation are examined, particularly since there is now available an "International Strategy for Development" that brings together in a coherent model the principal aspects of national and international action conducive to more rapid development.

There is a great variety of means of cooperation available to less developed countries, and for reasons of their own, which may be passing or durable, they may want to do without the help of international private capital. The very fact that alternatives often exist is in itself reassuring to these countries. Another advantage of the broader concept is that the contribution of international capital can be viewed and appraised against the background of the total capital flows. This is most important today when the debt burden of developing countries may very well set certain limits to the absorption of external private capital, unless public capital flows on concessionary terms increase.

This question of available alternatives is very crucial from a political point of view. The feeling of being captive to private interests for the acquisition of certain advantages is not easily accepted and generates a sense of frustration, which is not conducive to the normalization of relationships. This is observable particularly in the field of industrial technology. Developing countries find it strange that they can acquire technology for agriculture and health from the public domain, or through arrangements between public authorities, but that more often than not they must go to private companies for industrial technology. I am aware of the differences between different kinds of technology transfers, but I am also quite certain that a number of institutional devices and arrangements must be created so that the transfer of industrial technology does not have to depend exclusively on multinational companies. Such arrangements will help alleviate the suspicions and permit a rational comparative appraisal by the developing countries of the various means open to them. I am quite convinced that such comparative appraisal will, in many cases, show in sharp relief the advantages provided by the multinational companies and the package of goods and services they can deliver.

There is an area in which the United Nations forum may be useful in a very specific and new way. That is the area of energy resources and perhaps some mineral resources; here, the broad context is indispensable for various reasons. In the first place, if we are threatened with depletion or at least with severe bottlenecks arising from the changing relationship between known reserves, technology, and prices, then a good measure of cooperation or coordination for acceleration and exploitation is going to be necessary. And this will involve arrangements where multinational corporations have a role. Second, the opening up of the seabed for planned exploitation under a United Nations authority may play havoc with the traditional markets unless some measure of coordination is established. Guidelines for international policy and national action will be necessary. Problems of distribution will arise. The increase in the price of oil is certainly useful to producing countries and has proved acceptable to international companies and even to consumers of the rich countries, which are now giving so much attention to antipollution measures. But it has been harmful to nonproducing developing countries as their import bill is severely increased. So some more rational ways of doing things will gradually have to be devised.

Willis Armstrong commented that the national policy of the United States in regard to energy resources would free it from dependency on Middle Eastern oil. But pursuance of exclusively national policies in such matters cannot lead to an optimum situation in regard to very precious, if not physically exhaustible, resources. If there are going to be in the industrial countries, through subsidies and other encouragements, policies of autarky in regard to natural resources, and if at the same time there are very strict antipollution controls, then developing countries will see the disappearance of one of their few advantages on the international scene—namely, their possession of mineral and energy resources.

In fact, I believe that the subject matter within the United Nations forum will tend to be international production rather than multinational companies. International production, with a wide spectrum of forms of association and contractual arrangements being developed in countries of all ideologies and political systems. Presumably there will also be some prospective or futuristic approach, which in my view is very necessary. It would be surprising if ten to twenty years from now the forms of association that predominate today between multinational companies and other instances remain unchanged. On the contrary, one can count on the resiliency and inventiveness of the companies to develop the type of arrangements most suitable to changing situations.

I have spoken of power as an attribute of the multinational companies, and of the possibility of developing countervailing power within the developing countries themselves. Another way of dealing with power is through the development of some international or supranational form of surveillance and regulation. I have noted considerable skepticism at this conference in this respect. It is very difficult for an official of an international organization to accept the negative arguments that have been brought forward. To the criteria of behavior that Jack Behrman presented, one should add a sense of "accountability", which is what the United Nations is about and which should affect multinational companies as well as governments. In the light of the concept of accountability, there is a necessity to search for the forms and methods in which this concept can be implemented. I hope that when I talk about regulations or surveillance, I shall not be viewed as an obsessive, dirigist Frenchman. I would rather present myself as an admiring observer of the U.S. free market which appears to me to be one of the most institutionalized in the world. And therefore I cannot very well accept the idea that if we are strongly seeking some of the benefits of a free market, as I think we all are, we should give up the hope of institutionalizing it.

I previously mentioned the question of restrictive business practices and the possibility of a worldwide convention. I will not revert to it except to say that I believe it to be feasible. I think the elements are there. At the beginning, it may not be a very effective or forceful organization but it will provide a framework—a forum—where complaints can be investigated, where recommendations can be made, and where sanctions in the mild form of publicity may apply. It is also a way of rationally using the power of embarrassment, which is inherent in an organization like the United Nations and is part of a democratic way of life.

The field of taxes is also one where we should actively pursue our search for harmonization, or even for innovative institutional arrangements. One of the main grievances aired against the multinational corporations is precisely their ability to take advantage of accidental elements such as tax legislation. The OECD has drafted a convention on the question of double taxation which is of course based on the balance of mutual interests that exist, or may exist, between developed countries. Other forms and approaches must be sought in relation to developing countries where such balance does not exist. This is what we are trying to do in the United Nations through a standing group of very competent experts whose professional work has not as yet been backed by the needed political will. But I personally see no reason why such efforts should indefinitely be doomed to failure. In the United Nations we are now used to taking a ten-year perspective, with our decades of development, and in this perspective such objectives no longer appear unattainable. They would be the forerunners of other efforts, and would also help in increasing confidence in existing arrangements, such as the IBRD facilities for the settlement of investment disputes.

I believe that one can agree with Ambassador Korry when he so forcefully observed that changing market forces would in the long run force rules of good behavior on the various participants. This, in my view, does not abolish the need for international institutional arrangements. I would repeat: With such a complex phenomenon as multinational corporations today, laissez-faire cum good behavior will not be enough. It seems to me that the world is embarking on a decade of negotiations on international institutional arrangements for more concerted action on trade matters, monetary reform, capital flows. The multinational corporation cannot escape this trend, as the international community increasingly sees its problems as global ones and becomes aware of its common destiny.

* * * * *

COMMENT
John Evans

I want to make it clear in advance that I am not talking about the monetary problem but will limit my remarks to the question of trade and related problems arising particularly out of the activities of industrialized countries and multinational corporations.

First, let me emphasize the problem of discussing the form of international organizations before we quite know what it is we are attacking. This conference might have been entitled: "Fifty Characters in Search of a Problem." We have been groping for a problem to solve, and now we are about to discuss what kind of an institution we should set up in order to solve it, although we have not yet found the problem. I do not want to give the impression that I think we have been tilting at windmills, but I do not think we have yet found a problem that is internationally manageable at the present time.

I think you can understand what I mean if you contrast the situation with that which existed before the creation of the Bretton Woods complex immediately after World War II. There were very serious problems. Most countries maintained foreign exchange restrictions and quantitative restrictions on their trade. So long as these controls persisted, it was hard to contemplate that the world could get back on its economic feet. The difference between the situation then and the one that exists today with respect to the multinational corporation, I think, is a sense of urgency shared by all the governments that would have to participate in any solution. I would suggest that until such a sense of urgency arises, if it ever does, any attempt to set up an

228

organization designed to do more than study the problem would be a disastrous mistake.

When and if the principal actors feel they are faced with a genuine difficulty that must be solved, then I think we no longer need worry too much about the form of the organization that should be established. During the Korean War there was a serious shortage of many important commodities around the world, partly as a result of increased governmental consumption but also as a result of speculation and anticipatory stocking or hoarding. A very strange organization grew up almost overnight, one that was not based on any treaty obligations and had absolutely no power to dictate to governments; yet it successfully allocated these scarce raw materials among countries for as long as the crisis lasted. The situation created the organization and determined its form. There was not time to draw up elaborate blueprints or to draft and obtain ratification of treaties.

Another example goes back to 1947 when a large family of nations decided that they needed to build a great structure in which to house many problems they had inherited from before the war. While they were building the main house, they set up a small temporary shelter. As it turned out, they never occupied the house; they continued to occupy the shelter and they added to it as the family grew. They finally made the shelter so permanent that it looked very much like the original house although it did not have quite as many rooms. And the shelter so grew in importance that the family promoted the handyman, who had helped build and enlarge it, to the job of major domo. That house is GATT. It is not as prosperous today as it was a few years ago, but it operated extremely effectively during a very long period of history and accomplished a great deal. Yet it was created as a temporary, ad hoc organization adhered to only provisionally by the contracting parties.

I bring this up partly to give myself an opportunity to clarify a suggestion that I have made concerning the creation of an organization that would attempt to deal with the problem of restrictive business practices. This was in response to a suggestion made by Anthony Solomon that an organization be created to screen transnational takeovers. The point I had hoped to make was that if this problem is to be tackled in a substantive way, it would be much wiser to deal with the broader question of restrictive business practices in general, whether or not they involve multinational corporations, and to concentrate on the nature of the offenses rather than the kinds of enterprises that commit them. It would be an organization to deal with functions. I still think this would be the wise way to go about dealing with any trade problems likely to arise in connection with multinational corporations. But I would repeat that I do not think such an organization can be set up successfully until there is a conviction on the part of governments that they have a crisis on their hands that they must all solve in their own interests.

I do not think that that is the situation today. I would say that 1973, in any event, would be an extremely bad year in which to ask governments to take on the obligations involved in the creation of such an organization. They are already faced with difficult negotiations for the reform of the monetary system, and I suspect much more difficult negotiations in the international trade field where, among other things, they are facing the modest proposal by the United States that the developed countries abolish their tariffs on industrial products.

But the principal reason for not attempting to launch such an enterprise in 1973 is that no conviction of crisis exists among the governments concerned.

I hope no crisis develops. I would suggest that study is all right, but that any organization established for the purpose of studying the problems created by international investment and particularly the multinational corporation go a bit further and at least take on the functions of a forum to which complaints can be brought, even though there is no authority to deal with the complaints. Until such a forum is created, until somebody has received complaints from governments—or complaints from multinational corporations, for that matter—there will be no way of judging whether or not the time has ripened and whether it is now possible to establish an international organization that would deal primarily with restrictive business practices.

20

INTERNATIONAL ORGANIZATION
FOR CONTROL OF INVESTMENT
Luis Escobar

Excluding cases of ideological opposition to private foreign investment—which in most cases goes together with rejection of private investment in general—one can say that opposition to the activities of multinational corporations (MNCs) is due to the fact that occasionally their interests may not be the same as those of the host countries. Dealing with the subject of international control of investments, we want to discuss how—through the international mechanism—we can make both ends meet:

• We recognize that MNCs can make an important contribution to the development of less developed countries (LDCs).

• We recognize that occasionally there may be incompatibility of interests between the MNCs and the host countries.

• We recognize that, if left alone, the negotiations between MNCs and LDCs do not always end in the kind of balance conducive to a smooth, friendly, and dynamic partnership; the reasons for this are, on the one hand, the impressive financial power of the MNCs compared with that of many LDCs and, on the other hand, the relative lack of information, organization, and, on occasion, expertise in LDCs to deal with the highly sophisticated management of the MNCs.

The realization of these facts in many host countries leads, from the very outset, to a lack of self-confidence in negotiations with representatives of MNCs, and that attitude is not, of course, the most conducive to a good partnership.

The author is a member of the staff of the International Bank for Reconstruction and Development; however, the opinions expressed in this paper have not been cleared with the institution and, consequently, he is solely responsible for them.

Consequently, the idea of organizing international control of investments has been suggested. Is there a need for such organization? My answer is a qualified yes: The need is there. But the questions are: What kind of international mechanism is needed? What powers would it have? How would it be organized? Who would manage it? Let me briefly make some comments and suggestions on these questions.

I said that my answer to the question, "Is there a need for an international control on investment?" is a qualified yes. The qualification is raised because I do not believe that we will be able to control investments internationally. If any "control" is to be exercised, it will be done nationally. What we can aim at is to internationally monitor investment. If the question were formulated: "Is there a need for an international monitoring of foreign investment?" my answer would be yes with no qualifications. I think we need an information center, a reference bureau, dealing with all aspects of the activities of MNCs, a true data bank on the matter. I would say there is a need for an international organization to facilitate the national control of foreign investments. This international organization would do research work, would provide information and training facilities, and in addition should be able to provide, on request, advice to governments or private businesses about their prospective or present activities of an international nature.

Let us call this international organization simply The Office. The Office would be established out of the conviction that private foreign investment is needed to speed up the rate of economic growth of LDCs but that the foreign investors must adjust their activities to the true needs and priorities of the host countries with due respect to their sovereignty and national goals. In doing this, private foreign investors have the right to fair compensation and fair treatment as true partners in the development process.

The Office would have no powers other than that of persuasion if and when its advice is asked for. Also, The Office would be influential through its publications, which would enjoy the prestige of being supported by the best information center in the world on questions of private foreign investment.

The Office would deal with private foreign investment in a broad sense, with both developed and developing country questions. This means that The Office would be interested in problems of investments made by an MNC in an LDC and also in the investment made in another industrialized country (for example, U.S. investments in Latin America as well as in Europe and Canada). The Office would also follow the investments that an MNC based in a market-oriented economy might make in a socialist country and those made by a socialist country in an LDC, whatever its political system.

From the foregoing description it can readily be seen that The Office should be organized very much like a research institution that would monitor all activities of MNCs, studying, analyzing, and keeping up to date on their activities in host countries (regardless of their level of development or political system). In addition to the research aspect of its activities, it should have a well-developed information center; obviously the information function would be fed by the research activities. Training would also be an obviously important function, and according to what we have already suggested, The Office would have an advisory department to give services, upon request, to both governments and private foreign investors.

ICSID (International Centre for Settlement of Investment Disputes) is today conducting some of the initial, basic, research work that needs to be done. It is compiling all legislation of its member countries on private foreign investment, beginning with whatever is said in each country's constitution. This, of course, will provide a first basis for comparative analysis of the actual characteristics (legal, financial, economic) of investments made. This work would provide the information necessary as a basis to move toward the harmonization of local differences in the treatment of MNCs (local legislation, antitrust, pricing, profit repatriation, taxation, and national business practices).

It would be essential that The Office, from its inception, excite the confidence of both developed and less developed countries. This can be accomplished only if The Office is regarded as an independent research and information center (which can also, eventually, provide training and advisory services) and if The Office is managed by a truly competent and well-balanced international staff, sharing responsibilities between the managing and deputy managing director, and sharing in the work of the research, information, training, and advisory departments. Otherwise there would be no chance for The Office to have any impact on the problems with which we want to deal, for The Office would simply be considered an additional instrument of rich countries or a forum for LDCs. The image of The Office at its inception, its organization and management, will be The Office's first contribution toward a better dialogue and understanding between MNCs and host countries.

In order to recommend the kind of organization that might emerge to fulfill the functions described, my suggestion would be to appoint an institution or a small group of individuals. The appointment might be made by the United Nations. This group should undertake a study designed to assess the existing resources in the fields of research, information, training, and advisory services—the areas, in my opinion, where the new international center should be active.

Since a number of institutions are at the present time performing one or another of these tasks, obviously the first thing to do would be to determine who is doing what and suggest possibilities for coordination or absorption of related efforts.

The group might also explore possible contributions from regional banks and regional economic organizations on this matter—and of course the possibility of utilizing ICSID (with or without amendment of the convention that created it).

In brief, the group that would be in charge of this first job of evaluating the existing situation should come up with some suggestions for the future organization that would best serve the research, information, training, and advisory purposes indicated previously. It should also make suggestions on procedural questions as to the best way to go about organizing such an enterprise. Finally, since the financing of The Office would be crucial for its activities and image of independence, the group should explore this very important aspect of the question.

FORMAL AND STRUCTURAL PROBLEMS
OF INTERNATIONAL ORGANIZATION
FOR CONTROL OF INVESTMENT
Detlev Vagts

My function here, as I understand it, is to flesh out the proposed international organization by raising some of the issues that would have to be addressed by any lawyer assigned the task of preparing the first draft of organizational papers for such a body. This task is complicated by the fact that this lawyer has not been given the clear mandate that, say, a business client telling him to form a corporation would lay down.

Several versions of an agency governing the multinational enterprise have been proposed, both here and elsewhere. Each would pose somewhat different problems for the technician. Thus I feel it necessary to step back a few paces and look at the context of the task I am asked to experiment with.

First of all, consider the supposed dangers posed by the multinational enterprise to the world community. These are derived essentially from the great power those enterprises are thought to possess. That power flows not from the barrel of a gun but from the long purses—the enormous assets and income flows—they possess. That slumbering power is given special thrust by the flexibility and determinations their managements can give to the task of protecting and furthering the interests of their employers. They can, to an increasing degree, ignore territorial boundaries and plan on a global basis. They can concentrate on comparatively narrowly defined financial and material goals, subject to computation and evaluation in precise accounting terms. They can make most decisions thus indicated quite swiftly, autocratically, and privately without extensive and time-consuming electoral or political processess. These characteristics make multinational enterprises seem overpowering particularly to smaller nations that cannot match them in money, flexibility, or speed. Their reactive alternatives seem to be limited to the crude measures of exclusion or confiscation that, while hurtful to the enterprise, also have harmful consequences to the nation's economic and diplomatic interests. Even the home countries of these corporations, with all the advantages of having a grip upon the corporate nerve centers, are beginning to show concern about the capacity to bring corporate activities into harmony with what governments perceive to be the national interest.

The specific areas in which the powers of the multinational enterprise are thought to cause dangers are various. The economic plans of nation-states can be disrupted where they run against the grain of corporate planning. If enterprises refuse to place their new plants where and when national programs call for them, or if they dismantle or reorganize them contrary to the government's will, the economy of a country, particularly a small one, can be seriously disrupted. The nation's capacity to formulate and carry out a monetary policy, including taxation and currency control elements, can be impared. As a result, a less developed nation may be frozen into a position of subservience as a producer of minerals or bananas. Even national political and military security may be thought to be threatened by the presence of an intractable alien body.

The situation appears somewhat analogous to the status in the United States around the turn of the century when nationwide corporations such as U.S. Steel and American Tobacco confronted state governments that were unable to muster the will or the power to regulate them effectively. The deduction from the analogy would, at its most simplistic, say that some agency such as an international commerce commission should from an international level enforce a body of rules in the international interest. However, matters do not translate easily from the national to the international level, and indeed ingenuity is required to effect any transfer at all. Let us recall one important difference: The impotence of the states was in large measure created not by economic facts but by the restraints on state action imposed by the federal constitution; these same restraints protected the national corporation from hasty, erratic, or destructive as well as logical and purposive state reactions in a way that international law does not. Another difference is that nations are still trying to conduct independent sovereign operations—military and diplomatic—whereas the states had surrendered those claims. This increases the area in which conflicts can arise.

Thus at the international level we must think of a variety of different approaches to the problem. These have different levels of intensity and complexity. Listing a number of these, roughly in order of ascending intensity, they are:

1. A strictly consultative organization.
2. One equipped with power to compel the production of information, to investigate, and to make reports.

3. One equipped with power to arbitrate disputes between nations that involve multinational enterprises or disputes between nations and enterprises.

4. One fortified with the power to make decisions that the member nations would be obliged to effectuate.

5. One with the authority to lay down regulations directly governing the conduct of enterprises and having enforcement powers to see that they are observed, perhaps through a chartering power.

Obviously, each of these organizational levels implies a different solution to the administrative problems we will go on to consider.

MEMBERSHIP AND POWER

A basic question is who should belong to the organization, accompanied by the issue of relative voting power. As for choosing among nations, the basic initial question is whether membership will be open to all countries or only to the capital-exporting countries. This is a basic problem for upon it hinges the question of whether this is to be an organization to work out problems between the North Atlantic countries and Japan or whether it will include countries at all levels of development. Following down one avenue we have an association of countries all involved with multinational enterprises in much the same way. While the United States has, by a significant margin, the largest number of multinationals, there are an appreciable number associated with each of the major European countries and Japan. There would be relative ease in obtaining agreement on many issues in this circle of countries; each would have some capacity to see the other's point of view because there is some chance that the situation would be reversed on another occasion. This is not to say that European countries will not tend to think of themselves predominantly as hosts and America as a home base, but some mutual understanding should develop, particularly as the organization matures in experience. This organization would compare in membership with the Organization for Economic Cooperation and Development (OECD), which has formed fairly consistent patterns of bilateral treaties—on taxation and establishment—that ease the way for foreign investment.

On the other hand, such an intrafamily arrangement would not touch the most sensitive and explosive conflicts, those in which the multinational enterprise becomes embroiled as a bridge across the large and growing gap between the developed and the less developed countries. Thus, to get at the really menacing problems one would have to include all countries involved with multinational enterprises. A close question would be the admission of communist countries; those that refuse categorically to deal with multinational enterprises have no impressive title to membership, but there are those, like Yugoslavia, that enter into arrangements with outside firms that, whatever their form, look very much like foreign investments. The case for admission for the latter is very strong, even if it would complicate discussions.

The number of countries thus rises to a substantial number, one that could make the organization an unwieldy parliamentary body. In that event it would be necessary to separate out some smaller representative body that could sit more constantly and conveniently. A question would arise as to whether each country would have an equal voice (as among the contracting parties to the General Agreement on Tariffs and Trade) or whether the vote should be weighted according to members' stake in the matter (as is the case with International Monetary Fund). If the measure used—assets invested by multinational enterprises within the territory—took account of the interest of the host governments, it would not be fairly vulnerable to the charge of overrepresenting the home countries. The measures used to establish the weighting need not be so precise as to create serious statistical problems.

Another set of problems would arise if the multinational enterprises themselves were admitted to membership. In some senses this unprecedented step would seem to be called for by the theory on which the organization is to be formed: That these enterprises have grown so large and nation-like as to be beyond the capacity of nations to govern them fairly and effectively. On the other hand, the sensitivities of many governments would be offended by the elevation of private entities, whom they have legal authority to regulate and tax within their domain, to sit alongside them in a deliberative body. They would add, perhaps with some element of exaggeration, that the home countries will speak for their corporate creatures as much or more than they deserve, and they might also warn that the enterprises are apt to be indirectly represented through their ties with members of the agency's bureaucracy. Membership by corporations would also raise difficult and unanswered questions about assessments, immunities, and the many other burdens and requisites of membership in international agencies. Thus membership by corporations would seem to be both politically unsalable and administratively unwarranted.

THE EXECUTIVE BRANCH OF THE ORGANIZATION

The more duties that are assigned to the multinational enterprise control agency, the more serious will be the problems of limiting the agency's bureaucracy and keeping it under control. International agencies concerned with economic matters have already found signs of elephantiasis, enhanced by overlap and duplication with their fellow agencies. The complexity and scope of the multinational enterprises are such that simply devising, managing, and monitoring a reporting system will call for a highly trained staff of managerial economists and accountants, supported by a clerical force of impressive dimensions. If the maintenance of surveillance in one corporative system is a task for a full department of specialists, the work of keeping an eye on 200 to 300 of them will be Herculean, especially if the policy and administration of the international organization is such as to provoke opposition and passive resistance on the part of corporate managements—as it probably would have to be if it were to have much chance of being effective.

To operate successfully, the organization would have to be manned with persons familiar with the corporate way of doing things, at first presumably with people who had in fact worked in multinational enterprises, or at the least had been educated in the same way. The odds are that such ex-managers would retain at least a general sympathy for the enterprises they were regulating and would have a bias toward their interests. Likewise, there would almost inevitably be a shortage of qualified personnel from less developed countries who understood foreign enterprises. If there also developed a pattern of bureaucrats being lured away by multinational enterprises, the tendency toward a complacent harmony between the regulated and the regulators might even exceed that protested in regard to U.S. regulatory agencies. The international politics surrounding major appointments to the executive branch are likely to become both devious and ferocious. Furthermore, there may not be a parliamentary or executive body coherent enough to impose its will on the machinery. All in all, the potential bureaucratic problems of an agency capable of regulating multinational enterprises seem unattractive and even menacing. They seem to push one in the direction of limiting the functions one would want to bestow on such an organization.

RELATIONS WITH THE NATION MEMBERS

The nature of the relations between the international organization and the member nations depends very much on the scope of the responsibilities assigned to it. If what is involved is merely a consultative assembly, the questions in this area are the standard, easily resolvable ones about the possession of legal capacity by the agency and its immunities, and those of its personnel, vis-à-vis the members. Once we get past that point into genuine administrative or adjudicatory issues, we start to encounter real and perhaps insuperable conflicts. If the organization's functions include the production of information about multinational enterprises, that will not by itself produce conflict with the national bodies or the tax, exchange control, and statistical agencies that are studying the same transactions. Indeed, some of them would doubtless be glad of the additional data and might relax their own efforts in the field and rely on the offerings of the control agency, which would have access to more sources than any national agency.

However, pressures would probably grow for the information demanded of enterprises to conform to the international norm; enterprises would become surly about providing other data and appeal to the central agency for relief from such oppression. The categories used for assembling the data would begin to have normative effects. The figure used as manufacturing costs, for example, would begin to be regarded as, at least prima facie, establishing the starting place, subject to a reasonable mark-up, for export prices including transfer prices. There would then be pressure on tax authorities to accept such prices in calculating the portion of an enterprise's income that would be taxable within given borders. The same could be true of calculations as to the value of technology transferred from one portion of the enterprise to another. Such international uniformity of measurement, even if necessarily somewhat arbitrary and mechanical, would immensely ease the administrative burdens on both multinational enterprises and administrators. The price of the ease, however, would almost inevitably be some surrender of national authority both in the demanding of information and in the uses to which it is put. In particular countries that feel they have enough leverage on multinational enterprises to extract what they need from them in any case may feel that the exchange is not worth the sacrifices. For countries deeply attached to confidentiality, even with respect to private records, the activities of international agents may prove irritating; some recalcitrant enterprises will doubtless prefer those countries as bases for their most private operations. Thus, even at this most simple level of internationalization, difficulties may well be expected.

If one moves up the scale to regulation, even of an indirect and precatory type, one enhances the risks that national sovereignties will feel affronted. If the venture into international regulation is to gain any support or even acquiescence from the enterprises themselves and more than lukewarm support from their home governments, the quid pro quo will almost certainly have to include some limitation upon the right of countries to exclude enterprises that comply with the agency's regulations. This result follows from all nation-level analogies, from the concept of international incorporation, from the example of treaties of establishment, and, most significantly, from the balance of interests involved. Even if international regulation is tight enough to protect the major perceived interests of the less developed countries vis-à-vis the multinational enterprises, they would find irksome the surrender of what has come to be regarded as a basic attribute of sovereignty. This would presumably be true even if the system permitted a wide range of factors to be presented by governments as acceptable grounds for barring a multinational applicant from entering, for the attribute of discretion, even arbitrariness, that has accompanied the sovereign right to bar applicants is precious to many governments, including some in highly developed countries. Even having to state reasons might be a shock to many governments. Fewer might be upset at the idea that they no longer had unconfined power to change the rules as to enterprises that they had permitted to establish themselves. Many legal systems that regard the initial authorization as an entirely discretionary act contain principles inhibiting interference with rights that have been duly acquired. Still those systems do authorize extensive interferences with established foreign investors, going even as far as nationalization. It would be hard to tolerate the presence of an outside agency with the authority to review and evaluate the justification for such action.

Alongside the host countries, the home countries would have to yield some of their authority if international regulation escalated to this regulatory level. This would mean surrender of the right to control trading and production activities of overseas subsidiaries—such matters as the trade of such corporation with hostile powers. On the whole, this might not be as irksome to home countries as corresponding incursions on the regulatory rights of host countries. Host countries have long had to exercise their overseas regulatory rights subject to contrary instructions on the part of the host countries—as the United States learned in the Fruehauf case and in various endeavors to enforce antitrust laws abroad. The United States might well regard it as a fair exchange if it lost these fragile and nonessential regulatory powers but was in turn relieved of the responsibility of protecting and defending these emigrant firms. That would depend very much on the confidence of the United States in the capacities of the new entity as well as the extent to which its already discernible tendencies toward concentration on internal problems increase and make it anxious to relieve itself of such foreign responsibilities.

If the agency undertakes functions of mediating or adjudicating conflicts between host countries and enterprises, the likelihood is great that some nations will regard this as entrenching on their sovereign rights. Here we can gain some guidance from past history. Particularly in Latin America, countries have sharply resented having their conflicts with foreign enterprises become an international matter. The whole history of the Calvo Doctrine revolves around this theme—that relations with enterprises from abroad were and are purely local matters. It is true that this resistance was directed at intervention by the investors' own governments, intervention that inevitably tended to be partisan on behalf of the investors and all too often became interwoven with the territorial and political ambitions of the intervening state. Mexico had several occasions to feel the weight of all these factors in combination. As a matter of theory, an international agency ought to be in a position to offer disinterested and impartial sources toward peaceful settlement. It is not at all clear, however, that this disinterestedness will, in the minds of host countries, counterbalance the perception that the agency is an outsider. There is evidence that the mere fact an agency is international does not remove its alien quality. While obliged to accept the advice of the IMF as a condition to receiving aid in the resolution of foreign exchange difficulties, countries have resented the outside intervention—a feeling that has been enhanced by a judgment that, whatever their formal separations and whatever their divorce from an individual creditor country, these institutions have an overall attitude of complicity with the creditor countries as a group. In short, a banking organization is going to think like a lender and investor, and will fail to appreciate the problems of a country that is poor and in debt but terribly anxious to forward its own national goals. The uniform failure of Latin American countries to respond to the World Bank's convention on the settlement of international investment disputes precisely illustrates this attitude. Whether a world organization can escape the contamination of this sort of relationship remains to be seen.

Thus as we ascend the scale of possible intensities of operation by an international agency, we begin to encounter more and more likelihood that nation-states will resent its intrusions into areas they regard as within their domestic jurisdiction. It seems entirely likely that the result will be an unfortunate dilemma: Any agency with enough power to make a meaningful contribution to the problem will have to be so powerful as to make unacceptable inroads upon cherished aspects of national independence.

THE AGENCY AND ITS INTERNATIONAL
COLLEAGUES AND RIVALS

A multinational enterprise agency would have to find its place in the midst of a member of bodies founded in the hope that they would bring some measure of coherence and rationality to international economic affairs. Each has an established position, a bureaucracy, and a commitment. Fitting a new body into this scene is not as easy as if there were a tabula rasa as in 1945. Within the United Nations itself there are various committees and agencies that concern themselves with studying and debating social and economic questions that intersect with the sphere of interest of multinational enterprises. Then there are separate international economic agencies. The General Agreement on Tariffs and Trade (GATT) is one example. Its function is to attempt to free international trade from the restrictions that the years of autarky saw the nation-states apply. Much of what multinational enterprises do is encompassed under this heading; an impressive proportion of the overseas trade of the United States is carried on entirely within multinational enterprise systems in the form of transactions between affiliated corporations. Had there been no GATT and had tariff and other barriers remained at prewar levels, the multinational enterprise movement could hardly have reached the pace it has. A new agency would, of necessity, have to deal with the trade of multinationals. So long as it did no more than monitor such transactions and collect statistics about them, the problems of overlap should be quite manageable. Even at a more advanced level, one at which the new agency found itself laying down general rules about trade transactions or mediating or arbitrating specific disputes, say about transfer prices and customs levels, the conflict would probably remain manageable. GATT is, after all, a very loose and flexible organization, some would say too flexible to be effective in difficult situations. It has passed many of its problems on, either to working parties constituted within its own regular framework or, as in the "chicken war," to an entirely ad hoc tribunal. GATT has accommodated itself to the European Economic Community, to the Canadian-American automotive parts agreement, and to many other developments. Doubtless it could make room for the multinational enterprise agency as well.

The International Monetary Fund (IMF) designed to maintain relatively free currency flows among countries, also operates in areas of great interest to the multinational enterprise. While in the absence of free trade in goods such enterprises might have proliferated even more tariff factories to surmount local barriers, they would have found it impossible to pursue a global strategy without a fair amount of assurance that they could move their money around to meet investment needs or, ultimately, the demands of their shareholders and investors. Thus the IMF has made it possible to rely on the great likelihood that payments for goods and services can be made, free of unexpected restraints. Likewise managements have not had to divert as much of their energy into hedging against shifts in exchange rates or working barter transactions as they would have had to do in the 1930s. These impacts of the IMF exist even though the Bretton woods Agreement specifically left to the nation—and not just the less developed ones—the unrestricted power to control flows of investment capital. An effective agency for coping with the multinational enterprise would have to deal with problems of currency transactions and with charges that enterprises were undermining national monetary systems by disguised currency exports, that they were reaping and repatriating exorbitant profits on their investments, and, on the other hand, that national currency allotment programs were disfavoring and stifling firms' development. At times there would plainly have to be coordination between the IMF and our hypothetical agency; if, for instance, the IMF were consulting with a country facing difficulties with its exchange practices, it would be useful to have the agency exerting pressure on multinational enterprises to align their policies with that of the IMF (and that of the World Bank) in order to help pull the country out of its crisis. Thus although there would have to be interactions at times between the IMF and the new agency, there seems to be no very great danger of intense jurisdictional disputes. On the whole the IMF operates at a national level one step removed from the corporation level at which the multinational agency would function.

The work of the agency would overlap in a number of ways the activities of the OECD. This body does not have as broad a membership base as the IMF and World Bank, being restricted essentially to capital-exporting countries. The OECD also does not have as extensive an authority, being limited fundamentally to investigating, reporting, and recommending. The subject matter of its deliberations is very much in parallel with that which would be attributed to the new agency: technology transfers, taxation, antitrust, and so forth. Of these areas, antitrust is one that is critical to any action in the multinational enterprise field since much of the power of multinational firms rests on their market position and since there is considerable mutual distrust of the policies and fairness of national antitrust agencies. OECD has not made dramatic progress in this area, but it is not clear that a new agency would do much better. If any of the areas in which OECD has been functioning should be assigned to a new multinational enterprise agency, it seems desirable to exclude OECD from them since there would be no advantage in duplicating responsibilities.

The comparison with these three agencies raises an acute question that goes to the very roots of the idea we are discussing here. Is it preferable to continue to divide up problems strictly according to their subject matter—that is, monetary or trade matters—or is there really a special advantage to having an agency that will be more limited in scope in that small enterprises will not be subject to its controls but broader in that it can roam around different classes of subject matter? Should the gap rather be filled by a new agency structured along subject matter lines? If the problem is basically that international investment, as distinguished from international trade, is not now subject to internationalized controls or persuasion, could it be better to set up an agency responsible for that subject matter? Or do the advantages of dealing only with a relatively limited number of regulatees outweigh these problems?

CONCLUSIONS

Judges who prepare opinions and lawyers who draft contracts
sometimes find that the exercise of spelling out the details of their
undertaking reflects back upon their views of the substance. In this
case a closer look at some of the specific problems that would be
implied in the design of a special agency to control multinational
enterprises tends to make me skeptical of the wisdom of the undertaking, at least to the extent that it would go beyond information-
gathering. I have encountered a rather general consensus that it
would be good to have more information—in fact, hardly any body
seems to have a bad word to say about information exchange. The
administrative and bureaucratic problems at such a level would be
minimized. Problems of conflict with and duplication of the efforts
of other agencies would be minimized. Still, there are a few caveats
to be noted. Facts are not simply objects lying there in nature waiting
to be discovered—a view sometimes unfairly attributed to Francis
Bacon. Facts are created by human minds that have decided something
is relevant and then go out to dig it out of or impose it upon nature.
Normative factors and assumptions underlie much of this. In arguments over costs and prices, one finds not just facts but concepts of
fairness and justice. The question of the transfer price to the Colombia
branch of a pharmaceutical multinational enterprise for a drug that
is the only one of seven studied in its laboratory to prove useful is not
a purely statistical one. One cannot answer it by counting the number
of guinea pigs sacrificed or the hours spent by technicians. One must
decide whether it is just to burden the successful product with costs
of the further experiments. Then one must decide whether sales in
Colombia should bear a pro rata share of those costs or whether it is
entitled to be regarded as a marginal cost market.

These are questions as to which U.S. and Colombian authorities
are sure to have different answers, not to be settled by mathematical
proof. If the multinational agency does make decisions as to how to
report such costs and prices, those decisions will be important. The
history of the accounting profession and of administrative agencies
shows that standard reporting methods, standard forms, and particularly condensory figures such as "earnings per share" exert a powerful influence on substantive decisions. Thus we should not deceive
ourselves into thinking that an institution devoted to information-
gathering will have no substantive consequences. Still, it may be
beneficial to start in this direction for much is to be gained by grap-
pling with these issues and starting to have people from different
parts of the world wrestle with them. Only by sustained intellectual
effort and questioning can one hope to impose any sort of order upon
this field.

*   *   *   *   *

COMMENT
Seymour Rubin

Detlev Vagts suggests that spelling out exactly how an agreed principle will be put into practice sometimes casts doubt on the validity of the principle. The point is a valid one; it is a reason why decision-makers of all sorts should be compelled to write their own statements in support of their decisions, rather than relying upon expert staffs whose plausibility sometimes covers up what should be obvious defects.

I am in complete agreement with Mr. Vagts that the agency he describes is demonstrated, by considering how it would work, to be an impossible dream—perhaps more accurately, an impossible nightmare. In my opinion, however, this does not demonstrate that no advance from the present disorderly if not anarchical situation is possible. It merely demonstrates, very convincingly, that if one is to try for a global organization that will attempt to wrestle with all the problems he describes as "really menacing," one will arrive at an unworkable organization—one with too many members to be effective, where members are concerned not only with the numerous questions between the developed, nonsocialist nations but also as between the developed and less developed, and as between the capitalists and the socialists, and in all areas of the world. Moreover, it is implied, although Mr. Vagts mentions the possibility of "merely a consultative assembly," that the organization would have "genuine administrative or adjudicatory" responsibilities, perhaps even regulatory responsibilities. At this stage, one easily arrives at a compilation of difficulties that, based on the reductio ad absurdum principle, convincingly shows the impossibility—and I would think the undesirability—of the entire enterprise.

However, I do not believe that this impeccable logic necessarily negates the desirability and feasibility of any kind of organizational or institutional movement. More modest institutional arrangements than a global organization with extensive administrative, research, and possibly regulatory functions can readily be envisaged. Charles Kindleberger and Paul Goldberg have suggested a GATT for Investment—a concept that seems to contemplate the making of certain rules that would then be assigned to a GATT-like organization for administration and supervision. Perhaps the analogy to GATT is not entirely fortunate, in these days when others are writing about the twilight of the GATT—or perhaps, to steal a phrase from John Evans, the GATTerdamerung. I have previously suggested that the GATT analogy seems to me inappropriate since the formulation of rules, which is what the General Agreement on Tariffs and Trade is, is the most difficult part of any enterprise seeking to define and deal with the numerous questions arising out of the growth and the economic if not political power of the multinational enterprises. I would prefer as a first step the organization of a forum, perhaps several forums, in which the problems and, one would hope, the possibilities of multinational enterprise might be discussed, with the rules built up in discrete areas, more or less problem by problem, until a body of agreed policies has been accumulated.

To illustrate, it seems to me desirable to distinguish between the quite disparate problems of multinationals in developed nations, and those they face in operations in the less developed world. These are sufficiently different so that analysis, and possible subsequent accommodation, is confused rather than assisted by lumping them together under the rubric of the problem of the multinationals, or even the problem of conflicts of sovereignty, or the problem of the economic power of the multinationals. What France fears in connection with a Fiat-Citroen merger, or a General Electric acquisition of Machines Bull, or even U.S. government ability to direct Fruehauf-France to violate the terms of a politically sensitive contract, is not necessarily what the developing countries are concerned with in their attempts to keep or put what they consider national resources into national hands. The similarity is the worry about control by a foreign direct investor; the differences arise out of the vast gap between the nature of the economies of developed and developing states.

Moreover, there are quite distinct kinds of issues represented under the general heading of the extraterritorial power of the multinationals. One is whether the multinational corporation can be a transmission belt for the policies of a foreign sovereign—as in the attempts by the United States, and sometimes other states, to extend their trading-with-the-enemy concepts to foreign subsidiaries of their own corporations. Another is the possibility that the multinationals, rather than obeying the wishes of their home states, may instead dictate state policies. Unfairly or not, some American corporations have been accused of being able to influence the foreign policy of the United States so as to interfere in governmental matters abroad. In regard to the use of the multinationals as a transmission belt, accommodations have already been reached and it would seem that further progress might be made, perhaps by a generalized agreement. With respect to the influence of the foreign direct investor on his government's policies, inability to ascertain the facts, the less open nature of any influence multinationals may have on their home governments, the politically charged atmosphere of accusation and denial may make accommodation more difficult.* But it does not seem impossible that progress also might be made here.

There are also the range of problems of a more legal nature involved in the various current proposals for some form of international company law. These range from the long-standing and, it would seem to an outside observer, not particularly successful attempts of the European Economic Community to create an EEC company law to the more ambitious projects of George Ball for a "Cosmocorp." Whatever the prospects, these suggestions deserve analysis on some basis other than that of isolated scholarship. Perhaps, within the framework of a consultative organization, comparative studies could usefully be organized on the reasons for, the difficulties with, and the prospects of such proposals. An interesting analogy presents itself to the current suggestions in the United States for a federal corporation law, which for large multistate enterprises would replace the present system of state corporation laws.†

Given the issues, it is my feeling that a consultative organization could perform a useful purpose. It would necessarily have limited and relatively modest objectives. For that reason, it would avoid many of the obstacles pointed out by Mr. Vagts. It might well have to be several organizations; one might deal with developed country relationships, another with problems of the multinational enterprise based in a developed nation and with subsidiaries in the less develpoed nations. Within the latter category there well might be distinctions on an area basis; part of the work might be largely legal, part economic. As a result, what I am talking about may be more a series of groups or committees—organized preferably within existing organizations—than one global organization, with such groups undertaking to coordinate their activities, perhaps through an overall committee of liaison. One can think of existing organizations that might harbor this sort of loose consortium of working groups: The OECD already has before its council a proposal for more and better coordinated work by its several committees; the Organization of American States might take on the

_____

*An interesting discussion is contained in Dennis M. Ray, "Corporations and American Foreign Relations," of the American Academy of Political and Social Science, September 1972, esp. pp. 85-92. See also Emilio Collado, "Economic Development Through Private Enterprise," Foreign Affairs, July 1963.

†Note the essential analogy of the national corporation as it developed in the United States in the 1880s and 1890s to the growth of the multinational corporation in recent years. See Charles Kindleberger, American Business Abroad (New Haven: Yale University Press, 1969), pp. 33-35.

responsibility for work on the relations between Latin America and the developed nations, bringing into that work its expertise on such enterprises as the Andean Pact with its private investment code, as well as the relations between the integration effort in Latin America, the development of indigenous capital markets, and the external investor. Other organizations might make useful contributions on the relevance of investment to transfer of technology. And so on.

What would be new in this rather nebulous scheme would be:

• The commitment to seek to identify the problems; to deal with them dispassionately; to examine them in a noncrisis atmosphere; to do this work cooperatively and in coordination; and to work out a series of informal or formal understandings, codes, agreements, or whatever to alleviate the tensions that seem to be growing as the multinational enterprises develop.

• Establishment by international agreement of a coordinative mechanism.

The proposal is not grandiose. Perhaps for that reason I believe it is feasible. If something of this sort were put into effect, at least a first, and I think an important, step toward common analysis and mutual understanding would have been taken, in an area in which such analysis and understanding are of ever-increasing importance.

*　*　*　*　*

COMMENT
Charles Kindleberger

I am a little embarassed by the occasional reference to the fact that I have suggested that we need international rules for the international corporation, a sort of GATT. I do not really feel very strongly about this: I just threw out the suggestion.

The international corporation is a subject about which people are ambivalent. Peru will nationalize the International Petroleum Corporation one day, and advertise in the New York Times the next urging foreign investors to come on down and put their money into Peru.

We all feel ambiguous on the question. I do not want to go very far, and especially I do not want to disagree very deeply with Detlev Vagts, as to whether there should be an international agreement, or an international forum, or an international information center on international enterprise, and whether it should be in the UN, the OECD, or wherever.

Despite this lack of passion, it would seem to me useful to obtain some international agreement on a few simple principles for dealing with international enterprise, and then to deal, in an international body or forum, on practical questions as they arise. The principles would be simple, such as the elimination of overlapping and underlapping jurisdiction in dealing with international firms; a harmonization of tax rules, both rates and definitions, in the long run, or harmonization to eliminate investment not related to real economic values but to distortion, such as too little investment because of double-taxation, or too much and in the wrong directions because of tax havens; a dovetailing of rules about monopoly; and agreement that governments not use their national corporations to intervene in the jurisdictions of other governments.

The matter is not pressing. I see no strong necessity to produce such a basic agreement or machinery to build up a body of common law on its basis tomorrow. But we ought to work in this direction.

In addition to the overlap-underlap and the intrusion issues, we ought to agree that there is no compulsion to use markets when they do not function efficiently, and that it cannot be important to maintain competition within national boundaries but unimportant and even desirable to permit monopoly beyond the border.

I oppose, for example, the American attitude which holds that antitrust is a vital consideration as regards the U.S. market, and then accepts the Webb-Pomerene Act permitting American exporters to organize into cartels for selling abroad. Or the first decision of the European Court of Justice which said that the rules of the European Coal and Steel Community prevented price discrimination within the community but not between the community on the one hand and the rest of the world.

Admittedly we have a serious problem here. There are two rules in economics regarding price discrimination. One says that firms should make as much profit as they can, and the other says that they should not discriminate in price. When markets can be separated, and when each market has a different elasticity, a firm maximizes its profits by charging a higher price in the market with the lower elasticity. With perfect competition and infinitely elastic demand curves, there is no conflict. In the real world, however, the question is which rule prevails.

Economists are rendered unhappy by such a conflict. Lawyers tend to seek the rule of reason. But I have not heard the rule of reason mentioned by lawyers at this conference.

The economist's variant of the rule of reason is "workable competition." Pure or perfect competition is a will o' the wisp. But to apply the rule of reason, or to determine what is workable competition, we need a forum that looks at particular cases.

The forum probably should not be the OECD because it is not open to the less developed countries (LDCs). I doubt that the LDCs would want to join an international body concerned with multinational enterprise. On the whole, they are unwilling to discuss the issue of nationalization and compensation for nationalization. There is a wide gulf in attitudes, and in these circumstances it is idle to try to get divided parties into a single body, as they cannot agree.

No, opposite to my view that it is desirable to create an international forum among the developed countries, with agreement on a few principles and readiness to sit in judgment on cases as they are brought up by corporations or governments, is the view that with respect to the LDCs it is important to get governments out of the business. I should like to see the United States stop providing subsidies, insurance, and guarantees for investment in LDCs. The U.S. government has stopped sending in the Marines to collect debts, and stopped invoking the Hickenlooper amendment in periods of dispute. It is time to get the investors' government out all the way. I see no gain from having the issues internationalized. I would rather have them—if you will excuse the barbarism—privatized. Investors and host governments should work out such arrangements as they can, knowing the risks on both sides, without the paternalistic intervention of the developed country government.

Moreover, I see no gain from new gimmicks like planned disinvestment, as suggested by Albert Hirschman and Paul Rosenstein-Rodan. To plan today to liquidate an investment fifteen or twenty years from now at a price agreed upon today calls for better calculations of what a future equilibrium price will be than economists are able to provide. We are wrong on prices over five years in international commodity agreements; what an investment will be worth three or four times longer in the future is even less knowable. And the attempt to agree on a price today is dysfunctional, setting up disastrous incentives. The company will want to make sure that the assets are worth no more than the agreed price, and preferably less. The host government will apply pressure in the opposite sense, to ensure that the assets are worth as much as the price or more. When the end is in sight, both will start wrangling. The prime example is the action of the Venezuelan government in appointing conservators to safeguard oil properties on which the concessions lapse in 1985.

While I find these disinvestment arrangements unlikely to work, there is something to be said for the less developed countries' attempts—in the Andean Pact and in Southeast Asia—to limit competition among themselves in attracting foreign investors, so as not to erode their tax bases and find themselves all in the same relative position after competing, all having lost out to foreign investors through offsetting concessions. These regional cartels make sense for the LDCs, but I doubt they are ready to join a worldwide GATT for international investment.

My idea is that such an international organization should be open to all countries, but none should be pressured into joining against its will.

Finally, let me say a word about Jack Behrman's proposal for a world body to handle all trade, investment, research, and development problems at once, on the basis of efficiency and equity, not to mention equitable transfers from the rich to the poor. I believe in comparative advantage and the assignment problem. The assignment problem states that you do not try to solve all problems with a single weapon, but assign weapons to targets for which they are best suited.

My interest in the international corporation is one of effective resource allocation. I do not believe that the international corporation should try to correct inequities in world income distribution, or be used to assuage political anxieties, or strive to achieve worldwide political participation. Economic instruments have economic purposes, and political instruments political purposes. It is a mistake as a rule to mix them. To construct one hybrid world organization to solve all economic, political, and equity problems with one solution is romantic, as is belief in snake oil as the cure for every ill of man or beast.

The experience of the Concorde, ELDO, ESRO, and CERN is not reassuring. If we try to work out agreements in trade and investment problems that make each country in the world happy on equity and political grounds, we end up with trade and investment solutions like those in agriculture, where equity-political-cultural considerations dominate economic ones and inefficiency reigns supreme. If you want to feel badly about nationalistic solutions, look at agriculture, and if you want to feel especially badly, contemplate sugar. Sugar is the worst commodity in the world from the point of view of efficient resource allocation. Participation has dominated efficiency. Autonomy reigns supreme, and the hell with efficiency. It is a disaster.

* * * * *

COMMENT
Jack N. Behrman

In reply to Charles Kindleberger, I might say that I agreed with him as long as he was analyzing, but he lost me when he started preaching. Politics, of course, is the art of compromise in the fields of economics, sociology, science, technology, and so forth. His comment that politics should be left to the politicians and economics to the economists in essence is a reductio ad absurdum.

Such a statement implies that we would leave war to the generals, genetic changes to the biologists, and the problem of 500 dialects in India to the linguists. Of course investment is a social and political phenomenon—witness the fact that high-rise apartments have increased the crime rate proportionately with the number of stories off the ground, increasing the need for police protection. In addition, investment in automobiles means that we are moving metal—a very inefficient way of moving people—which involves sociological concepts of mobility, individualism, and individual power, each affecting the sense of community among people and involving an increase in rootlessness. Finally, political decisions affect the creation of infrastructure, such as roads, which can attract different industries.

Of course, economics was historically called political economy and developed out of an ethical concept of man's purpose and progress. The idea that economics can provide technical and a-ethical solutions to critical problems is the basis for increasing comment that economists are irrelevant for the problems the world is facing today. For example, the extension of special drawing rights involves both equity and participation problems: equity as concerns the in distribution, and participation as concerns who decides the distribution.

The problems the world is now facing include problems of sharing and the benefits of growth, which will be exacerbated by any diminution in the rate of total world growth. They also include a sharing in directing the growth—that is, the decision as to what should be produced to meet man's needs and desires. Not all these decisions are appropriately made in a market on the basis of individual desires; they also involve political measures for the benefit of the community in terms of its present needs and its projected future.

To achieve man's goals, no institution is sacrosanct nor removed from adaptation or control. As to the multinational enterprise, it is likely to mutate before it matures.

CONCLUSIONS

22

ROUNDTABLE DISCUSSION
Seymour Rubin, William Rogers,
Lincoln Gordon, Philippe de Seynes,
Kurt Biedenkopf,
and Don Wallace, Jr.

OPENING STATEMENT by Seymour Rubin

One of the slogans that goes around the world is that there is nothing that can stand in the way of an idea whose time has come. Nothing in that slogan indicates that there is necessarily merit in the idea whose time has come. And I have sometimes felt that the various propositions put forward with respect to international organizations, to do something in connection with multinational enterprise, are an idea of this sort.

Nonetheless, a sufficient amount of respectable authority exists for the proposition that some kind of international organization supplement should be put together. So I think one should address oneself to the proposition that perhaps something might be done in the way of international organization beyond that existing at the present time.

Here I think it is desirable to note the valuable suggestion of Luis Escobar that a survey be made of all the existing sources of information in operation at the present time, under the aegis of the United Nations and United Nations organizations like UNITAR (United Nations Institution for Training and Research).

What could or should such an organization do? The discussion here has indicated that the information and training functions most appeal to the majority. It seems to me that information is not a commodity that one mines, takes out, and distributes. It requires a certain amount of analysis. I have in mind the vast amount of information that pours into every foreign office in the world and goes directly into wastepaper baskets or, what is worse, into large file cabinets and therefore contributes to the paper pollution of the world. It is, I suppose, one of our major problems of pollution. Information must be used if it is to be of any particular utility.

Given this kind of situation, and given the vast discrepancies between the developed countries on the one side and the less developed countries on the other, it seems to me that an organization we might reasonably talk about must be a rather informal organization, perhaps no organization at all.

Perhaps it could just be an agreement that there would be some kind of coordination of the information-gathering, the trading, the other activities of the various international organizations presently engaged in some work in this field.

Let us terminate this conference with the so-called roundtable discussion.

STATEMENT by William Rogers

First a comment with respect to the restrictive trade practices discussion. I have been gratified that this group has spent so much time on that subject. I have written on the relevance of antitrust or restrictive trade practice considerations to the problems of the relationship of the international corporations to LDCs. It has been my judgment for some time that a number of the compunctions and apprehensions that the LDCs have demonstrated with respect to foreign investment have been fears as to the excessive and overweaning power that foreign investment can bring into what are ordinarily not very well structured and not highly competitive markets. And the consequence of that often is, at least in the eyes of the concerned host country, the suppression of local enterprise, primitive as it may be.

I have long felt that more effective programs within the LDCs, antitrust, for example, along the lines that we understand it in the United States, would go far to ameliorate some of the concerns these countries have displayed with respect to particular foreign investment. I think that still is true, and I am delighted that this conference has spent much time on that aspect. However, I think that the basic problem is not going to be the organization of an international regime for antitrust—I regard that as quite unlikely and unreal at this stage. The really important work will be harmonization, as Charles Kindleberger has described it, the avoidance of both overlap and underlap. As anybody who has been working in the antitrust field for the last ten years knows, the problems of overlap and underlap are really quite serious at this stage of the game, and will grow more serious as the affronts to national competitive values by international activities of multinational corporations increase.

I would now like to move into some broader perspectives. It seems to me that the two really successful institutions on the world scene today are the nation-state and the corporation for profit. All the rest, at least in Kissingerian terms, can be discounted as lacking power and consequence. And again to oversimplify, it is the nation-state that monopolizes political power and it is the corporation for profit that monopolizes economic power. The two are relatively un-controlled except to the extent that the corporation for profit is oc-casionally regulated by the nation-state. Of course, that regulation is only limited to the small patches controlled by each respective nation-state. A good deal of this conference has been dedicated to the proposition that the mediation between these two institutions can be improved, their capacity to cooperate and continue to conduct the world's business can be enhanced, and the conflict between them can be reduced, and indeed I think we all want such conflict to be reduced.

I think this suggests one point, and you may take it as "Rogers' Rule," that we will not see any effective new forms of regulation or control of international investment, or of other practices, until this is regarded as in the interests of both institutions. Furthermore, I think that the day is coming when this will be regarded as in the inter-ests of both institutions. To work out some harmonizations of national regimes, as Charles Kindleberger pointed out, may be on the way with respect to antitrust. It certainly is overdue in certain tax areas. Finally, some techniques for avoiding competition between incentives offered by various LDCs may also inspire an effort to harmonize. But it seems to me that harmonization, control, and regulation, in whatever form, will come only when they are regarded as in the inter-ests of both the corporation for profit and the nation-state. I think that observations made at this conference raise some interesting questions about the future of these two institutions.

One need not spend too much time detailing the aspects of a corporation for profit, and the consequences that flow from the fact that its mandate is limited to economic efficiency. The fact of the matter is, both the nation-state and the corporation for profit may appear less and less satisfactory to the world community as we begin to face problems that take on more and more comprehensive and global character: the environment, the problems of overall growth, and particularly the rationing of energy, minerals, and other resources.

STATEMENT by Lincoln Gordon

Much of the dialogue in the literature, in prior conferences, and I suppose behind the inspiration for this conference, comes from the cliché Raymond Vernon made into the title of his book, Sovereignty at Bay. I was very skeptical of that title when I first saw it, and I was amused when a student of Raymond Vernon pub-lished in Fortune a review entitled "The Multinational Corporation

259

at Bay." In teaching about this subject, I have found myself constantly impressed by the fact that sovereignty is not doing so badly, and that rumors of its demise have been distinctly premature.

I did want to make one specific point in defense of an idea that was attacked rather vigorously by Piero Sella on behalf of the World Bank, and then by Ambassador Martin. And that has to do with the question of what kind of useful role the World Bank, and also the regional banks, might play in one aspect of this field.

My suggestion was that they might play a role in information-gathering; obviously that would not be an exclusive task. Second, I suggested—at least in international investments in less developed countries where the World Bank and regional banks participate in the financing through loans or participation in equity—that they make a formal analysis of the potential benefits from the investment and the way these benefits are to be divided.

The World Bank in particular, and the regional banks, which have copied a good many of its analytical methods, have put a great deal of money and intellectual talent into refining analyses of public investments. I do not myself regard all of those refined methods as necessarily constituting truth, but for the reasons that Detlev Vagts has suggested, they do constitute prestige and sanctified wisdom. It seems to me that, despite the observations Ambassador Martin made about the actual or apparent bias of the World Bank as essentially an instrument of the developed countries, at least in these particular cases its role comes closer to being a neutral role than anybody else's. Neutral in the sense that its charter and its business is development, and I think one should not underestimate the extent to which the management and officers of the World Bank in particular have managed over the years to come to be regarded as formally institutionalized champions of the cause of development of their less developed member institutions. They want financial security for their own participation, but they presumably want the proposal to be a good economic proposition.

If the World Bank and regional banks are engaged in that kind of analysis and accept it as a regular charge, it seems to me that the judgments expressed at least tacitly by their participation in financing, are a possible positive contribution, despite the objections that have been raised. I think particularly of investments in the extractive industries.

My last point is that I have been struck by the wisdom of the remarks that any issues of international control in this field really do not break down very well by object, the object in this case being the multinational corporation; they break down far better by function.

In regard to less developed countries, I am impressed by all kinds of needs for improvement in international organizations dealing with various developmental issues. My hope would be that existing institutions do make it a point to systematically include the potential role of the multinational corporations in their scope of exploration. This is something that has not always been done, and it seems to me that they do have a lot to contribute to any of the functions concerned with development with which the international community is charged.

STATEMENT by Philippe de Seynes

The comment of Lincoln Gordon, his particular proposal, and the allusion he made to the respectability that goes with certain international institutions is, I think, an important one. I have had the privilege of dealing with individuals from multinational companies in the last three or four years, as we developed our activities in the United Nations. And it seems to me there is something like what the sociologists call "felt need," which might be described as a need for legitimacy or legitimization. It is very difficult to know where it comes from, but probably from the extraordinary attempts at adaptation these companies have been subject to. I think the desire to come closer to the United Nations is perhaps not always just functional but has something to do with the idea of getting into what is considered "respectable society." I hope that we can continue this dialogue. If one considers the UN as a sort of generalized ombudsman, not for dealing with specific cases but for voicing apprehension and finding, in a very general way, certain areas of reconciliation, then perhaps the multinational companies will be considered less predators and more as forms of social organization in the modern world. In this very general way and without being at all specific, I think some institutionalization in this area could be of benefit. I do not say that it is easy.

Second, since Charles Kindleberger has sharpened the issues, I will follow him. Our experience in developing countries shows that there is growing hesitation between microeconomic efficiency and macropolitical organization, if I may use that sort of jargon. And while the tradeoffs there are not really easy, I think they are a reality of life. We see that in certain countries the problem is not so much efficiency as organization capable of finding both an equilibrium and a way of progressing for that society. I think the problems as stated by Jack Behrman are very relevant.

One point that must be mentioned is that the calculus of economic efficiency is one of the most difficult tasks when it comes to multinational corporations. When it comes to such questions as pricing, rates of return, balance of payments, and so on, statements made in these respects are almost universally unreliable, and certainly this is not a field where one can hope to be very normative. But one can hope to give certain tools of analysis to parties that lack those tools. The contest then becomes one of forces, but at least now it is done with greater knowledge than would otherwise be the case.

I would agree with Mr. Kindleberger that we should not rush into decisions and institutional arrangements, but I think there is absolutely no danger that this will happen. I think we have some idea of the maturation process of international agreements right now. But I would have some reservations about John Evans' suggestion that we should wait for the crisis before we start working.

Finally I would concur that there is a growing area where problems will have to be attacked globally. There is one big chance of being able to pursue a global policy in the interest of mankind in the question of the seabed, although this will have some effect of disruption on markets and resources, and might tend to increase the need for a wider area of international planning in the field of resources.

STATEMENT by Kurt Biedenkopf

I would like to start off with a comment connected to what William Rogers said about the two institutions that have proven to be of consequence, namely, the nation-state and the corporation for profit. I would like to include a third one that has been mentioned at this conference, namely, the labor union. If you define the relevant organizations as those holding power and capable of exercising that power, the labor unions will have to be included.

During the last couple of years the labor unions, both in the United States and increasingly in Europe, have been the organizations pushing the issue of multinational corporations. Now if the "Rogers' Rule" is correct—that we will only have regulation in this area if both powerful institutions, namely the nation-state and the corporation for profit, find it in their interest to have such regulations—it is quite possible that the labor unions will function in some way as a catalyst and will force both to agree on some kind of regulation.

We find within the scope of the international labor movement the creation of international organizations, and I am tempted to mention the parallel that has been drawn between the development of the multinational corporations internationally, and the development of the corporation within the United States. I think the same applies to the labor union movement. Within the United States the labor unions followed the corporations west, and found a need to organize in new markets occupied by the corporations as they moved west in order to retain their power. Right now the labor movements are doing the same thing at the international level, since they find the corporation moving beyond the nation-state. The labor unions so far have been entities within the nation-state because their autonomy was guaranteed by the legal system of the nation-state. Labor unions now find themselves confronted with the necessity of international organization and they are using pretty much the same tools as the multinational corporations, with the one significant difference that they cannot use private property as a vehicle of control. To substitute for this, they are entering into contracts based on the autonomy granted to labor movements in practically all the larger industrialized states.

I was impressed by the clear distinction made at this conference between the problems of direct investment in developed countries, and in less developed countries. I think this is a significant difference and must be kept in mind when analyzing the problem, and here again analysis as well as the effort toward regulation should be directed not at the object but at the functions.

The functions of direct investment of multinational corporations in developed countries and less developed countries are distinctly different. I would agree with Mr. Rogers that the antitrust aspect of the problem is important. However, I am not sure whether the position of the multinational corporation in less developed countries can be handled successfully through the application of antitrust rules, because of the very reason that Secretary Rogers has pointed out: These countries do not have well-developed economies and hence do not have the ability to apply well-developed antitrust regulations. So the question arises: Who will be the attorney representing the less developed countries' interests in respect to the application of antitrust? I think that here we have a situation where the industrialized countries can offer some kind of development assistance by applying antitrust to situations such as the exportation of oligopoly into less developed countries by the multinational corporations.

In conclusion, I would again like to direct myself to something Mr. Rogers pointed out. He doubted whether the nation-state and the corporation for profit will really be the vehicles for future development. As to the nation-state I would not want to comment, but I would like to comment on the corporation for profit. As we know, the corporation for profit still turns on the idea of private property and production facilities, and the control that goes with shareholding. The multinational corporation seems to me to be the vehicle to extend control to third parties and third countries by way of recognizing the control that goes with property. It is not totally impossible to conceive that this control can be transferred or changed; perhaps investment in less developed countries could be connected with control only for a certain period of time. I think one of the less developed countries' major objections to foreign investment is the fact that it means permanent foreign control over the investment, even after the transfer of technology and know-how and the return of the invested capital profits have been completed. The less developed countries feel that the retention of control after the profit has been realized is no longer justified.

I could envision a development where multinational corporations put more emphasis on the service that goes with transfer of technology and capital into less developed countries. I am not sure whether this will happen; maybe it would in a competitive investment market. Therefore, I think it is essential to maintain a competitive situation in less developed countries, because only if we have a competitive situation can we hope that new institutional vehicles to solve the problems will develop. It is, after all, the competitive process from which we expect the initiative for development of new institutions.

I would concentrate on maintaining this competitive situation also as far as international regulation is concerned because I think that if you regulate the multinational corporation as it is, you will create a vested interest in the multinational corporation on the part of the regulators. Then the regulators will be the last to permit changes in the institution.

STATEMENT by Don Wallace, Jr.

There has been some debate as to whether the idea of this conference is timely, or indeed has merit. I have the feeling that we may be talking about an idea whose time has not yet come, rather than one that has come but is not of merit. Philippe de Seynes referred to a felt need, and that is where I come out in my own mind: I am torn between real skepticism and some active enthusiasm and interest. There is a feeling about this subject but I do not believe it has reached the level of an idea yet. John Evans said we were looking for a problem; in fact, we are trying to define the problem.

What we have been doing is considering a whole range of problems under what Mr. de Seynes has called a normative aspect. I think this has been valuable because it pulls one out of the rut of debates as to whether private investment is good or bad, or what its contribution to development will be. I come away with the impression that something modest ought to happen. The question will remain whether that will be a start on something less modest, or whether that will be the end of it. One way to find out is by doing something modest.

We have considered at length whether one should deal with the developed and developing countries together or separately. I think a technical point we might want to examine in years to come, not only in this area but in other areas as well, is whether international efforts should deal exclusively with nation-states, or whether they should deal with private actors such as the multinational enterprises, and the unions of which Kurt Biedenkopf has spoken. It is interesting that so many people have accepted the lawyers' assumption that international organization must be international or interstate. I think that is a point we might want to think about, especially if we are talking about the provision of information.

It has been suggested that multinational corporations might submit forms to an international organization. But it is quite uncustomary for the citizens, the subjects, of nation-states to deal directly with an international body, although there are some analogies, for example in Intelsat and in the International Labor Organization. I think this is really one of the interesting questions in this area.

One wonders what the role for lawyers will be in the general area defined by this conference. I have been asked to review Raymond Vernon's book, Sovereignty at Bay, and I have a title for my review: "Lawyers at Bay?" Certainly there are technical issues for the lawyers. One that has not been mentioned goes to the investment protection issue rather than the matter of an overall control regime. It has been raised in the United States by a case called Sabatino, with which all American lawyers are familiar and about which they have probably written almost as much as economists have written about the multinational corporation.

In Sabatino, the Supreme Court of the United States said it would not look at the question of what was an appropriate standard of compensation for an expropriation abroad, in this case in Cuba, because it was a court in the world's principal capital-exporting nation and would therefore be so distrusted that it would not pass on the matter. The action of Cuba was said to be a political matter, an act of state, that the court would not review. Why, rather than duck the issue, should not U.S. courts define a more moderate, middle-of-the-road standard of compensation and begin to move away from the prompt, adequate, and effective compensation standard, which is concluded to be the standard of capital-exporting countries? So, too, in the contract area, the courts might begin to move from the Latin formalisms of pacta sunt servanda and clausula rebus sec stantibus toward a more flexible scheme of renegotiation. I think that this sort of action could help.

Finally, in their concluding observations, William Rogers and Philippe de Seynes have touched on a key point that did not come out before. I agree that we live in a world of a kind of double laissez-faire. A laissez-faire in economics, which I tend to believe in, and also laissez-faire in politics, namely the laissez-faire of the nation-state. This world, as Mr. Rogers suggested, is faced with a whole set of new issues. We have talked about growth and redistribution of income on a new and really massive scale. And what of the whole problem of industrial and economic planning, something the United States has to some extent inflicted on many developing countries, but not on itself.?

There are some who think that sooner or later planning must be done on a coordinated and global basis, and this set of issues is not unrelated to the issues considered at this conference. If we do not consider these issues this year, then we should consider them at least by ten years from now, the date Jerome Levinson mentioned as possibly more timely for this conference. Because the nation-states and the industrial corporations, and perhaps the unions to a lesser extent, are powerful and do have an impact not only on the extent of growth but also on its shape, character, and style.

And I would think that at some point someone is going to have to look at these matters, and I do not believe that GATT or the IMF or the World Bank has. But I would think that perhaps someday the public international organizations of the world would be concerned with this question.

*   *   *   *   *

COMMENT
R. Krishnamurti

On the suggestion that the developing countries should enact laws on restrictive business practices, I would like to point out that this is not such a simple solution. Very few developing countries, among them some Latin American and Asian countries such as Brazil, Mexico, Argentina, Colombia, India, and Pakistan, have enacted restrictive business practices legislation. Most of them are of recent origin, and very little knowledge or experience of the administration of these laws is available. There is hardly any case law.

The great majority of the developing countries do not have any competition legislation, and it is not realistic to recommend to them that they should all enact such legislation on any particular model. If the developing countries wish to enact competition legislation, such legislation would vary from country to country in its scope and objectives. These laws would be influenced by such factors as the level of economic development, the degree of private enterprise, the role of foreign enterprise in development, the concentration of economic power and wealth within the country, and, above all, the attitudes and policies of the country concerned toward private investment both at home and abroad. In these circumstances it would be difficult to recommend any one model or pattern of legislation. UNCTAD has the subject under study.

*   *   *   *   *

COMMENT
Edward Korry

I would like to comment about a misunderstanding, it appears, over my use of the term "market forces." By that term, I include political as well as economic factors. I am thinking of the processes and forces by which an equalization of bargaining power is reached in order to achieve what Philippe de Seynes described as "an integrated world society." That is why I persist in my optimism when I consider the interplay of the political and the economic.

Those who say the world is becoming more nationalistic and regard it negatively in political terms do not perceive that this could be a constructive step toward integrated world society. Power that was limited to a few superpowers is being dispersed and thus adding to the diversity of mechanisms that can equalize the bargaining process.

There are five major centers of power today in the world and others are in the process of evolving. Some observers have pointed out that a good many of the so-called less developed countries are already quite capable of defending themselves in a bargaining situation. Moreover, one should distinguish between the number of LDCs and the populations of individual LDCS. Brazil, Mexico, Argentina—those are the big tickets in Latin America.

The countries with the thorniest problems are the small and intermediate ones with limited resources, small populations, and particular problems of one type or another. In some instances, such countries have begun to identify the factors that affect their development and the flow of resources they need.

The Andean Group, for example, did not come into being primarily to deal with MNEs. It emerged because Brazil and Argentina were major powers in South America. The smaller countries wanted a balance to the weight of those two. A market had to be created, a market large enough to sustain industries. The dimension of that potential market provoked new relationships with the MNEs. We should not be discouraged by this sorting out of essential factors, this move toward equalization of "market forces." It is encouraging.

Nationalism certainly was behind the internationalism of the United States. We never proclaimed it, but now it is out in the open. This is a healthy phenomenon. The fact that some MNEs engaged in political activities in LDCs was well known. Now it is in the public print. That too is healthy. It is a cause for optimism.

Similarly, the acceptance by socialist countries of the superiority, in many ways, of the packages MNEs can offer must surely have an effect on their own perceptions of their societies, of their internal organizations, and of what will be required in the future to make their societies more efficient. That too gives me cause for optimism.

INDEX

223; markets, 24, 32, 38, 53, 56, 63; market institutions, 92; movements, 61, 111, 130, 183; outflows, 34, 46, 66, 67; private, 30; public, 225; receiving countries, 141; repatriation, 116, 379; restrictions, 42

Capital flows, 23, 32, 45, 228: inward capital flow restrictions, 45; long-term, 47; official, 30; outward capital flow restrictions, 45; short-term, 34

Cartegena Agreement on Common Treatment of Foreign Capital, Trademarks, Patents, Licensing Agreements and Royalties (Andean Code), 82, 101, 117, 175, 199

Castro, Fidel, 164

CECLA (Comision Especial de Coordinacion Latino Americano), 162

Central American Common Market, 162, 183, 194

Central Bank, 32, 42, 99

Cerro Copper Company, 166

Charter of the Economic Rights and Duties of States, 120

Chateau de la Muette, 57

Chile, 91, 95, 107, 111, 116, 117, 148, 149, 152, 159, 164, 165, 166, 167, 169, 196, 213

China, 124, 153, 161, 184

CIAP (InterAmerican Committee for the Alliance of Progress), 158; Annual Country Reviews, 154

CICYP (Inter American Council of Commerce and Production), 154

Colombia, 111, 116, 117, 128, 129, 152, 196, 245, 266

Commission on International Trade and Investment Policy, 87

Committee of 20, 248

Companies: American-based, 77; foreign-based, 76, 77; foreign-owned, 185; international, 158; international holding, 185; locally owned, 185; national, 54, 55; sister, 53, 56; U.K., 217; U.S., 217

Concorde, 252

Conferences, 4, 5, 8; Düsseldorf 1973, 88, 202, 258, 264, 266; on International Trade Organization Charter, Havana 1948, 152

Conglomerates, 53, 55, 56

Copper, 166; companies, 166; technology, 167

Cosmocorp, 248

Cruft, Edgar, 93

Cuba, 147, 148, 149, 161, 164, 215, 265

DAC (Development Assistance Committee of the OECD), 110, 154, 158, 217

Danish Kronor, 41

Defense, 63, 67, 347

Delaware, 64

Detroit, 60

Deutsche mark, 31

Devaluations, 34

Development, 68, 127, 222, 261; aid, 42; finance, 30; finance institutions of developed countries, 117; industrial, 187, 194; LDC, 82; local, 187; national, 187; objectives, 204; regional, 189; resource, 189

Disinvestment, 8, 9, 166, 180, 251; formulae, 167; 174; voluntary, 166

Dollar devaluation, 35

Dominican Republic, 164

Dumping, 26

Dunlop-Pirelli, 64

ECOSOC (Economic and Social Council), 121, 126, 163, 221

Ecuador, 91, 116, 117, 128

ELDO (European Launcher Development Organization), 252

Electronics, 185, 192

Employment, 45, 53, 76, 205

IFC (International Finance Corporation), 131
IMF (International Monetary Fund), 42, 44, 47, 238, 242, 243, 244, 266
India, 111, 116, 187, 253, 266
Indochina, 190
Indonesia, 111
Industries: basic, 187; foreign dominated, 107; key, 191, 194; national security, 190; resource based, 107
Inflation, 6, 60, 63, 149
Intelsat, 265
Interest: Equalization Tax, 34; of foreign investors, 207; rates, 61, 62; restrictions, 61
International: agencies, 5, 9, 27; Code of Investment, 139, 140; Company Law, 248; financial institutions, 92, 137, 139, 140; 170; Industrialization Institute, 191; Labor Movement, 262; law, 207, 236; law commission, 137; pricing behavior, 19; private banks, 155; Registry or clearinghouse, 85; Reinsurance Program, 139; Textile Agreement, 192
International Association for Research in Income and Wealth, 200
International Center for the Settlement of Investment Disputes (ICSID), 76, 135, 136, 137, 139, 140, 155, 233, 234; convention, 140, 155; secretariat, 140
International Chamber of Commerce, 158, 225
International Chemical Workers, 59
International Council of Copper Exporting Countries, 81
International Labor Movement, 59
International Labor Organization (ILO), 265
International Monetary Fund (see IMF)
International Monetary System, 60
International Petroleum Corpora-

tion, 249
International Trade Organization (ITO), 76, 144; Articles 11 and 12 of the ITO Charter, 144
Investment, 23, 24, 53, 68, 202, 208, 243; area, 48; benefits, 85; bilateral, 142; code, 79; control problems, 5; controls, 30, 33, 34, 36, 37; direct, 31, 36; 101, 111; Direct foreign private, 104; disputes, 135, 155; effects of foreign, 138; flow of, 57; foreign, 57, 62; Incentives, 87; Laws and Planning, 101; manufacturing and service, 79; manufacturing, 111; multinational, 132; multilateral, 142; patterns, 182; portfolio, 30, 101; position, 50; problem, 252; process, 167; promotion seminars, 119; protection issues, 265; provisions, 145; reciprocal, 174; short term, 30; Third Country, 52; U.S., 129; West German, 112
Iran, 111
Istel, Yves-Andre, 44
Italian lira, 41
Italy, 46, 63, 102, 113
ITT (International Telephone and Telegraph), 166

Japan, 19, 24, 34, 38, 61, 68, 75, 79, 87, 91, 102, 130, 145, 153, 159, 160, 163, 166, 168, 187, 192, 237
Javits, Jacob, U.S.S., 224

Kennecott Company, 152, 164, 167
Kenya, 111, 116
Kindleberger, Charles, 18, 62, 224, 246, 249, 252, 258, 261
Korry, Edward, 158, 168, 172, 180, 198, 213, 228, 267
Krishnamurti, R., 130, 266
Khrushchev, Nikita, 164
Kuwait, 111; Fund for Arab Economic Development, 138

Labor, 186, 197; intensive indus-

Spain, 149
St. Gobain Workers, 59
Standard Oil of Ohio, 20
Statistics, 10, 49, 97, 104, 113, 115, 175,
Steel, 185, 192, 236
Stock exchange, 45; commission, 56
Stockholm Conference on the Ecology and the Environment, 180
Strikes, 54, 186
Subsidiaries, 10, 18, 59, 69, 115, 128, 143, 200, 217, 219; American corporate, 87; wholly owned foreign, 59
Surveillance Agreement, 19; of international cartels, 21
Sweden, 114, 197, 199, 213
Switzerland, 61, 102, 114

Taiwan, 24, 82, 84
Tariff: barriers, 243; exemption, 116; walls, 66
Tax: authorities, 240; basis allocation, 88; behavior, 54; concessions, 99, 116; control, 55; duplication, 77; evasion, 77; harmonization, 37; haven, 64; incentives, 185; legislation, 227; losses, 54; mechanism, 34; policies, 191; payer, 167; rates, 186; returns, 127; revenues, 55; treaties, 55
Taxation, 52, 236, 244; direct income, 128
Technology, 23, 50, 54, 66, 96, 97, 129, 190, 191, 222; exchange of, 62; flow of, 223; imported, 129; industrial, 225; transfer of, 218, 225
Telecommunications System, 162
Texas, 63
Thailand, 111
Tokyo, 225
Trade, 23, 24, 53, 201, 221, 228; barriers to developed countries

markets, 151; flows, 16; multilateral, 181; non-discriminatory, 181; offs, 183, 192, 261; overseas, 243; patterns, 23, 190; preferences, 163; policy, 123; problems, 5, 252; transactions, 243; unions, 55; with developing countries, 16; with industrialized countries, 16
Transportation, 16, 190
Treaties, 142, 145; bilateral, 237; of establishment, 240; of friendship, commerce and establishment, 145; on taxation and establishment, 237

U. K. (United Kingdom), 111, 113, 123
UN (United Nations): Economic Commission for Africa, 161; Economic and Social Council, 119; Regional Economic Commissions of the, 137; Third Conference on Trade and Development, 221
UNCITRAL (United Nations Conference on International Trade Law), 137
UNCTAD (United Nations Conference on Trade and Development), 11, 82, 101, 108, 115, 119, 126, 133, 134, 208, 209, 216, 221, 266; resolution 56 (III), 120; III, 120, 208; Trade & Development Board, 121, 208; secretariat, 211, 216
UNDP (United Nations Development Program), 210, 211
Unions, 60, 265, 341, 354
UNITAR (United Nations Institute for Training and Research), 257
Uruguay, 146
U.S. (United States): Congress, 165; Department of Commerce, 10, 15, 17, 89; detente with the USSR and China, 153; firms in Latin America, 129; investment controls, 35; regulatory agencies, 239; Supreme Court, 265; treasury, 167

274

DON WALLACE, JR., a graduate of Yale and Harvard, is Professor of Law at Georgetown University and Director of the Institute for International and Foreign Trade Law. He is currently on sabbatical leave as Senior Fellow at St. Anthony's College, Oxford. He has practiced law in New York from 1957 to 1962, worked as Deputy Assistant General Counsel for the Agency for International Development, and spent a year in Turkey as a Fulbright scholar. The author of articles and books including an Introduction to Turkish Law, he is an active member of the American Bar Association.

HELGA RUOF-KOCH, a German citizen, is Assistant to the Director at the Institute for International and Foreign Trade Law. Before joining Georgetown University, she worked for the European Economic Community in Brussels, and for the Federation of German Industries. She is a graduate of the Universities of Cologne and Munich, where she received her M.A. in economics. Together with the Director, she works on all aspects of the Institute's programs.

KURT BIEDENKOPF is now General Secretary of the German Christian Democratic Party. During his distinguished academic career he was Dean of the Law School and President of Ruhr University. He has written extensively on questions of labor law, antitrust, energy policy, and many economic-political subjects.

PETER ADY is a Fellow of St. Anne's College, Oxford, a tutor in economics, and a lecturer in development economics. She has worked on international assignments in developing countries, United Nations technical assistance, and as a consultant on development questions. She is a co-author of Systems of National Accounts in Africa and edited Private Foreign Investment and the Developing World.

WILLIS ARMSTRONG is Assistant Secretary of State for Economic Affairs. He has pursued a long and distinguished career in the U.S. government and diplomatic service, notably in the embassies in Moscow, Canada, and London (where he served as Minister for Economic Affairs). Formerly President of the U.S. Council of the International Chamber of Commerce, he has published numerous professional articles.

FRANZ BALLMAN is Vice President of the Bank of America. After being in private law practice, he became Director in the Federal

Ministry of Economics in Bonn. He has served the German government as Senior Counselor to the International Monetary Fund and as Consultant to the Ministry of Finance in Singapore.

JACK N. BEHRMAN is Professor of International Business at the the University of North Carolina. He has held research positions and professorships at several universities including Delaware, George Washington, Harvard, and Princeton, and was Assistant Secretary in the Department of Commerce. Among his many publications are National Interests and the Multinational Enterprise and U.S. International Business and Governments.

FERNAND BRAUN is Director-General for Internal Markets of the Commission of European Communities. A citizen of Luxemberg, he served the Commission of the European Economic Community in Brussels in 1958-67, when he was Director of Industry, Commerce and Small Business, and industrial negotiator. In 1969 he became Assistant to the Director General of Industrial Affairs of the Commission, and then was promoted to his present post. He is also a journalist and has worked for Radio Luxemberg and the Associated Press, and is the author of numerous articles.

EDGAR CRUFT is a British citizen. He has had a distinguished international career as a geochemist in Africa, Canada, and the United States. Formerly Associate Professor of Geology and Geochemistry at the University of New Mexico, he is currently President of Nord Resources Corporation.

LUIS ESCOBAR, a citizen of Chile, is currently Special Representative for Inter-American Organizations at the International Bank for Reconstruction and Development. He has been both Professor and Dean of the Faculty of Economics at the University of Chile. In 1961 he became Minister of Economy, Development and Reconstruction and left this post to come to the United States as Executive Director of the International Monetary Fund and the World Bank. He is an expert on Latin American affairs and has written numerous articles and books including Organization for Economic Development and The Task of the University.

JOHN EVANS is a retired Foreign Service Officer. He has been Director of the Office of Economic Defense and Trade Policy, and Economic Minister and U.S. representative to the Council of the General Agreement on Tariffs and Trade in Geneva. He has also served as Assistant Special Representative for Trade Negotiations in the Executive Office in Washington. His publications include U.S. Trade Policy and The Kennedy Round in American Trade Policy.

LINCOLN GORDON has followed a distinguished career in academic and government posts. He has taught economics at Harvard University and was President of John Hopkins University in Baltimore. He was Minister of Economic Affairs in London, U.S. Ambassador to Brazil, and Assistant Secretary of State for Inter-American Affairs. Now a Fellow at the Woodrow Wilson International Center for Scholars, he is the author of several books, including Government and the American Society and A New Deal for Latin America.

RAINER HELLMAN is Editor in Chief of the German Economic News Agency VWD (Vereinigte Wirtschaftsdienste) at the European Communities in Brussels. A distinguished economist, he has written books and articles on subjects concerning European and international affairs, including The Challenge to U.S. Dominance of the International Corporation.

YVES-ANDRÉ ISTEL, originally from France, is now a U.S. citizen. He is a general partner of Kuhn, Loeb & Co., responsible for the International Department in New York. Also a director of Dreyfus Intercontinental Investment Fund, Industria Electrica de México, Société d'Investissement et de Gestion, Transatlantic Securities, and others, he is a frequent speaker on international economic affairs.

NICHOLAS de B. KATZENBACH is Director, Vice President, and General Counsel of International Business Machines. He was formerly U.S. Under-secretary of State and U.S. Attorney General. He has been a Professor of Law at both Chicago and Yale Universities, previous to which he was in private practice.

CHARLES KINDLEBERGER is Ford Professor of Economics at the Massachusetts Institute of Technology. He has been a research economist and Adviser and Vice President of the American Economic Association. He is the author of many books including International Economics, American Business Abroad, and Power and Money.

EDWARD KORRY is President of the United Nations Association. He was formerly U.S. Ambassador to Chile and Ethiopia, and was associated with the United Press for thirteen years as an international journalist and diplomat.

R. KRISHNAMURTI is an Indian citizen. He is currently Director of the Manufacturer's Division of the United Nations Conference on Trade and Development, and has been with the United Nations for twenty-five years, working in the UN Economic Commission for Asia and the Far East and the Asian Development Bank.

MILIC KYBAL, originally from Czechoslovakia, is Adviser in the Technical Department of the Inter-American Development Bank. Previously he was an economist with the United Nations, the Federal Reserve Bank of New York, and the U.S. government. His latest publication is Capital Markets in Latin America.

JEROME LEVINSON is Counsel to the Subcommittee on Multinational Corporations for the Senate Foreign Relations Committee. Previously he worked as Special Adviser to the Office of the President of the Inter-American Development Bank, Assistant and Deputy Director for Capital Development, Agency for International Development, in Brazil and Washington, and was in private practice in New York. He is a co-author of The Alliance That Lost Its Way and has written many articles on international economics.

EDWIN MARTIN is Chairman of the Development Assistance Committee of the Organization for Economic Cooperation and Development. He has held many posts in the field of government economic affairs. He has been Special Assistant to the Secretary of State, U.S. Economic Minister in London, Assistant Secretary for Economic Affairs, Assistant Secretary for Inter-American Affairs, and U.S. Ambassador to Argentina.

ROBERT NEUMAN is a partner of Arent, Fox, Kintner, Plotkin and Kahn and a member of the Bars of New York and Washington, D.C. He was Legal Adviser in the U.S. Department of State in Near Eastern and South Asian Affairs, in Politico-Military Affairs, and in Ocean Affairs. He is the author of "Oil on Troubled Waters: The International Control of Marine Pollution."

J. A. OYELABI, a citizen of Nigeria, is Research Fellow at the Nigerian Institute of Social and Economic Research at the University of Ibadan. He has been a lecturer in economics at Ibadan University and at the Bronx Community College in New York. He has written several articles and reviews, including Tests of Factor Substitution In Nigeria's Manufacturing Sector.

JOHN R. PETTY is Managing Director of Lehman Brothers, Inc., in Washington, D.C. He worked for the Chase Manhatten Bank from 1953 to 1966 and for the U.S. Department of the Treasury, where he became Assistant Secretary for International Affairs.

RAUL PREBISCH is an Argentinian national and presently Director-General of the Latin American Institute for Economic and Social Planning. He acts as Special Adviser to the President of the Inter-American Bank and to the Secretary-General of the United Nations.

His many distinguished posts in Latin America and the United States include Executive Secretary of the United Nations Economic Commission for Latin America and Secretary-General of the United Nations Conference on Trade and Development. He is the author of many books and publications, including Change and Development: Latin America's Great Task.

WILLIAM ROGERS is a partner of Arnold and Porter, Washington, D.C., and President of the American Society of International Law. He was formerly Deputy U.S. Coordinator of the Alliance for Progress, and President of the Center for Inter-American Relations. He is the author of The Twilight Struggle—The Alliance for Progress and the Politics of Development in Latin America and numerous reviews and articles.

SEYMOUR J. RUBIN is a counsel for Surrey, Karasik and Morse and Professor of Law at American University. He was with the legal staff of the U.S. government before going into private practice in 1948. Since then he has been General Counsel for the Agency for International Development, U.S. Representative to the Development Assistance Committee, and U.S. Representative to the United Nations Commission on International Trade Law. He is the author of many articles and several books including Private Foreign Investment: Legal and Economic Realities, and the editor of Legal Problems of Development Lending.

WALTER SEDWITZ is Executive Secretary for Economic and Social Affairs of the Organization of American States. He is also Executive Secretary of the Inter-American Economic and Social Council, and of the Inter-American Committee on the Alliance for Progress. He has worked with the United Nations and the U.S. government, and is the author of many publications on economic and Latin American affairs.

PIERO SELLA is an Italian citizen and Assistant General Counsel at the World Bank, where he has worked since 1959 as an attorney and Secretary for the Legal Committee on Settlement of Investment Disputes.

PHILIPPE DE SEYNES, a French citizen, has been Undersecretary-general for Economic and Social Affairs in the United Nations since 1955. Previously he was Inspector of Finance in the French Ministry of Finance, a member of the French Delegation to the United Nations, and Adviser to Pierre Mendès-France, the French Prime Minister.

IBRAHIM SHIHATA is Senior Legal Adviser to the Kuwait Fund for Arab Economic Development and Professor of Law at Ain-Shams University in Cairo. He has frequently represented the Egyptian government in international meetings, and has written many articles and books on air and space law, multinational economic ventures, and other subjects, both in English and Arabic.

ANTHONY SOLOMON is Special Consultant to Chairman Wilbur Mills and the House of Representatives Ways and Means Committee. Following an international career in which he was, among other things, Lecturer at the Harvard Business School, President of Rosa Blanca Corporation in Mexico, and Chairman of the Agency for International Development mission to Bolivia, he became Deputy Assistant Secretary of State for Latin America, Assistant Secretary of State for Economic Affairs, and President of the International Investment Corporation for Yugoslavia in London.

SAMUEL STERN is Resident Partner of the European office of Wilmer, Cutler and Pickering. He is a graduate of Harvard and the University of Pennsylvania, has had an impressive legal career, and was appointed as Assistant Counsel to the President's Commission on the Assassination of President Kennedy.

DETLEV VAGTS is Professor of Law at Harvard University. Previously he was in private practice with Cahill, Gordon, Zachry and Rendall in New York. He is the author of many articles and co-author of several books including Transnational Legal Problems Casebook and Secured Transactions under the Uniform Commercial Code.

CONSTANTINO VAITZOS is the Secretary of the Andean Group in Lima, Peru. He is a frequent speaker at international meetings and conferences.

RELATED TITLES
Published by
Praeger Special Studies

MANAGING FOREIGN INVESTMENT IN SOUTH-
ERN ITALY

> Douglas F. Lamont

THE MULTINATIONAL CORPORATION AS A
FORCE IN LATIN AMERICAN POLITICS: A
Case Study of the International Petroleum Com-
pany in Peru

> Adalberto J. Pinelo

STRATEGIC AND LONG-RANGE PLANNING
FOR THE MULTINATIONAL CORPORATION

> John Snow Schwendiman

THE CHILEAN RESPONSE TO FOREIGN
INVESTMENT

> Stephen F. Lau

PRIVATE FOREIGN INVESTMENT AND THE
DEVELOPING WORLD

> edited by Peter Ady

RECENT FOREIGN DIRECT MANUFACTURING
INVESTMENT IN THE UNITED STATES: An
Interview Study of the Decision Process

> John D. Daniels

FOREIGN INVESTMENT: The Experience of
Host Countries

> edited by Isaiah Litvak and
> Christopher Maule